From
34 Great Su

Monica Sjöö was born in the north of Sweden in 1938. Since the end of the 1950s she has lived mostly in Britain and has been active since the end of the 1960s in the Women's Liberation Movement. She sees herself as a radical Goddess feminist and artist. Her paintings have been exhibited throughout northern Europe as well as in the USA. She is the co-author, with Barbara Mor, of *The Great Cosmic Mother: Rediscovering the Religion of the Earth* (Harper & Row, San Francisco, 1987, new edition 1991) and has contributed to many anthologies, including *Walking on the Waters: Women Talk about Spirituality* (Virago, 1983), *Glancing Fires: An Investigation into Women's Creativity* (The Women's Press, 1987), *Voices of the Goddess: a Chorus of Sibyls* (Aquarian Press, 1990) as well as the feminist art books *Visibly Female* (Camden Press, 1987) and *Framing Feminism: Art and the Women's Movement 1970–85* (Pandora Press, 1987). She has written numerous articles which have been published in British journals such as *Arachne*, *PAN* (now *Pandora's Jar*), *Wood and Water* and *From the Flames*, as well as in *Womanspirit*, *Calyx* and the *Woman of Power* in the USA. Some of her paintings have recently been used as book covers.

New Age and Armageddon

The Goddess or the Gurus?
Towards a Feminist Vision
of the Future

MONICA SJÖÖ

The Women's Press

First published by The Women's Press Limited, 1992
A member of the Namara Group
34 Great Sutton Street, London EC1V 0DX

Copyright © Monica Sjöö 1992

The right of Monica Sjöö to be identified as author of this work has been asserted by her in accordance with the Copyright, Designs and Patents Act 1988.

British Library Cataloguing in Publication Data
Sjöö, Monica
  New age and armageddon : the goddess or the gurus?
  1. Occultism
  I. Title
  291.1783442

ISBN 0-7043-4263-4

This book is sold subject to the condition that it shall not, by way of trade or otherwise, be lent, resold, hired out, or otherwise circulated without the Publisher's prior consent in any form of binding or cover other than that in which it is published and without a similar condition including this condition being imposed on the subsequent purchaser.

Phototypeset by Intype, London
Printed and bound in Great Britain by
BPCC Hazells Ltd
Member of BPCC Ltd

This book is dedicated to my two sons in the otherworld: Leif, whose sudden and tragic death in 1985 changed my life from what it then was, and Sean, with whom I explored aspects of the New Age movement as we struggled through his illness from lymphoma cancer and were both of us in desperate need of healing and help. This book was written for him as I owe it to him and to his great courage to tell the truth as I see it. He died on the full moon, 10 July 1987.
I love you both.
Blessed be in the Mother.

Monica Sjöö

Contents

	Acknowledgements	viii
	Introduction	1
1	Questioning the New Age Movement	17
2	Dreaming the Sacred Land	51
3	Explorations of Consciousness	75
4	Banishing Darkness: Findhorn's Plan of Light	89
5	Reclaiming the Dark Mother	126
6	The Lord is a Consuming Fire	151
7	From the Rebirthing Movement to Biological Engineering	178
8	Traditional Shamanism and its New Age Manifestations	217
9	The Harmonic Convergence	248
10	False Transcendence: the Gurus or the Goddess?	278
	Notes	291
	Bibliography	312

Acknowledgements

Without the experiences I went through with my son, Sean, who died in 1987 from lymphoma cancer at the age of twenty-eight, I would not have written this book, nor would I have been at all familiar with New Age thinking.

Writing this book has been a long and painful and often depressing task, but it had to be done. I have many friends to thank for help, inspiration, written material and encouragement and for keeping me going.

An early inspiration was meeting up with Daphne Francis many times at Greenham Common during actions there during 1983–4. I was aware of the article she was writing about having lived in Findhorn and being a 'New Age survivor'. This article has been invaluable for my book. While in Brighton in February 1988, I was given Matthias Neitsch's paper on what he calls 'Plastic Shamans', by Richard Cupidi, the Italian-American who owns and runs the radical Public House bookshop. Richard introduced me to important books by Paula Gunn Allen, and other radicals. This was a significant meeting in terms of 'midwifing' this book.

In March 1988, I, together with Maggie Parks and Jill Smith, ran a workshop called 'New Age Patriarchy' during a conference called 'Angry Women's Conference' in Malvern. This conference was organised by a group of Malvern women who, together with Maggie Parks, have all read the manuscript of this book with enthusiasm and good energies which have been very helpful to me.

The three of us also organised and led a workshop/discussion on 'New Age Patriarchy' during 'The Goddess Re-emerging' exhibition in September 1989 held in the Assembly Rooms in Glastonbury. Jill Smith and I took part in this exhibition with Philippa Bowers and Joanna Gorner. Jill Smith, who wrote the article 'Unharmonic Convergence' that I draw on in this book, has been a friend and inspiration to me for a number of years. She is a wise woman artist and poet of Earth mysteries and my pilgrimages to visit her on the Isle of Lewis on the outer Hebrides have been magical highlights in my life. We have been together at Greenham and also took part (with Philippa Bowers) in the incredible journey across Salisbury Plain in 1985 which I write about in this book.

Reading Serena Roney-Dougal's papers and research on the pineal gland and parapsychology has been important, as well as being able to stay with her many times when I have visited Glastonbury. A source of strength.

I was given encouragement early on from Wren Sidhe and Lindsay River who both read the manuscript for this book, from Asphodel (Pauline Long), from Jenny Goodman and from Jean Mountaingrove. Jean was the editor and mother/creator of the no-longer-published *Womanspirit* journal in Oregon, USA. She has the manuscript which she also passed on to Cher McKee of the Massachusetts-based *Woman of Power* journal. Cher used a section of it as a long article entitled 'New Age or Armageddon?' published in March 1990, in the *Women Re-visioning History* issue of the journal. (This article was included by Bob Stewart in his anthology *Psychology and the Spiritual Traditions*, published by Element Books.)

In this context I want to thank my dear friends Leila and Chris Castle who invited me in August 1988 to give a workshop at their West-coast moat of Earth mysteries in California. Thanks to their hospitality, love, support and great patience, my journey to the USA became very powerful and inspired. It was also important from the point of view of giving me further insights into the Californian-based New Age movements. In May 1990, Chris Castle and I exhibited together in an exihibition entitled 'The Stones and the Goddess' during the Californian Earth Alive festival in Berkeley.

Many thanks also to Val Remy who retyped and edited, thereby teaching me a lot, an unpublished manuscript that I called 'Spiral Journey: Pilgrimages to the Sacred Sites' which I wrote in 1983-4 whilst still living in a cottage in Pembrokeshire. I have included sections of that manuscript here, notably on pilgrimages or journeys in the Celtic world, on holy wells, the bleeding yew and treading the maze at Glastonbury Tor.

Many thanks to Daniel Cohen and Jan Henning who published my article 'Some Thoughts on the New Age Movement' in their pagan newsletter *Wood and Water* and also to Daniel for making it possible for me at the time to buy a reconditioned electric typewriter.

Thanks also to Tom Wengraf for lending me his typewriter when I was stuck and to Gill Hodder, former national secretary for Compassionate Friends (bereaved parents), for her loving friendship, for her expertise in mending typewriters that go wrong, and for helping me over times full of grief.

Gill Hodder has laboured many long hours to unravel and type out my manuscript. She lost her beloved son Martin in a tragic accident more than ten years ago and she witnessed my oldest son Sean's struggle with cancer and his death. Without friends such as Gill I don't think that I would now be alive or at all sane. Thank you for being who you are.

My New Age article was also published during 1989 in PAN (*Pagans Against Nukes*), now called *Pandora's Jar*, that is created and sustained by my friends Nicola Beechsquirrel and Phil Cousins, as well as in *Greenline* and in *Everywoman* (edited by Barbara Rogers).

In September 1989 some of us called a conference of women entitled 'Challenging New Age Patriarchy'. It was held in Malvern and 150 women came. Out of this has come a new journal called *From the Flames* about our spirituality, politics and lives. It is published in Nottingham by Vron MacIntyre.

I do not know how to thank all my so loving friends in Bristol who have, over the last years of grief, given me so much love and healing. I thank you all and I love you.

A source of knowledge of ancient cultures, the universal and primordial religion of the Goddess, is my own and Barbara Mor's book *The Great Cosmic Mother: Rediscovering the Religion of the Earth*. Without the grounding of that book, a source always to draw from and refer to, I would not have had the confidence to embark on this present project. Thank you Barbara Mor for your passion, wisdom and word-magic and for our collaboration now over many years as our book expanded.

I finally want to thank Ros de Lanerolle of The Women's Press for taking on my book for publication, and my editors Diana Scott and Loulou Brown for working on and shaping my somewhat amorphous original manuscript. Diana is a friend and a fine poet. Loulou Brown, who has had the gruelling and long, hard work finally to put this work into shape is a radical thinker and a meticulous and experienced editor to whom I am eternally indebted. I have found it very inspiring working with both her and Diana. Thank you sisters.

I hope that you, the reader, will enjoy this book and find it thought-provoking.

Blessed Be, August 1991
Monica Sjöö

Introduction

We are fast approaching the millennium. The question now facing us all is whether the Earth – Mother, spirit, planetary psycho-physical being – will be able to renew and transform Herself, or whether She is by now so abused, polluted and choked in Her very blood/water arteries – from rainforest devastation, acid rain, ozone-layer destruction and the direct poisoning of the oceans and underground waters – that she will die.

If She dies, so do we; if She transforms and survives, so might we. If Her immune system breaks down, so does ours.

I am a visual artist but also need to communicate through the written word. I passionately love the Great Mother, our beautiful Earth, and all my work, whether painting or writing, has always been done on Her behalf. Probably because of this my work seems to merge in magical, uncanny and sometimes quite terrifying ways with my lived everyday experience.

While living in Pembrokeshire between 1980 and 1985, I became involved with radical ecopagans, with CND, with actions at Greenham Common and with the Women for Life on Earth network. It was the sudden, tragic death of my youngest son, killed by a car when he was only fifteen years old, and then my oldest son Sean's illness with cancer which brought my life to a complete standstill. At that time I lost my faith in the Goddess and even feared her. During this time of great need I found myself exploring spiritual teachings that until then had not interested me.

I moved back to Bristol to care for my sick son throughout chemotherapy treatments and hospital visits, until he too died in 1987. Together we became involved in healing and meditation circles, spiritualism, joined the Cancer Help Centre, explored near death and paranormal states, read widely and were present at many New Age events.

After my initial amnesia following the death of my youngest son, barely alive and wanting to die, it slowly began to dawn on me how reactionary and patriarchal much New Age thinking is, in spite of its deceptive façade of niceness, love, light and claims to Earth healing.

This book comes out of my sense of outrage and of feeling betrayed.

Having looked deeply into many aspects of the New Age movement I feel I have to share my misgivings, to warn the many women who are tempted to get involved in that so seductive movement; I also want to speak of what I see as its sinister, hidden agenda. I want to see a discussion and a questioning of the aims and politics of New Agers and hope that this book will provide such a contribution.

There are major differences between White Light New Agers, who have forgotten that their 'Sons of Light' are also sons of the Mother, and pagans/ecofeminists who still remember that Earth is Gaia, the living and self-creating Great Mother.

Paganism has no fixed creeds or dogmas, no self-proclaimed gurus or prophets, no holy books or saviours.[1] Earth Herself is our teacher. Pagans, like all natural peoples, desire to live in harmony with Earth and see all Her manifestations, whether animal, plant, insect, rock or mountain, or, as Native Americans say, four-legged, two-legged, crawling and flying,[2] as our relations and as ensouled. This is recognised by New Age shamans who go on vision quests and communicate with animal spirits. (See chapter 8.)

The European Craft-tradition (Wicce) still practises some of the aboriginal Neolithic as well as Celtic shamanism, as in Britain. Pagans believe that the creative force of life does not originate from a transcendent outside force (God), but is immanent in nature and the Earth; that we are spirit and consciousness because She is so; that the powers of transformation are inherent in the Earth Spirit. To us, as to the ancients, the natural environment is a psychic and spiritual entity, and we are aware of, and honour, the inter-connections between the material world and the otherworld. Physical and spiritual events are indeed interwoven. Ancient peoples communicated freely between the different realms, and the Goddess, who is both light and dark, the giver of life and the giver of death, the giver of immortality and the giver of rebirth, awaits us now. Bob Stewart, the author of many books on the Celtic faery and underworld tradition,[3] writes that there is a powerful relationship between humans and the energies of the land, and that the Celts believed that the faery realm is beneath the Earth. It is the source of all primal powers such as sacred waters and magical springs. (See chapter 5.)

Those New Agers who persist in dualistic thinking yet again rend apart spirit and matter (*mater*/mother), this and the otherworld. To them, spirit is, as to all patriarchal men throughout history (not herstory), an omnipotent and disembodied transcendent male mind which controls matter. 'He' is not immanent in creation and therefore cross-communication with nature is forgotten and forbidden. Many New Agers make the absurd assumption that this anti-sexual, distant 'God' is somehow able to bring forth and sustain the fruitfulness and fertility of the Earth. The myths of divine fatherhood, which are inversions of the original creation myths, have caused a dangerous split in our psyches and have set us warring against ourselves and against the Earth Mother who is punished for giving us the gift of life.[4] The alienated male mind experiences the physical body as a prison of the spirit and seeks redemption from 'sin', from a saviour undefiled by femaleness. To him the Earth is expendable; to many eastern gurus She is 'Maya' or an illusion to overcome which therefore can be exploited and abused. (See chapter 6.)

The western Christian industrial world has treated Mother Earth as simply a resource to be used for political and economic ends, and every atrocity – war, rape, exploitation, imperialism – has been sanctioned by its God and his male priesthoods. (See chapter 1.)

In this book I explore the New Age movement's hidden agenda, as I see them. Many covert ideas are racist, misogynist, reactionary and right-wing, inherited from a mishmash of both eastern and western occult sources, ranging from the Theosophists to Christian mystical thinkers such as Rudolf Steiner and Teilhard de Chardin. Spiritual techniques have been borrowed from natural peoples and distorted to accommodate western New Age shamans and reactionary thinking.

I find it impossible to write of the New Age movement without discussing US politics, since so much New Age thinking originates in north America amongst the children of the white and privileged. In January and February 1991, the USA clearly set itself up as the policeman of the world as it waged total hi-tech remote controlled warfare in the Gulf, an electronic armageddon. Is this the true meaning of the 'global village', a concept so beloved of New Agers? White north Americans are set upon creating a new world order – with themselves in control. Many New Agers appear to look forward to such an outcome and see the north American continent as the home of a forthcoming neo-Atlantean civilisation. This was prophesied by Helena Blavatsky, the founder of the Theosophical movement at the end of the last century. In the interest of western economic and political aims, a network of electronic communications media is encircling the globe, with computers 'speaking' from city to city, polluting our environment with electromagnetic overload. This in New Age speak is called the development of a global brain[5] and Earth transformation to higher states of awareness. The peoples of the Pacific have been sacrificed in the process. (See chapter 1.)

I ask whether some New Agers actively co-operate with the CIA (the US Central Intelligence Agency). I have seen some very strange statements in New Age writings. (See chapter 10.)

Reactionary politics, government by authoritarian, hierarchic male élites and the creation of the atomic bomb appear to have been encouraged, welcomed and even instigated by 'Secret Masters', the Hierarchy/Mahatmas/ White Brotherhood, who are said to rule and direct our destinies from their secret, occult realms. They are also said to be overlords of planetary evolution and a 'civil service'[6] for the absentee land/Lord who resides away from 'his' creation. Such thinking is taken very seriously by many New Agers, particularly those who reside at Findhorn, the White Light community in Scotland, who are influenced by Blavatsky and Alice Bailey, a former Theosophist who, in the 1930s and 1940s, was the medium for one such Master. Both Blavatsky and Bailey were obsessed with fire and light, which are also regarded as very important by New Agers. Bailey's many 'channelled' books and her 'Great Invocation', which is intoned as a hymn at many New Age gatherings, were popularised by her disciple David Spangler at Findhorn.[7] Blavatsky, a woman of great occult and mediumistic powers, was in contact with Secret Masters who supposedly reside in the mythical Shambhala under or beyond the Gobi desert, the legendary homeland of the 'Aryan race'. Blavatsky's *The Secret Doctrine* was admired and studied by the Nazi élite who found her racial theories useful.

Unfortunately, such misogynist and racist thinking is common today in the New Age movement. David Spangler, for example, wrote in 1977 that 'the Aryan race (Indo-European/Caucasian) is the first race in the evolutionary progression of man to come to full grips with the power of the mind'[8] and that with this event the spiritual hierarchy of the Masters came into existence. Spangler consistently advocates that 'man' stands apart from the natural cycles of nature as in '. . . unlike plants and animals we do not need to wait upon rain and sun and soil for our growth', and that it is because 'man' is the seed of Christ-consciousness that he was given domination over nature. According to Spangler's even more sinister scenario, 'man' will move out from the solar system to create other worlds, and to prepare for this, 'man' must be weaned from Earth and Her magical clairvoyant powers. We are not to communicate with the ancestors and the spirits of nature, but must free ourselves from the 'group consciousness of the natural world' and step free of the Earth into cosmic experience where 'the voice of nature will no longer be heard'. This will, according to Spangler, be facilitated by the 'Lord of the World, King of the Hierarchy of Masters'.[9] (See chapter 4.)

Much of the writing that came out at the time of the 'Harmonic Convergence', held as a worldwide event from 16–17 August 1987, is similar in tone. People gathered in their thousands on sacred mountains and places of power around the world, supposedly to do Earth healing. The writings by some New Age men who initiated the event were, in my opinion, highly dubious, such as those of Robert Coon, Sir George Trevelyan, Vincent Selleck, José Argüelles and the New Age shaman Harley Reagan Swiftdeer. The New Age movement speaks a lot about 'Earth healing', but being patriarchal and male-initiated, overall it sees spirit as transcendent and male by definition and *not* as inherent in nature or in the Earth. Many New Agers believe that some humans, the élite, are star people [10] or intergalactic travellers who originally came here from the Pleiades or Sirius. A common New Age expression is 'spaceship Earth', and I have even heard Earth described as a 'hostess'. A second coming is anticipated: not of the Goddess but of assorted male saviours or 'Sons of Light' – the 'Father' not the Mother is obviously the source of light to them – and a spiritual élite believed to be physically immortal, having transformed their bodies into light and able to materialise and dematerialise at will,[11] is expected to transcend and survive coming cataclysms, even a nuclear holocaust. This belief is shared by fundamentalist Christians who believe that the elect will undergo a bodily resurrection.

Sir George Trevelyan believes there is a battle being waged between the forces of light and the forces of darkness on both a cosmic and human level. The forces of light are led by Christ and the archangel Michael, 'the dragonslayer'. The dragon or serpent is, however, the Great Mother and the sacred places that New Agers shun are those expressing Her watery and chthonic Earth dragon energies. Michael is popular with New Agers and the attempted slaying of the dragon energies has been described as 'solar, chivalrous, victorious day against lunar watery and reptilian night'.[12] (See chapter 9.)

So the Lords of Flame set out to slay the Moon Mother and Her lifegiving waters and want to deprive us of our lucid dreams and dark, menstrual, clairvoyant powers. Considering that our bodies consist of at least 75 per cent water, that we think with our watery brains, we are surrounded by amniotic fluid in the womb and that women bleed, such actions seem somewhat suicidal for the human race. (For a discussion of our menstrual powers and the sacred waters, see chapter 5.)

Light and dark first became associated with good and evil in Sanskrit.[13] This reflected the invading Indo-Aryans' contempt for the aboriginal and conquered dark Dravidians of the Indian continent who had created the great, advanced Mother-centred Neolithic cultures of Mohenjo-daro along the Indus valley and the city of Harappa in the Punjab during the third millennium BC, or earlier still.[14] The Indo-Aryan 'heroic' warriors, the Sons of Light, delighted in their shining metallic weapons and worshipped the fires which smelt the ores ripped out of the Earth's belly. Their bright, fiery shining gods were formed in their own brutal image as they set out to defeat the gentle Goddess people of darkness and the serpent, and to introduce the caste system based on colour of skin. (See chapter 6.)

By creating a God who is all light and transcendent, the rest of creation is demonised. The Devil is truly the projection of those who have abandoned the Goddess who is both dark and light. The stronger the light, the darker the shadows. It is almost as if the light-obsessed New Age movement is rehearsing a near-death state as we now approach a new millennium and live through the ever-present threat of nuclear holocaust. It is in such states that the great white light of the spiritworld is experienced. As never before, the death of nature is now a distinct possibility.

A nuclear catastrophe seems, however, to be welcomed by some millennial New Agers who see this as light being released from within the atom and the Earth transformed and made light-radiant. In this scenario, the passive and submissive Earth, subject to divine male will, sacrifices Herself to transcend on to another and higher octave of creation. The French Jesuit and mystical Christian, Teilhard de Chardin, so admired by New Agers, believed that Earth and the biosphere is evolving a new level of consciousness which he called the Noosphere. The planetisation of 'mankind', aided by global electronic communications and machinery, extends this consciousness. Chardin thought that until now mind had not been manifest on Earth except in a static state, that 'mankind' is now building a composite brain and that finally we will cease in space-time and become trans-human. He described the detonation of the first atomic bomb in New Mexico as 'super-creativity', and wrote that 'it disclosed to human existence a supreme purpose: the purpose of pursuing further to the very end, the forces of life.'[15]

It would seem that when men see themselves as most godlike, they become the most demonic, as they tamper with the very fabric of life to our total detriment.

New Age men's obsessive denial of darkness is founded in their fear of women and of the Goddess. The sons of patriarchy are forbidden by their jealous and possessive 'God' to merge ecstatically with nature, the Mother, or with women, and must at all times muster a non-participatory consciousness which allows them to be forever in control, a control that is also killing them. Light was born from the dark cosmic womb of space; space is full of dark matter; and it is in the dark and fiery womb of the Earth that creation takes place. The embryo gestates in darkness and so does the seed in the dark soil. It is the dark and radiant night with its lunar and star light which gives us deep knowledge and lucid dreams; all ancient people believed that the Lunar Mother gave us mind and wisdom.[16] We lived for many millennia within the dark caves and always knew that without the dark winter season, with its rotting vegetation and recycling of life, there is no rebirth, and so the most ancient Dark Mother was revered and honoured above all. (See chapter 5.)

Patriarchal men see themselves as deeply spiritual, even when they hold the most anti-life and fascist views, because their Godhead is not seen to be immanent in the physical universe. Women, however, know full well that all life is sacred. As we give birth from our living and bleeding bodies, we know the cost of that life which patriarchal men so easily expend in murders, wars and desecration. Women know that spirituality cannot be divorced from struggles against oppression, and that to be truly free we must free our Earth Mother from further exploitation.

The New Age movement claims to be non-political while it embraces reactionary views. It preaches that one must never at any time resist anything, not even those who rape and plunder the Earth and its people and creatures. This is said by those who are well fed and well off and who live in the western world. New Agers claim that the individual mind in lone majesty has the supreme power to create reality; a catchphrase of the New Age is that 'you create your own reality'. In fact, our minds and nature's interact at all times; we are instructed from the spirit realms and there are innumerable interconnections between inner and outer realities; this quite apart from oppressive political realities we might have been born into. But as patriarchal New Age men assume that mind and spirit are not inherent in nature, they therefore cannot be acted upon or formed by Her. If the individual mind is all powerful, then the oppressed poor of the Third World or the ghetto can comfortably be blamed for their own oppression, and everything, however unjust or atrocious, is created by oneself and one's own lack of 'positive thinking', another New Age catchphrase.

New Agers, with ideas based on the ancient Eastern doctrine of Karma, explain that people suffer in this life as a result of what has happened in their past lives, which implies that no way must one interfere and try to change a world full of racism, misogyny, poverty and exploitation as this was already ordained and has to run its course. Collective karma is not considered, nor are other mind-created realities that constantly impinge on us. If we live sheltered, well fed and protected lives in the west while the rest of the world starves and burns, that is only because of our well deserved karma. New Age thinking is full of such dishonest, smug, self-righteous and right-wing doublethink paraded as 'spirituality'. New Agers such as rebirthers can then cynically claim that they deserve to be rich and even physically immortal. Money flows towards those who have plenty of 'prosperity-consciousness' and make the proper affirmations. They don't have to think about living in a world rampant with western imperialism, that poverty and starvation are on the increase in the Third World, and that as westerners they are the most privileged people on Earth. (See chapter 7.)

The New Age movement is, in my opinion, fundamentally flawed because New Age men cannot come to terms with women's real powers, or with the Goddess who is both of this world and of the otherworld, both immanent and transcendent, and behave as if the Women's Liberation Movement and Goddess awareness had come and gone without a trace. New Age men see the Goddess as merely a manifestation of 'God', and to them a divine male is the ultimate purpose of creation. Like all patriarchs, they imply that the Mother, both physical and divine, is the giver of material things, and therefore of illness, old age, death and all things 'dark', passive and ultimately evil. They deny consciousness and divine powers to the Earth Mother, even when they call Her 'Gaia'.[17] (See chapter 6.)

It cannot be a coincidence that now, when women are reawakening worldwide and the Goddess is speaking through us, along comes the New Age movement with its innumerable male gurus, teachers, masters, shamans and therapists (the rapists) telling women yet again who we are, who we should be and what we are to believe. We are to aspire to 'Christ consciousness' and identify with the 'Sons of Light' and solar fathers — never mind that to the ancients the sun was most commonly a Goddess.[18] We are to act out 'the feminine principle', popularly called yin, as defined by heterosexual patriarchal men. Many of these self-proclaimed authoritarian and misogynist New Age gurus could be mistaken for reincarnated Old Testament prophets. The rebirthing movement which emerged in California in the 1970s, encapsulates many of the most reactionary aspects of the New Age. Rebirthed women, it is claimed, should aspire to become as one with Babaji, an Indian yogi, who is seen by the rebirthers as the 'Father' of the world, a modern Christ and as physically immortal.[19] (I explore this movement in detail in chapter 7.)

I find it fearful that all monotheistic patriarchal religions set out systematically to sever our umbilical psychic cord to the body-mind of the Earth Mother or Spider Woman. It is as if they are attempting to tear apart the very web of life. During the European witchhunts or burning times, the Inquisition prodded into women's very dreams and country people were punished for communicating with the spirits of nature at their holy places. The powers of nature were demonised by the church and later denied entirely by western reductionist male science which declared there are no mysterious forces in nature and that Earth is but a mechanism.[20] Patriarchies have desecrated and desacralised the Earth, and as a result we are now all endangered. Men who see birth as an obscenity and loathe having been born of a mere mortal woman, and therefore become subject to illness, old age and death, also see death as an enemy to be overcome. Such men think they can achieve immortality by conquering and slaying the Goddess/nature. This is called 'progress', 'transcendence' and the birth of (male individualistic) consciousness. New Agers do not want to know about the ancient tantric beliefs of India that characterise death as Mother Kali/Shakti's transforming touch which brings freedom from limited time-space consciousness. Tantrikas believe that Kali, the Black Mother, manifests the worlds and dissolves them back again into Her great cosmic womb of self-luminous light and consciousness.[21] (See chapter 3.)

I have been a lifelong feminist and active in the mainstream and grassroots of the Women's Liberation Movement since 1969. For a number of years I have been involved with the emerging womenspirituality, as well as feminist and Goddess, arts movements. I have always believed that only if women rise up worldwide will there be a future. I felt this most urgently after an initiatory experience, in a state of heightened awareness, at Silbury mound which is the pregnant womb of the Earth Mother.[22] This was in 1978, and I experienced then the Earth's terrible anguish and grief at the increasing violation, pollution, exploitation and rape that She suffers. I felt this deeply in my own body-mind. As a result I left the city and went to live in rural Wales/Cymru. I was drawn again and again to the ancient Neolithic Goddess sites that have ever since informed and inspired my dreams, thoughts and images.

In Britain alone there are some 900 stone circles, sometimes called lunar temples or observatories[23] that can be understood as etheric energy centres or chakras, linked by pathways of the spirit or leylines, across the living body of the Earth. At these stone circles, as at other sacred places – wells, trees, mounds, mountains – peoples of old communicated freely with the ancestors or fairies, were initiated, healed, dreamed lucid dreams and entered into shamanic journeys into the otherworld realms, bringing back knowledge and the powers of healing, prophecy and pre-cognition. Today we have forgotten that we were always instructed and taught from those realms. Some of us are, however, beginning to re-member, and many people are feeling increasingly drawn to the ancient places of power[24] where we listen again to the voices of the spirits and hear the warnings of the Mother as she speaks of the imminent death of all nature if patriarchal societies continue. (See chapter 2.)

British Earth mysteries researcher Paul Deveraux thinks that Earth communicates with us through Earth lights[25] (and perhaps now through crop circles) which emanate from deep within the subterranean caverns of Earth's womb. In past ages these white lights, often in the form of floating globes/spheres/balls or columns of varying sizes and glowing in different hues ranging from orange to blue, were thought to be spirits, ghosts of the dead, fairies or shining ones, white ladies, fiery dragons and, most recently, UFOs. The lights are, according to Deveraux, trance-inducing, they imprint human thought and are an intelligent energy-form unknown to science. They appear at faultlines in the Earth's crust – window areas into the spirit realms – and here the Neolithic peoples raised the stones and mounds of their sacred sites. We ourselves are sensitive to invisible energies and have a geomagnetic sense which we share with animals and plants. We are linked as by a radiant electromagnetic umbilical cord to Mother Earth, or, as the Hopis say, to Spider Woman's web as She weaves the universe, as well as the bones and the tissues of the child in the womb.[26]

Patriarchal, western city cultures have instilled a fear of the natural world and have taught that ancient peoples, as well as present indigenous peoples, were/are 'primitive', brutish and superstitious. This is blatantly untrue. The Kogi people have been able to protect themselves from 'civilisation' and Christianity and live in the high sierras of Columbia in South America. They have retained their belief in the Great Mother, who to them is the ultimate source of being, and, like the Hopis, another ancient people, they see themselves as the guardians of the Earth and as the elder brothers (and sisters?) of the human race. Their priests, women and men, are called the 'Mamas' (Mothers?) and seem like awesome spiritbeings, long-haired, gentle, white-robed, with aged, genderless faces. They agreed to be filmed for one television programme only[27] to warn the Earth's peoples of forthcoming catastrophes of which they can see the signs in their sacred mountains. High in the sierras, the heart of the world, they see the waters dying, the vegetation drying out and the snow and clouds disappearing. The Mamas warn that the Great Mother is sickening and weakening, that the radiant web that keeps the world alive is being torn apart and that its spirit guardians are diseased. They intone that the Great Mother conceived spirit in the dark waters and spun the worlds from Her spindle; She is memory, darkness, possibility, and Earth has mind, eyes and heart. She has taught us everything and nourishes the world. They warn that the 'younger brothers' must stop mining and taking oil, minerals and ores out of Her because She needs these within Her body. There must be harmony in the spiritworld and in this world, and the pathways of the spirits must be kept clear and open. The Mamas, who as children were trained for the priesthood within the darkness of the cave/womb, hear the voices of the otherworld and never lose that connection.

In the New Age movement, there is no recognition that women were the creators of the most ancient cultures and that the original mother of humanity and ancestor Goddess was African and black. Hers is the luminous darkness that creates life. There is no recognition of women's shamanistic death and rebirth every month when we bleed, that women are the guardians of the twilight zones between life and death as we risk our lives giving birth, bringing spirits from the otherworld womb into the Earth plane. Women are always the communicators with the great unknown.

We are so because the rhythms of our body-minds are in tune with those of the Earth; the tides of the oceans in our very beings as we rhythmically menstruate with the moon, the radiant queen of heaven, in Her changes. The moon, home of the spirits and the maternal giver of mind, knowing intelligence, wisdom, visions, psychic powers and lucid dreams. She who is both dark and light – anathema to New Agers who fear the dark maiden, Mother and crone.

We are in conversation with the Earth all the time – She is, after all, our Mother, and there is a silver astral umbilical cord that joins us to Her – whether or not we are aware of this. She speaks through our bodies and what we do to Her we do to ourselves. Within Earth – in Her internal fires, ores, minerals, crystals and waters – there are mysterious life-creating powers that we no longer understand.

I have been writing this book with a great sense of urgency because I know in my very bones that the Earth is suffering and that we must now use our Second Sight which is our birthright and be still and listen to what our Mother the Earth is telling us.

Since we are of Her great mind and being, we *can* know what must be done now to heal Her and ourselves. We have reached a time nearing the millennium, when the 'ring of fire' – the active volcanoes of the Pacific basin – is awakening within the Earth. Within the Earth, there is an enormous and sometimes dormant coiled serpent/dragon of electromagnetic powers. She is Kundalini, the rainbow serpent, the fiery she-serpent that also dwells within the etheric chakra system of our subtle bodies. She is now awakening and rising within us, shifting our consciousness to a new and faster level of transformative energies. The Goddess is returning . . . as Brigid of the sacred internal fires, serpent and mother of wells and springs – as Hawaiian Pélé of the active volcanoes – as White Buffalo Woman of the Native American peoples bringing vision quests – as the African Goddess Oya of the wild winds, tornadoes and uncontrollable forces of nature.

We now have to channel these fierce energies or be destroyed.[28]

The time has come when all of us, who in past ages were burned as witches because we loved and cherished the lunar (sometimes solar) Mother and magically communicated with our Mother Earth, have to fight anew on life's behalf.[29]

1
Questioning the New Age Movement

My Young Son in the Spiritworld

I saw my youngest son Leif being run down by a car and lie dying on the road in the South of France.

I spent thirty anguished hours by his brain-dead body, in the hospital in Bayonne in the Basque country on a beautiful late August day in 1985, and experienced flying with him on great white wings into a great loving light-presence.

Lament for My Dead Son

My son, only fifteen years old, has journeyed into the otherworld.
Leif, oh why did you leave me, oh why . . .?
Violently killed by a car
bleeding your lifeblood from your damaged head
there on the road in the South of France, 26 August 1985.
Powerless to save your young life
overwhelming pain, pain and remorse, gripping my heart.
Panic and unbelievable horror when realising it was you my love,
lying there on the road
like a wounded animal in its death throes.
   Replaying in my mind again and again and again
   why did it happen, why did you cross the road?
   why were we in this place outside Bayonne?
   why had I no sense of impending danger?

why was I lulled into a false sense of security?
we were happily going to a beach with a friend –
why didn't you wait for the lights of the zebra-crossing
to change?
Did you look the wrong way?
Why, oh why? . . .

Always so impatient, my son, so reckless and careless
with your life,
extreme in tempers and feelings; inquisitive, intelligent
and eager to learn and to experience life to the full.
Oh, how I grieve for all the things you had no chance to
experience,
I, who knew your longings so well.
  This summer you had flowered, learned to play the
  drum
  amongst the tipi people in Wales who loved you,
  enjoyed the sun, riding bareback on the horses
  and helping with the hay on our friend's farm
  in the South of France, in the skirts of the Pyrenees,
  feeling good about your increasingly beautiful body
  relaxing from the stresses and paranoias.
  'I am growing up, Monica,' you said to me.
  You received so much healing this summer . . .
  Why did the Dark Mother take you back now
  when you envisaged a future and dreamed of things to
  come?

I long so for you, want to hold you in my arms
feel as if my heart has been amputated,
the psychic umbilical cord cut, suffer from shock.
I want to touch and smell your curly afro-hair,
look into your deep black eyes . . .
Oh, my sweet baby Leify, where are you now?
  In death you were so serenely and peacefully beautiful,
  you were at rest in the arms of the Cosmic Mother
  I thought then: 'You are innocent Leif, you have done
  nothing wrong'

and we felt you soaring and flying. You are free and I
am not.

We stayed at your bedside the thirty hours before
your heart stopped beating . . .
I felt a gentle touch across my head as your spirit parted,
as if you were trying to comfort me in my grief.
I had asked your forgiveness and had wailed and cried
for the disappointments and frustrations I hadn't been
able to protect you from or help you through.
> I had always loved you intensely . . . but it was not
> always easy to show it to a teenage son in our culture
> which sets out to divide son from mother and causes
> divisions.
> My friend asked me 'Was he forgiving?' and I said
> 'He always was' . . . and wild and generous and angry
> too.

Never have I experienced death like this . . .
so close and so peaceful in spite of the violence
that had caused the passing of my son's life.
Feel as if I hover between different realities,
feeling pulled to follow you into the infinite space
of our Mother's womb. Unbearable to continue living,
each day a strain to live through.
> Must I descend into the underworld to seek my young
> son
> journeying into the darkness of my soul,
> shadows gathering round me?

Leif . . . I will soon join you when my work is done,
work I still have to do with many women and also some
men,
for the Goddess . . . for our Mother the Earth
whose body is now under seige.
I still have two older sons.

I love you, Leif . . . always did, always will do . . .

> Goodbye for a little while . . .
> Rainbow Leif, Rainbow Leif
> go where you are going to
> do what you need to do
> because love is guiding you.[1]
>
> 17 September 1985

A few hours before the life-support machine that had kept his heart beating turned itself off, a message came telepathically flooding into me from my son, telling me that 'the only thing that matters is love . . . absolutely the only thing that matters is love'.[2]

I had, at the time, not yet come across accounts of near-death and journeys out of the body experiences. Even though I believed in the living 'dead', in the Goddess otherworld, this experience overwhelmed me. Since then I have come to understand that women shamans always were the mediators or threshold guardians between different realities, with birth and death as a coming forth and a returning back into the dark/light womb of the universal Mother.

The big question is: How does one live the 'love' that my young son communicated?

My son, whose biological father is Afro-American, would surely mean that you must actively work for and defend what you love and that this might even mean picking up a gun and fighting back against overwhelming and intolerable oppression and injustice. Che Guevara said that 'the true revolutionary is motivated by great feelings of love', and Denise Levertov, the American poet, once said: 'There comes a time when only anger is love.'

In this exploration of the New Age movement, I set off in the spirit of both anger and love.

Women as Mediums

As I had to come to terms with the experiences of my son's death, for a while I became involved with spiritualism. I see spiritualist women mediums as the direct descendants of the wise women of the Craft (the witches). I want to explain how I see the historical evolution of psychic women, who were originally ancient oracles and prophetesses and who became the wise women or shamankas of mediaeval Europe, and finally, after hundreds of years of persecution, re-emerged as spiritualist mediums.

The spirit-ancestors communicate with us through signs, omens, dreams and trances. The ancients believed that dreams originate in the realm of the blessed dead and in the magical effects of sleep within the ancestral tombs such as Newgrange in Ireland and West Kennet Long Barrow in Wiltshire in England. The priestess healers on Malta dreamed in clairvoyant sleep, deep in underground chambers which evoked the dark womb of the eternal Mother. These were the antechambers of the under/otherworld and here the voices from the spirits could be heard bringing knowledge of healing and prophecy. Women oracles were associated with subterranean powers originating from within the Earth Herself. At Delphi, within the underground cavern temple of Gaia and her python, the oracle inhaled the sulphurous fumes from the underworld. To the Goddess peoples, the Christian inferno was a realm of great fertile and supernatural power.

In Greece from 500 BC to 500 AD, sick pilgrims took part in rituals in Ascelepius temples, of which more than 200 existed. The god of medicine was expected to visit them during the dream state or in the strange state between sleeping and waking, and either heal them or prescribe drugs, diet or ways of treatment. The goddesses of healing, Hygeia, Panacea and Iaso, had by then become the 'daughters' of the god.[3]

In Scandinavia, prophetic utterance, healing and shamanism belonged to the Goddess Freya, the great disa of the earlier Vanir people.[4] Her priestesses practised 'Sejd' and entered into ecstatic trances communicating with the spirits of the dead. To Freya belonged the magical bird costumes that were used by the women to fly into the other realms. The inspired state of the shaman women was seen as dangerous and uncontrollable by the god Odin's Iron Age priests, who were set on gaining ascendancy over the people in the troubled times of inter-tribal warfare before the Viking era. Odin was then called the great shaman and originator of runic magic – knowledge taken from Freya's priestesses and tamed.

Shamans (women and men) amongst the Sami people of the north and their relatives, the Inuit of Greenland and Alaska, as well as shamans in the Americas, use *peyote*[5] and sacred mushrooms to enter into other realities. Everywhere they were outlawed, persecuted and murdered by the ascetic priesthoods of the Christian God who condemned any ecstatic state and carried on warfare against the sexual body and the clairvoyant and dreaming mind.

To the Celts, the spirit realm was 'the land of the Everlasting women' and their druids taught belief in reincarnation and the survival of the soul. The shining ones, the people of the Sidh, were fairy women – the ancestors, or the beloved dead, who lived on in the luminous summerland or on invisible islands out at sea. They were thought to live within earthworks and mounds such as Newgrange and they were immortal and existed in a halfway state between this world and the next.[6] Their fairy queen is the white Goddess, giver of immortality, poetic inspiration, transmutation and magical skills.[7] To the Scandinavians and the Germanic peoples, Frau Holle, or Hel, was the fairy queen or Goddess of the otherworld and one entered Her realm through the neolithic mounds and long barrows, or the sacred mountains such as the Brocken in the Harz mountains in Germany, or Glastonbury Tor in Somerset in Britain. To the Christians, Her uterine fiery shrine or cauldron/well became hell. The Celts believed that the winds were the spirits of the invisible dead who control the weather. It seems that in Welsh, words for the forces of nature are feminine, as are the words for oak and dragon. There is a great unbroken continuity between this world and the next; some of us are in a physical form and others in luminous bodies – worlds that co-exist and interface.

The ancestors exist in all the elements: in fire from cremations, in air from the smoke of the fires, in earth from burials and in water from drownings at sea. We form a single community.[8]

Spirit possession is an ancient African tradition which was carried with the African slaves to the USA, the West Indies and Brazil. Amongst ecstatic dancing and drumming, the spirits are called up by voodoo priestesses and priests. To the Fon people of Dahomey (now Benin) in Africa, voodoo means creative genius and protective spirit as well as that which is inherently known.

Luisah Teish, an Afro-American feminist who is a practising voodoo priestess and medium of the Yoruba goddess Oshun, has written a book called *Jambalaya*.[9] Teish says that the Africans believe that those who go before us make us what we are; that they continue to exist and create in the spiritworld. They exist on another level within the creative energy and are to be treated with loving respect and reverence. Teish herself is a 'mother of the spirits' in her tradition.

The Christians, who were truly the cremators of the souls that dream, outlawed the doctrine of reincarnation as heresy in the fourth century and denied the existence of the spiritworld. They cut us off from the realm of the dead and murdered European shamans, the Wicca or wise women and men of the Craft by the million. We are only now beginning to realise what we have lost in diminished psychic powers and sensitivity. We also have a devastated Earth whose voices we no longer hear.

Christians believe the 'angels' are male and of a separate creation, while in fact the archangel Michael was originally the winged Goddess. She is the white Goddess of death and rebirth who carries souls into the air in her mantle of light, pale ghosts awaiting the next life – She whose hair is white feathers and whose face shines like the full moon and the white snow.

In the USA in 1988, I was fortunate enough to attend a slide-illustrated talk by the brilliant feminist archaeologist Marija Gimbutas, who is Lithuanian but lives and teaches in Los Angeles, given at an arts institute in San Francisco. She pointed out that the stiff, stark, abstract and bonelike cycladic Goddess images, in white marble or alabaster, represent the Goddess of death and the underworld as well as of rebirth and regeneration, and are always found buried with the dead in the tombs.

Marija told us that the colour white in fact symbolised death to the pre Indo-European or old peoples of Europe and Asia. White as the bleached bones, as the white hair and white snow, as ashes and 'ghosts', the white light of the astral world. To the old peoples, on the other hand, black was the colour of the dark and fertile soil of the Earth in whose dark womb seeds germinate during the winter months, the nourishing and protective womb of the mother who carries her child, the cave homes within the mountain Mother, the darkness of cosmos that gives birth to light.

It was the warlike, horse-riding, pastoral Indo-Europeans – the Kurgan warriors as Marija calls them – destroying the old cultures in their path, who worshipped the bright sky and fire, who sacrificed to male gods and denied any autonomous powers to the Earth. Everything light and white was good and pure to them and everything dark and black was bad and evil. This highly anti-Goddess and racist thinking is embedded in our language and consciousness.[10]

Whoever defines the past also defines the future and its possibilities. Patriarchy is not just about economic and political control in the present, it is also about the ancestors. *The Language of the Goddess* by Marija Gimbutas is no less than the alphabet of the metaphysical in the neolithic period.

Her research and conclusions are ridiculed and put down by patriarchal archaeologists who want to preserve the status quo and who wish to see women as expendable throughout human history.

I was blessed to be able to spend some time with Marija when in the USA, as well as with Luisah Teish with whom I spent a full moon day. In a mediumistic trance she communicated with both my dark son and my light son in the spiritworld. It was wonderful to behold the love, intimacy and respect with which Luisah communicated with the ancestors – the Egun and the Orishas who live on in the spirit realms.[11]

Spiritualism

In October 1985 I went to live in Bristol in the South West of England because my oldest son, then twenty-six years old, was suffering from virulent cancer and had to have chemotherapy treatment at Southmead hospital there. He also wanted to be able to attend the Bristol Cancer Help Centre.

We naturally gravitated towards people, both men and women, from whom we could receive support and understanding. We took part in meditation and healing circles and New Age gatherings. I also attended spiritualist churches where I found people who, although in most other ways were very conventional, take the spiritworld and continuing communication with the so-called 'dead' for granted and believe in other realms beyond this one.

The modern spiritualist movement was born in the USA through the mediumship of the Fox sisters, then twelve and thirteen years old, in 1848. In tribal shamanistic cultures it is at puberty when it becomes clear whether a girl or boy will be a future shaman of the people and it is often through strange dreams and illnesses that this shows itself. In repressive patriarchal cultures, where the strong tribal and loving bonds, so favourable to shamanism within the community, have been torn apart, poltergeist phenomena are common around potentially psychic girls and boys passing through puberty.[12]

Spiritualism has been known in Britain since 1852, and many of the country's greatest mediums have been descended from Celtic families with a tradition of 'second sight'. It seemed as if messengers from the spiritworld had decided that the time was right, at the height of the mechanistic and materialistic time of the late-nineteenth century, to give irrefutable evidence for survival after death and the possibility of communication with spirits. From the start it was clear that women were favoured by the spirits. These mediumistic women had, however, grown up in the patriarchal and sexually repressive Victorian world and were no longer the free and orgiastic/ecstatic shamankas of the great Mother.

Great women writers during this era often had to publish their work under male pseudonyms so as not to be dismissed out of hand. In the same way, women mediums could not speak with their own voice or those of spirit-women.

So began the tradition of passive women clairvoyants and mediums channelling the messages given from supposedly male spirit guides – a tradition that has distorted what we are hearing from the spirits.

Alex Owen explored in her book, *The Darkened Room – Women, Power and Spiritualism in Late Victorian England*,[13] the herstory of women's mediumship in recent times. Among spiritualists it is recognised that women are more open to mediumship and psychic awareness because we are more conscious of the mysteries of birth and death. As Alex Owen points out, however, there was an inherent contradiction between the clairvoyant powers and spiritual authority and wisdom displayed by many women mediums and the doctrine of self-renunciation and passivity they were supposed to adhere to. Spiritualist women both undermined and confirmed male ideology concerning women's roles in the family and society at large.

Because spirit guides were, and still are, predominantly seen as male, it followed that women were supremely suited to be 'invaded' and to have their psyches and minds taken over in totally passive trance states.[14]

For a time, women mediums performed extraordinary feats of physical materialisation of the spirit beings of the dead from 'ectoplasm', a substance like living and luminous white cobwebs that emanated from the body of the medium.

I have read some extraordinarily poetic and almost hallucinatory descriptions of 'life in the world unseen'[15] that remind me of LSD visions in their perception of the colours, light and forms that exist there. And these accounts were written down by perfectly 'straight' and 'respectable' people at the end of the last, or early in this, century.

Christian spiritualists looked back with longing to the early Church and gnostic teachings[16] of healing, prophecy, direct communication with the divine, greater equality between women and men, and speaking in tongues. Many spiritualists who believed in reincarnation and who followed eastern doctrines later became Theosophists.

We have forgotten how important the spiritualist movement has been in breaking the way for a far more open spiritual climate.

Spiritualist mediums were persecuted by the law. The Witchcraft Act of 1735 declared there to be no psychic powers and that therefore anyone who claimed the powers of mediumship was lying and/or fraudulent.

The Scottish working-class materialisation medium, Helena Duncan, a woman of rare powers it seems, stood trial in 1944 for 'fraudulence', and died soon afterwards as a result of the injuries she sustained at the hands of investigators who attempted to grab hold of the materialised form.[17] After this, most mediums have worked with the far less draining or dangerous healing and conscious clairvoyance, giving messages from spirits that are 'seen' or 'heard' in a semi-trance state or when fully conscious. It was thanks to the horrendous trial of Helena Duncan and the public outrage at her death that the repeal of the Witchcraft Act was finally brought about in 1951.[18] Since this trial the spiritualist movement has bent over backwards to prove itself to be 'respectable' as an organised church with a congregation. Most present-day spiritualists do not want to be associated with pagans and Wicce,[19] although a few spiritualists will use the term father/mother when speaking of 'God'.

Since the repeal of the Witchcraft Act in 1951, there has been a revival of the pagan movement.

Because most spiritualists are not Christians (they consider Jesus to have been a great teacher and healer but not the son of God come to redeem humanity), present-day Christian fundamentalists accuse them of 'communication with demons' when they commune with the spirits of the dead.

The first two principles (there are seven in all) of spiritualism are 'the fatherhood of God' and 'the brotherhood of man'; a feminist awareness and Goddess-consciousness are not welcomed. The spiritualist movement, which is predominantly working-class and grassroots, and led by some powerful women mediums, is not part of the New Age. Nevertheless, without it there would not now be the fashion for 'channelling' spirit guides, so prevalent throughout the New Age movement. Here, however, the trend is to use mediumship for personal power, prestige and financial gain. There is also the temptation for mediums in the New Age movement to pronounce that their own prejudiced and often reactionary views are voices from the spiritworld, and are therefore beyond questioning. They are monologues that no one takes any responsibility for.

A quote from *Psychic News* is relevant here: 'The craze of "channelling" currently sweeping America shows no signs of abating . . . ordinary New Yorkers are now claiming their bodies can be temporarily taken over "by former incarnations or spirit guides who need a pipeline to speak to the world".'[20] Channelling originated in California. Shirley MacLaine a few years ago held a working seminar on reincarnation and channelling which sold out – at over

£100 a ticket.[21] The actress explained to 1000 people why she had to charge for helping people to find their power within. 'It is karmically unbalanced to do something for nothing,' she said. *Psychic News* feels she has 'sanitised the supernatural' for Americans.[22]

Another medium, Mrs J Z Knight, has been 'channelling' the spirit guide 'Ramtha' who claims to be 35,000 years old, since 1977. She charges people $400 to attend her meetings and the sale of video tapes and other items brings in millions of dollars each year. She has said: 'I am not a guru or someone's saviour. This is business.' As a result of Ramtha's apocalyptic teachings, rich followers are moving to the Pacific north west, building pyramid houses in preparation for catastrophes to come.[23]

This is in contrast to the loving service given by ordinary spiritualist healers and mediums in Britain who ask only for voluntary contributions and who believe that their powers come through them from the spirit and must not be abused or used for personal gain.

There are many spirit guides beloved by the movement, especially 'Silver Birch' and 'White Eagle', both supposedly Native American. During my own long, dark nights of despair, I found 'Silver Birch' a wise and loving being.

After Leif's tragic and premature death, I experienced a darkness of my mind. At times I could barely see in this literal darkness around me and, for a period, I hated people for still being alive or for having reached old age. Nothing made any sense any more and I did not want to be in my physical body. I longed to fly with my son into the great loving light of the otherworld. Death seemed a great release. I several times set the date for my own death.

Women are the guardians between the realms – we create life and we grieve the dead ones. Our children are woven from our very life-blood. Never have I experienced such a thing as smelling the blood of my dead son and seeing my own body in his. A pain beyond description and a longing to go with him.

Questioning the New Age Movement

I had a difficult childhood during which I grew up in poverty with my (unsupported) mother in Sweden. She was a talented artist, a loving and beautiful woman who had married 'beneath her' and, therefore, was rejected by her class. (My father was also an artist but from a peasant/working-class background.) My mother suffered much pain because of a physical disability. My parents divorced when I was three years old.

My experiences as a child in no way sheltered me from harsh and often brutal realities. I know what poverty does to one's psyche and expectations of life. At the age of sixteen, I left school and was homeless. Middle-class women are protected to a certain degree from seeing men's sexually predatory attitudes and power over women in its undisguised and naked forms. This was not so in my case.

During the 1960s, I worked full-time for several years with the anti-Vietnam war movement in Stockholm and organised exhibitions on Vietnam. During that time I learned about American imperialism and racism. I got to know Afro-American radicals who spoke of the USA as Babylon. I was also involved in the anarchist movement. When I lived in Britain in the late 1960s, I helped to found the Bristol Women's Liberation group with which I was deeply involved for many years. During that time I worked in WACC (Women's Abortion and Contraception Campaign), in the Claimant's Union working with unsupported mothers, in Wages for Housework[24] in the Gay Women's group and lesbian movement. Nationally I am part of the Matriarchy Research and Reclaim Network and helped to found feminist and Goddess arts movements. I have written a great deal on feminism and women's art. I work with the Radical Pagan Movement and was involved with CND and women's actions at Greenham.[25]

My first experience of the New Age movement came in 1978 when I found myself taking part in the Festival for Mind and Body. I had recently finished my important painting, *The Goddess at Avebury*, which came into being as a result of my heightened experience at Avebury and Silbury during my initiation to the Goddess (see chapter 2). My friend Beverly Skinner, with whom I have held many exhibitions over the years, had been invited by the organiser, Grahame Wilson, to take part in the Festival with some of her paintings, and she brought me along with her.

It was clear that Wilson felt threatened by me because I was a feminist and because physically I do not conform to the type of beautiful young women he was surrounded by. He also didn't seem to consider patriarchal religious groups, such as Hare Krishna, which believe that woman worships God by worshipping him in man, as being 'political'.

I learned a great deal from this festival which seemed to be a 'spiritual supermarket' at vastly inflated prices. Ironically, Beverly and I ended up having free stall-space, my painting of *The Goddess of Avebury* was displayed and I was selling my feminist posters. We seemed to be the only haven there for feminist women who felt bewildered at this event which passed itself off as spiritual whilst firmly adhering to entirely patriarchal notions of godhead and spirit.

Another unpleasant experience of the New Age Movement for me was when I lived for a year (1979–80) in a large squat called the Durdham Park Community in Bristol.

I still feel, as do many others, that the Community, which had been started by a group of unsupported mothers and their children, was the best thing to happen in Bristol for many years.

We came to dearly love the huge old house, a former 'free school', and its beautiful grounds. Throughout the two years of its existence, it was a centre for all kinds of grassroots activities involving a large number of people, and was a welcoming place for travellers and tipi-dwellers. We shared cooking and cleaning on a rota basis; the children took decisions at their own meetings and were very free. We ran workshops and arts events. Many homeless people came to us. In short, it functioned as a real arts and community centre and almost everyone who lived there was from a working-class background.

We were, however, threatened with eviction and found that Dartington Hall in Devon owned the property and wished to convert it into luxury flats for the rich.

Dartington Hall was set up by the very wealthy Leonard and Dorothy Elmhurst who had been inspired by an Indian village project founded by the great poet Rabindranath Tagore. The idea was to raise the energy level within a geographic district and to attempt to balance cultural and commercial projects. Dartington Hall is very rich and has thriving arts and crafts centres. Considering that they professed to believe in communal living and alternative activities, we naively assumed that the Dartington Trustees would be sympathetic to what we were attempting to achieve, so we presented them with our plans for running a 'mutual aid' centre.

Maurice Ash, who headed the Dartington Hall Trust, writes books on Green politics, is an associate of *Resurgence* journal and was involved, together with Satish Kumar, in the Schumacher lectures held yearly in Bristol, refused point blank to consider our proposal or to take us seriously.

In desperation, we (that is, three women and our children) went to Dartington Hall and ended up having confrontations with the Dartington Hall trustees who had refused to speak to us. Ironically enough, one of them, Lord Michael Young, has written a book about mutual aid centres.

When we found we could not communicate with the trustees, my friends, Sandy (who then had four children) and Alison (who was pregnant), decided to squat in the toilets of the Elmhurst Centre, starting on a day when the trustees were having a party, to alert the press and people in Bristol. We stayed at Dartington Hall for more than a week, supported by members of the Durdham Park Community and students at the Dartington Hall college who fed and looked after us.

During this time we witnessed the weird spectacle of plummy, upper-class male trustees arguing by the toilet windows in front of TV cameras with people from our community. We came across as the landless and disinherited peasantry confronting the landed gentry who believe that might makes right.

In the end we were violently evicted from our Bristol community, in spite of promises given by the trustees that they would call the bailiffs back and allow us a month's respite to discuss things with them. We felt that we had been tricked.

Living at Durdham Park brought home to me just how much can be achieved when we have land and buildings and how unfocused and scattered we are otherwise.

It has become clear to me that there is very little political questioning, no awareness of race, sex, class and imperialism within the New Age movement. It seems not to have heard what women have been saying for so many years.

Asoka Bandarage, a Sri Lankan teacher, writer and freedom fighter, wrote an article called 'Spirituality, Politics and Feminism' which was published in the American journal *Woman of Power* in 1986. In it she says:

> At the present time the New Age philosophy and life style is dominated by the white upper middle class. Only members of this class can afford to shop at health food stores, eat at macrobiotic restaurants, attend expensive retreats or pay for healers and therapists. Furthermore, this movement, which draws so much of its inspiration, its ideas and even many of its names and symbols from non-western cultures – Hindu, Buddhist, Native American – gives little if anything positive to those cultures in return. Divorced from a broader political struggle towards social change, the New Age effort feeds into the cash nexus and materialistic values and behaviour of the

> status quo. It has largely been absorbed by the narcissism of the 'Me Generation'. It looks for individual nirvana at the expense of all else. Spiritually without politics. It does not seem to work . . . It remains focussed on a single issue, inner fulfilment and healing, and there is little effort made to relate personal change to social transformation.[26]

New Agers lack the cosmology of the Goddess (Earth to be revered and defended) and therefore attempt to undertake social transformation and Earth spirit healing without being grounded. And so they flit from Zen Buddhism to Gestalt, to rebirthing, to Native American shamanism to the latest trend or craze, and pillage eastern and native peoples for spiritual support and iconography in the way that the British pillaged material and artistic wealth from Africa and the Orient two centuries ago.

I do not think that the New Age is apolitical. It fits in very well with capitalism, which it in no way fundamentally challenges. The New Age wants change but no revolution and believes that humanity must somehow evolve into a better way of life.

The big question not being asked is whether positive changes are possible as long as the present military–industrial complex exists.

The most insidious of the New Age ideas is the one that claims that 'you create your own reality' – you, yourself, in isolation from oppressive realities. From this it follows that if you choose to believe that 'I am no longer oppressed' (as a woman, black, gay, etc.) then that oppression is suddenly gone. This is blatantly untrue since eliminating oppression cannot be brought about without collective and organised struggle.

Marilyn Ferguson's *Aquarian Conspiracy*[27] is a book written in 1982 about the New Age that had an enormous following when it was published. Ferguson is locked into the thinking of Marshall McLuhan,[28] whose thesis is that the electronic revolution will create a universal 'global village' and 'electronic brain', a single consciousness, that will make everyone emotionally aware of the total dependence of each person on the rest of the human family. Psychic communication, integrated and made possible by the electronic media, will ultimately create an inclusive universal consciousness – 'a new interpretation of the body of Christ' in typical New Age speak. This type of technology, however, is made in the west. Wealth in Europe, the USA and Canada goes hand in hand with vast electrical energy consumption and developing nuclear power stations, and is dependent on cheap labour and raw materials from the Third World. It can only be spread across the globe through US and other western intervention and domination.

Films and videos from the USA are watched on television screens across the world and create a desire for the north American way of life: luxury, consumerism and selfish irresponsibility. Colonised peoples are taught to despise themselves and their own culture which is destroyed and replaced by that of the coloniser. These cultural transplants were, in the past, carried out by missionaries, but today are achieved through the Coca-Cola culture and television. (In the USA itself, by the age of seventeen, the average child has seen 300,000 commercials!)

The German socialist thinker, Hans Magnus Enzensberger, writes in *Raids and Reconstructions – Essays in Politics, Crime and Culture*[29] about what he calls the 'industrialisation of the mind' and the 'consciousness shaping media' of today's world. He says that Marshall McLuhan is the prophet of the apolitical avant-garde and that his is a reactionary doctrine of salvation devoid of any sense or understanding of class, race, sex and economics. He claims that it is in fact our awareness of exploitation which is now being abolished. In the west we live in societies controlled by a universal system of electronic media which thrive on the immaterial exploitation of the mind. McLuhan assumes we are able to determine the conditions of our own existence – an assumption now common in the New Age movement – but this is meaningless if people are subjected to poverty, sexual harassment and physical intimidation.

McLuhan's global village describes the web of electrical circuitry that we now live in as if it were an extension of our own nervous systems. We are being pulled together in a shared wiring, the effects of which are subliminal. 'The medium is the message' and information is seen as an end in itself. We have come to mistake information for knowledge. Television feeds the world with images and sounds and information-gathering has become a prime commodity.

Our lives are being manipulated and polluted; we become addicted to new thrills which never actually satisfy; our minds become caught in the electronic circuits around us; we are mesmerised by the blue, flickering television screen. As the Earth becomes enmeshed in an electrical web, it is being depleted of its vital, natural energies and electromagnetic overload affects our immune systems, causing ill-health and allergies of all kinds. Mass tourism enables westerners to pollute every corner of the Earth. We have cars that destroy the air we breathe and cause the greenhouse effect. We are surrounded by chemical and electrical pollution as well as by radiation, and we have no idea what long-term effects these will have on either the Earth or on human well-being. The 'global village' lacks both humanity and compassion and serves predominantly western male patriarchal interests, such as those of US multinationals.

Marilyn Ferguson's explanation of the class basis of the New Agers is as follows: the affluent youth and adults in the USA and the western world, who no longer need to struggle for a material existence and have achieved the wealth and security their ancestors fought for, have now reached a point where, though they have got all this, they are still unhappy and disillusioned and have now set out on a quest for spirituality and a meaning beyond materialism. Marilyn Ferguson fervently believes that a great 'psychic revolution' is happening in the USA and enthuses about research projects on meditation, biofeedback, psychic phenomena and alternative medical approaches funded by the Department of Defense and other military and governmental bodies. She has an optimistic conviction that New Age ideas and thinking will influence, and radically change for the better, men who are in control of management, the military, technology and science.

In both west and east the military are funding 'innovations', such as ESP, and could benefit greatly from psychic mind-control over entire populations. Just as the majority of scientists now work for and are financed by military and drug industries, so might parapsychologists and psychics be in the future, and this is, in fact, already happening.

I found it extremely depressing to watch Jerry Rubin on television recently, the former 'leader' of the Yippies in the USA and a wild, long-haired revolutionary, now very 'straight' and advocating Yuppiedom. Apparently he had undergone therapy and soul-searching in the 1970s and now, using the New Age language of 'networking' and 'overcoming his resistance or negative attitudes to money', he advocates entrepreneurial acquisition of wealth, even to the extent of participating in the stock exchange. People (mainly men) in non-productive work seem to think that 'money is just an energy' that you may or may not attract to yourself according to your positive or negative atttitudes to it. Rubin never mentioned people who actually produce the commodities which these brokers buy and sell, or women's unpaid work in the home.

In the USA at least 20 million people – mainly blacks, Native Americans and Hispanics – live below the poverty line. The USA, with only 6 per cent of the world's population, is ripping off 60 per cent of the world's raw materials. These two facts place in context its apparent and real wealth and prosperity.

I feel that the interrelatedness of the social and the psychic is ignored by New Agers and Marxists alike. Both concentrate on just one side of the coin: simply to speak of economics without a spiritual perspective is futile, while to talk of spirituality without also taking into consideration the economic and social bases of society is equally futile.

Women and Patriarchy

Strong women-identified women are seen as a threat to patriarchy and every attempt is made to silence us. Peggy Kornegger, the American anarcha-feminist, wrote an article for *The Second Wave* in 1976 called 'The Spirituality Ripoff'.[30] In it she says that feminists in the USA, who got caught up with the New Age patriarchal spirituality that spread like wildfire in the 1970s, were no longer into 'politics' or such 'narrow concerns as feminism'. Instead they were choosing which man to follow or obey – god, father, priest, therapist or guru.

Radical lesbian women are the greatest threat to patriarchal power as they are redefining the meanings of politics and spirituality and are attempting to abolish the godfather both within and without. Feminist spirituality is extending consciousness. Women's liberation is a spiritual revolution in which we are exorcising the internalised godfather in his various manifestations as he drains our energies and sets us against each other and ourselves. We live in a society where reality and truth are male-defined. Women know that both psychic and physical energies are needed to change the world and ourselves, that we must leap beyond male-perpetuated barriers to become whole spiritual/sexual/political beings in a permanent process of be-coming.

Re-naming ourselves and the world means that we no longer have to separate the spiritual/cultural and political action. The women at Greenham are a clear example of this. We must, like them, develop the psychic/intuitive powers and confront daily oppression in concrete and direct action. We do not have to believe that the only alternative to mind is its annihilation, as advocated by assorted eastern gurus. Kornegger says that the typically patriarchal dualistic mind-set of either/or is leading men and women from a political to a spiritual solution when in fact they are disillusioned and frustrated by both realities.

One result of excluding women from the patriarchal language that speaks of man, mankind and he is that when human communities are planned the women who are their mainstay are actually forgotten. This means, for example, that in the Third World when development aid is given, the economic aid is given to men's projects, and women, who are the real food producers, are disempowered and are unable to feed themselves, their communities and their children – the increasing feminisation of poverty worldwide.

Most of the hard and gruelling work on this Earth is done by undernourished and starving women (in Africa 80 per cent of food is produced by women and 70 per cent of all firewood is gathered and carried long distances by women) whose weakness and ill-health often jeopardises the survival of their children and yet who desperately try to keep their children alive. (One person in three who starves to death in the Third World is a child under the age of six.)

Susan George[31] writes a most damning condemnation of the activities of the west in the so-called 'under-developed countries' and especially of the disaster of the so-called 'Green revolution' which has plunged those nations into huge debt and made them even more helplessly dependent on multinational US-owned corporations and agri-farm businesses. The 'Green revolution' introduced varieties of high-yield grain to countries where they do not naturally grow and, therefore, to survive need vast amounts of chemical fertilisers, insecticides and machinery which can only be supplied by the west. All of this has only benefited the ruling élite in the Third World and the multinationals in the west, and has plunged the poor peasants and women into even more abject poverty and starvation and landlessness. Women have been hardest hit as they do most of the work that feeds the families and villages. They grow the subsistence food crops and sell their produce at the markets, while, in the 'Green revolution', it is the men who are given the training in the newer techniques of farming and economic aid. They grow the cash crops and receive the money, and it is they who get to drive the highly esteemed and costly tractors. It is thought that not only is mass starvation in Africa and universal hunger 'man-made' (the true word here) because the west uses grain and foods as a weapon and bargaining tool – the west also feeds valuable grains and soya-bean products to its animals for the meat market rather than feeding starving populations – but also because women, who were always the main and respected food producers, have been utterly undermined and are no longer able to support themselves and their hungry children. The situation is now worsening rather than getting better, thus the 'feminisation of poverty'. Unless women are empowered, given back their land and livelihoods, world hunger will increase and the dispossessed will rise up.

The New Age now grotesquely parodies the tragedy of the 'feministation of poverty'. It offers young women 'happiness' – 'happy' women, barefoot and pregnant, cooking brown rice in ashram kitchens – and 'romantic/ spiritual love' where women become 'brides of Christ' and substitute god or guru for husband. They are offered mystical joy, to be blissed out with the perfect master, while fulfilling traditional roles as housewife and mother. Women struggling to develop an identity are taught the benefits of 'non-ego'.

Blissed out followers of gurus are no threat to the status quo. It is no surprise that the US government has funded Transcendental Meditation (TM) teachings and research programmes, as well as Erhard Seminar Training (EST). Peggy Kornegger finds this particularly pernicious. The methods that modern technology is developing for social control of 'deviants', especially women, are very subtle and provide new mind-control/brainwashing techniques for the godfather.

In 1975, TM cleared $20 million in the USA alone. Because it is classified as a non-profit educational organisation, all of that money was exempt from tax. Transcendental Mediation functions as a non-chemical tranquilliser to 'cool out' 'anti-social behaviour', and is used by both those who make the laws as well as those who are punished by them. TM helps to make us placidly accept the iron bars of our lives and keeps people 'out of trouble'. It pacifies inmates of prisons and 'self-actualises' workers to become more committed to the company they work for. 'A fully functioning employee with a healthy "self image" is money in the bank', wrote Marilyn Ferguson.[32] She adds enthusiastically that 'the entrepreneur is the new non-violent change agent',[33] a statement that takes on a dreadful irony when read in the light of 'achievements' of the Thatcher–Reagan–Bush era.

This kind of 'spirituality' which helps both government and big business to function more effectively – a calmer, happier capitalist is more adept at ruthless and cut-throat competition – makes workers co-operate more and complain less and lessens student unrest or questioning/rebellion. What people are not supposed to become aware of is where the profits go, what is being produced and who is being exploited, either here or in the Third World.

According to Peggy Kornegger, EST is a multi-million dollar corporation headed by Werner Erhard, a former salesman of 'such diverse products as used cars and mind dynamics'. Erhard established the EST trainer style: visually hip, cool and casual while verbally authoritarian, manipulative and militaristic. The purpose of the training is to 'tear you down and put you together again', leaving participants at the mercy of the EST group leaders.

Verbally abused and psychologically browbeaten to the point where they are so confused and will-less that they will accept anything, the participants are finally told that 'you are perfect the way you are' – and for this they pay about £200 each for a weekend.

EST promises passivity and well-adjusted lives in authoritarian patriarchal societies. Kornegger calls it a kind of 'soft fascism' and an education for submission.

I have in my possession a pamphlet advertising the EST Forum Seminars Centers Network. Its blurb says that Werner Erhard 'has been engaged by major corporations, charitable enterprises, city administrations and federal agencies around the world as a consultant in management, corporate culture, productivity and leadership'. The forum has ninety locations all over the world and claims to 'provide you with direct access to being itself'. The forum seminars are personal development seminars for large institutions – like management of transnational corporations, and it teaches how to handle workers more subtly, to be self-fulfilled and less stressed, and for management to be more personally effective and able to achieve.

Movements such as TM and EST have both interacted with and influenced New Age thinking in its reactionary attitudes to money, politics and self-development.

White North American Ideology

To understand white north Americans' attitudes to money and power, it is necessary to look at their puritan Christian heritage and what this sets out to destroy.

European history is written from the point of view of the male ruling class. Women are now rewriting that his/herstory in the same way that radical Afro-American and Native American writers are now telling the true story of how the USA was built on the oppression and slavery of the black peoples, and on the genocide of the indigenous peoples.[34]

The Puritans came from the old world to the new to do the Lord's bidding, to build Zion in the wilderness, a place where the light could shine and where Christ could usher in the kingdom of the millennium. The massacre of the indigenous peoples and profits from the African slave trade were justified in the name of the Lord's will and 'manifest destiny'. American Protestantism damned the 'Indians', reduced the blacks to 'soulless animals' and made a virtue of expanding capitalism; racism and 'democracy' went hand in hand; might was right.

White intellectuals moulded a 'god' to reassure these Puritans that what they were doing, no matter how bloody, as they occupied Indian, Inuit, Mexican and Hawaiian lands, was right and necessary.

The Christian religion was traded to the 'natives' because it was thought that the influence of the Gospel would make them more submissive. It was said by both Native Americans and Africans that: 'The missionaries came and they had the Bible and we had the land. And then they said, "Let us pray". And when we opened our eyes, we had the Bible and they had the land.'[35]

All indigenous peoples, with their belief in a mystical relationship between Earth, sun and collective land, were seen as obstacles to 'progress' and expansionism. The natural peoples, for whom there was no separation between daily life and religion, saw that the whites both hated and wanted to possess the Earth and nature.[36]

The white north Americans are the first people in history to have entirely ignored the ancient sacred pathways and centres of the native lands. Cut off from their psychic roots, they created a society that is violent, mad and utterly alienated, a culture that believes that anything artificial or synthetic is superior because it is 'man-made' and not created and nurtured by mother nature.

Paula Gunn Allen, who is part Laguna Pueblo/Sioux as well as of Lebanese and Scottish descent, writes in *The Sacred Hoop – Recovering the Feminine in American Tradition*[37] that it was under the influence of the white man and enforced Christianity that some Native American men slowly came to accept a patriarchal version of the world and ways of living. She says that white American feminists did not have to look to early Greece, Sumeria or Crete for evidence of early matriarchal cultures as these already existed in the USA until relatively recently, and to some extent still do. The Native American communities were, until very recently, tribal, matrifocal and matrilinear, respectful of all that lives on the sacred body of the Earth Mother and for the most part peaceful. 'The great spirit', now assumed to be male to accommodate monotheistic Christians, was originally Spider or Thought Woman who thinks beings into life as well as biologically creating them and the entire universe from the electromagnetic web spun from her cosmic body. Thought Woman's power of mind gives rise to biological organisms as well as cultures and transformations of all kinds.

The puritan work ethic went hand-in-hand with the belief that wealth and success were blessed by 'God-the-Father'. Prosperity is next to godliness. This is today believed by fundamentalists and New Agers alike. Not for them Jesus' message that 'the meek will inherit the Earth' and 'blessed are the poor'.

Today we find some New Agers solidly behind US politics and its economy – which depends on its weapons industry and needs wars and hunger in the Third World. They believe that the USA is the 'land of the free, and home of democracy' and has a special role in the 'coming planetisation of mankind'. There seems, indeed, to be a strong link between some New Age advocates and US power élites.

Nuclear Power and Destruction of the Earth

The USA, the anticipated initiator of the New Age global neo-Atlantean civilisation prophesied by the Theosophist Helena Blavatsky and others, has, amongst other things, provided the world with nuclear weapons and nuclear waste.

Colonialism and nuclear power go hand-in-hand. In the west the build-up of nuclear power stations and weapons strengthens the police state and there is a corresponding curtailment of freedom and information which comes with the dangers and secrecy inherent in a nuclear world. There is hardly a part of the world, outside of the eastern bloc and China, where the USA does not have military and nuclear bases. Indigenous peoples from the Inuit (Eskimos) in Alaska where nuclear weapons are stored, to Hawaii (once a Polynesian queendom and now the fiftieth state of America), headquarters of the US Pacific command and full of military installations, including the naval base of Pearl Harbor, suffer most.[38]

The education for submission and the colonisation of Afro- and Native Americans in the name of white imperialist power is happening in the Pacific region in the world today. The Pacific peoples are being sacrificed for the sake of the 'nuclear deterrent'. While the western world is preparing for the possibility of a nuclear war, people of the Pacific are dying from the results of nuclear weapons testing. For the past forty years, they have lived through a nuclear nightmare.

There have been something in the region of 250 nuclear-bomb tests in the Pacific, instigated by the USA and France, since the end of the Second World War. These tests in the Pacific have devastated entire cultures, destroyed whole islands, caused the island peoples to die from radiation illnesses and have made women give birth to deformed babies not recognisable as human.

The US network of bases in the Pacific region is vast; its power is economic and political as well as military. The military safeguards the trading routes as more than 40 per cent of US trade passes through the Pacific.

The USA maintains an island-based defence line running in an arc from the Indian Ocean to Japan; a satellite operations centre links the Philippines (which was forced to allow the USA a rent-free lease on twenty-three bases in exchange for aid) with Hawaii, South Korea (where the USA backs a dictatorship) and Diego Garcia. Japan dumps vast amounts of nuclear waste from its thirty-one nuclear power stations into the Pacific. The USA also has plans to incinerate or dump chemical weapons.

After the Second World War, the USA engineered the administration of Micronesia which was designated a 'strategic trust territory'. It was agreed to protect the peoples and promote their development towards independence. This was to be overseen by the United Nations Security Council.

What has happened?

A nuclear apartheid prevails throughout Micronesia. The US military motive for keeping control there is to provide a base for 'star wars' anti-satellite testing at Kwajalein in the Marshall Islands which is the USA's major testing ground for long-range ballistic missiles. The people of Kwajalein have been forced to move out to Ebeye Island, five kilometres away, where 8,000 people live in squalor on only sixty-six acres of land.

From 1946 to 1958, the USA conducted sixty-six atmospheric tests on the Marshall Islands, leaving fourteen islands uninhabitable, and vaporised another six. The weapons included the hydrogen bomb: the largest was called 'Bravo' and had a destructive capacity a thousand times greater than that of the Hiroshima bomb. The small population of the islands served as a human laboratory where the effects of radiation and nuclear fallout could be observed and analysed.

When 'Bravo' was exploded, the people on Rongelop, 160 kilometres away, and on nearby Uterik, were not evacuated or warned, although the US authorities knew full well that the wind was blowing in their direction. The weather conditions were, in fact, anticipated. Children played with the radioactive white ash from the fallout, thinking it was soap powder. The entire population suffered from radiation burns and is now dying from leukaemia and thyroid illnesses, while the women suffer innumerable still births and give birth to 'jelly babies'.

A US Atomic Energy Commission report in 1957 said: 'The inhabitation of these people in the island [Rongelop] will afford most valuable ecological radiation data on human beings.'[39]

Because the sea around the Pacific islands is polluted, the indigenous people's livelihood is in jeopardy. Their lands are taken from them to make room for US installations and they are forced to live in utter squalor and poverty in slums, dependent on handouts, while the US military personnel live in western-style luxury and comfort.

In Micronesia, people are organising for a nuclear-free Pacific. Belau became the first nation in the world to create a nuclear-free constitution in 1979. In 1987 New Zealand/ Aotearoa also became nuclear-free. Ever since then these islands have been harassed by the USA which has resorted to murder and victimisation as the islands are wanted as military harbour bases for Trident submarines.

In 1962, following Algerian independence, France moved its test site from the Sahara to Moruroa Atoll in French Polynesia which consists of 400 islands, including Tahiti. From 1966 to 1975 the French conducted forty-one atmospheric tests. Moruroa Atoll is now sinking into the lagoon, its structure totally destroyed. In 1975 France switched to underground tests which have continued to the present time. The nuclear policy has not changed with Mitterand as a 'socialist' president of France. There is now a great struggle in both New Caledonia (Kanaky) and in Tahiti for independence, but as up to 40 per cent of the world's nickel deposits, vital for arms manufacture, are to be found in the land of the Kanaks, this would seem to be an unlikely possibility.

The British conducted twenty-one atmospheric nuclear tests between 1952 and 1958 on Aboriginal lands in Maralina and Monte Bello in Australia without the peoples' consent. The Aboriginal peoples were not warned or removed. Many have since gone blind and have died from cancer. The British left the land devastated and contaminated. The suffering of the Aboriginal people went unnoticed by the whites, until it was discovered in the

1980s that many of the 20,000 British and Australian servicemen who were exposed to radiation and fallout were also dying from cancer.[40]

Joan Wingfield, an aboriginal woman activist of the Kokotha people, and Charlie Ching, a leader of the independence movement in Tahiti, spoke in Bristol in May 1988 with great grief about the genocide of their gentle peoples and of the utter indifference of the white western world. (Joan has also given evidence to the Sizewell enquiry, and Ching has spent many years in and out of French prisons for opposing French nuclear policies in Polynesia.)

That meeting in Bristol was organised by Women Working for a Nuclear-Free and Independent Pacific, which is a nationwide network of women's groups in Britain, initiated originally by Zohl, an Australian woman, and other women living at one time at the women's camps at Greenham Common. From their newsletter, meetings and publications,[41] I have learned all I know about what is happening in the Pacific and for which I have a great sense of shame, as I am myself a westerner.

Australia has 30 per cent of the world's uranium reserves. Under pressure from mining companies, the Labour government has backtracked on its electoral promises to the Aboriginal peoples on land rights legislation. Roxby Downs Mine is situated on traditional Aboriginal land which belongs to the Kokotha people. To the Kokotha it is land of which they are the guardians, and part of the 'dreamtime', or otherworld consciousness of the relationship with the ancestors and the sacred land. The mine is jointly being developed by BP (British Petroleum) and Western Mining of Australia. Some of its uranium is destined for Sizewell and from there plutonium goes to US nuclear weapons production. Many of the sacred sites have already been destroyed, and the central mining shaft goes through a particularly important site – straight through the multicoloured belly of the 'dreamtime lizard' as Joan Wingfield told us, while the airstrip goes right through the ancestors' burial ground.

Aboriginal culture has known for thousands of years that the ability to destroy the planet lay dormant under their sacred sites in the rock called uranium.

The Roxby Down mining companies are pretending that uranium is incidental to the gold and copper extracted there. Uranium is found in the copper. The mining of uranium is extremely dangerous and lung cancer is caused by the radon gas and decay products released during mining. It permanently devastates the environment and the tailings (the ground rock remaining after uranium has been removed) stays radioactive for some 80,000 years.

I once heard Shorty O'Neil of the Aborginal Commission to Europe speaking about present-day uranium mining and British nuclear bomb testing in the 1950s in Australia. He said that the underground waterways of the Earth are the blood vessels of Her body and that if the waters are interfered with in one place, a whole forest fed by the waters might die many miles away; that radiation discharged into the waters from the uranium mines poisons all the streams, is carried away far underground and finally out into the oceans which are dying as a result.

He also said that the Aboriginal peoples consider themselves the guardians of the Earth where they were born and where they also want to die, that we are here to cherish the sacred land and take care of Her, that if we die away from our ancestral burial grounds, we will become lost spirits and will not be received back into Her.

A Warning . . .

Nuclear scientists and the US government are gambling not only with our present lives and with those of the coming generations but also with our souls and our bodies of rebirth through our Mother the Earth for all eternity.

An Australian Aboriginal woman Oodgeroo Noomical (Kate Walker) has this to say:

> But time is running out
> and time is close at hand,
> for the dreamtime folk are amassing
> to defend their timeless land . . .

The experience of the womb is the source of extrasensory powers; the Mother's womb is a condensed experience of the cosmos. An old Jewish myth says: 'In his mother's womb man knows the universe and forgets it at birth.' But patriarchy has created violent contradictions between life and death, womb and tomb.

If we cannot now regain a vision of the symbiotic relation between us and nature/cosmos, as that between a mother and her children, we shall surely die.

2
Dreaming the Sacred Land

My Initiation to the Goddess at Avebury/Silbury

I want to write of my own experiences of dreamtime in the sacred and timeless landscape. The word 'dreamtime' comes from Aboriginal Australia where this otherworld consciousness of the connectedness with the ancestors and with the sacred tribal land is an all-creative force. Ancestor-spirits created the ancient places of power and by following in their journeying and performing rituals where they still dwell, the people relive the sacred which is not only of the past but also of the present. Peoples such as the Aboriginal Australians retain an experience of the creation and the sacred as now and of the ancestor spirits as forever present and to be experienced in the land itself. There is a benevolent, collective and nurturing relationship between the spirits, the people and the land.[1]

The neolithic peoples who lived in the British Isles and who created the great stone circles, the mounds and long barrows, had a very similar sense of the sacred. To them, the land was the body of the Great Mother who is the original creator and ancestress, and at such sacred places as Avebury, Silbury and West Kennet Long Barrow on the Wiltshire Downs in the South of England, the entire peasant population would have journeyed with the land and lived the sacred year cycle,[2] the birth, death and re-birth of plants, animals, humans and of the Goddess Herself as experienced in dreamtime.

The ancients followed the wheel of the year with its eight festivals, four of which were solar (the solstices and the equinox) and four of which were lunar and fire festivals. The lunar festivals (that were celebrated by the Celts and still are by the people of the pagan Craft tradition) are Imbolc or Bride's Day around the time of 1 February, Beltane on 1 May, Lammas or Lughnasadh on 1 August and Samhain on 1 November. They are about the dissolution of the boundaries between the physical and the spiritual that lead to higher states of consciousness and are times of shamanic journeys into other realms.

Imbolc or Bride's Day is the time when the Goddess re-emerges as the young Brigid/Bride bringing the greening of nature; she is the corn maiden, the warming of the waters of wells and rivers, the lambing of the ewes and the abundance of milk from cows. Beltane was celebrated at the time of Her sexual fullness and as May Queen. She performs the sacred marriage with Her lover, the horned god. This was the time of orgiastic sexual rites within the Avebury stone circle. At Lammas, the Goddess of Earth becomes Mother. Silbury mound is Her great pregnant womb and here the peasant population would gather as they did until the last century to watch the birth of the Lammas or harvest child and the first fruits were given to Her. This was the time of the cutting of the corn and therefore also a time of sacrifice. Silbury is the primordial navel of the world, the sacred mountain that generates an energy that inspires high states of madness and gives oracular powers. Everywhere in the world there are such sacred mountains of the Goddess. On Crete they are still called the 'Mothers' and in Germany sibyls or prophetesses dwelled on their heights.

Samhain, to the Celts, was the beginning of the new year because, to them, darkness comes first and gives birth to the light. They had a calendar of thirteen lunar months.

Night-time was, to them, a source of, and not the death of, light. The Dark Mother, Cailleach, was the source of inspiration and visions. At the time of the waning moon in November, the crone or hag Goddess retreated into Her mountainfastness or into Her tombs as at West Kennet Long Barrow where She becomes the womb of death and rebirth. The Celts believed that the stone circles, standing stones and cromlechs were dropped out of the apron of the giantess Cailleach who, in the spring, re-emerges as Bride. The daughter and the ancient Mother are one and the same, and this is the mystery.

I now want to relate an experience I had at Silbury/Avebury in 1978 that had a profound effect on me and utterly changed my life. I wrote this down a few days after what happened in what can only be described as a prophetic or trance state.[3]

> Five days after Imbolc/Bride's Day, the ancient quarter-day fire festival of the pre-Celtic Brigid who was worshipped by the Celts until very recently. Imbolc means 'ewe's milk' and was celebrated by the Celts as the first day of spring when the penned-up animals were let out in the fields and the first lambs were born. Brigid/Bride was the Goddess of healing, of the flocks and of plantlife, of childbirth, the waters, fire, smithcraft and poetry. Perhaps ancient Avebury/Silbury was Hers – or belonged to Anu/Danu. Danu/Bride was probably the original mother/daughter unity. They were the same as Demeter/Kore of the ancients and of the Celts of these isles.
>
> We arrived on a beautiful late winter's day at Avebury village, parked the old post office van and ate our mushroom salad. The village is built, and contained within the stone circle. (The neolithic stone circle at Avebury is the largest one in northern Europe.) Amazing, rough, squat, colossal stones, seeming like human bodies and gigantic heads. Here one feels is the centre of the Mother Goddess. What would it be like living in this village, being part of Her living body? The earth around the stone circle is shaped and moulded in ridges and ditches. Many of the stones are mutilated, like half a head chopped off – painful to see. Many are missing and ugly-looking

triangular-shaped stones have been positioned to mark where they fell or once stood. They look like gravestones. During the witch-hunts of the burning times the stones were deliberately destroyed, split apart and buried, the Church fearing their power. That great power still remains, and there is a beauty and mystery in this whole space and its stones.

We follow the earth-works around the entire circle and then slowly follow the remains of West Kennet stone avenue as it winds its way across the fields.

The magic mushrooms (in the salad we had mixed in some psilocybin) have now taken effect. I long to arrive at Silbury Mound, the pregnant earth womb of the Mother. We have seen Her in the distance from the road and from the village. I clutch a stone in my hand for safety and we plod across the ploughed and muddy fields, continually having to cross barbed-wire fences. Gripped by panic, unable either to remain or to cross over the ugly, offensive fences; wanting to find comfort and refuge with the breast/eye/womb-belly rising out of the landscape, naked and vulnerable. We scramble through what seems like marshland and wilderness, and I feel as if transported thousands of years back in time. We come closer to Her womb and discover that on the road by Her side there is parked a square bright red lorry with the name 'Peter Lord' written on its side . . . Lord . . . oh no . . . is there nowhere, not even in Her presence when one is allowed to forget about patriarchy and its deadly godhead?

Nearer Her mound we discover notices that say, 'The monument is closed due to erosion'. Her womb, surrounded by water, is everywhere shut off by treble layers of barbed-wire fences. Feeling stunned . . . the earth around the mound appears to move and flicker . . . some swans are frozen motionless . . . I feel caught in eternity. Some teenagers scramble past us up the mound. We follow them, hoping they won't talk with us, we who are from another century. Feelings of fear at daring to trample on Her belly, the grass matted and unkempt.

A man shouts from the road: 'Get down from there!' We sit down on the side of the mound furthest away from the road; the teenagers disappear out of sight and hearing. I am overtaken with a sudden and enormous grief . . . the Mother . . . the entire mound cries through me. I am at one with Her, grieving at our lost women-cultures . . . the pollution and death of Her land all around us.

What have they done to you, Mother, what have they done . . . what have they done . . . ? I feel overwhelming fear . . . am a hunted female animal . . . got to flee . . . got to get down from Her womb and away from the road, away. The road appears to stand for everything alien and evil: motors, men with patriarchal authority, oppression. Shots are heard regularly in the distance. (The nearby Salisbury Plain is Ministry of Defence land and is used for army exersises.) . . . Aeroplanes fly continuously overhead . . . evil, evil, danger . . .

Almost run, slide down Her side . . . walk slowly . . . great effort, fear . . . tracing our way around the water-moat, back into the fields whence we came. Feeling of victory; we had avoided the road we are safe . . . we are still within Her nature. I look at Her mound . . . so exposed . . . like veins on a breast streaking Her sides . . . again overwhelmed by tears and sorrow. I now understand what Mother Earth means . . . something so enormous, powerful . . . also so painful in my own woman's body which is like Hers . . . violent but gentle . . . powerful but vulnerable.

Slowly we follow the river, feeling myself floating with Her . . . flowing with the wonderful water formations . . . dancing along with Her serpentine rhythms. Sudden sharp halt at the sight of the pollution of the waters and the rubbish accumulated there . . . anger, anger. More barbed-wire fences . . . We follow the direction leading to West Kennet Long Barrow and walk up a long mud track. We see the Long Barrow at the summit and the enormous stones covering the entrance. We walk around the stones . . .

and *suddenly* . . . we see the stark blackness from the entrance of the cunt/mouth into Her underground womb. Fear at being swallowed up by the so-intense darkness . . . but I overcome the fear and enter . . . totally another world in there . . . of mystery . . . of power . . . of peace. Sounds are amplified in here and the stone chambers appear for a timeless moment to breathe. I feel like gyrating . . . I feel like a spiral . . . then feel a great urge to sleep on the floor in the uterus-room at the end of the passage . . . great stillness in Her living darkness. Feeling infinitely 'higher' within the tomb temple than when re-entering the world outside . . . strange and powerful vibrations (perhaps emanating from powerful underground waters?) . . . here no feeling of sorrow and vulnerability. This is the place of the winter/death/cosmic waters/rebirth/the dark aspect of the Goddess . . . we are here within Her season and we are welcome . . . We walk down the mud track . . . feeling an enormous tiredness and exhaustion . . . just want to sleep . . . to sleep. We trace our way back to Avebury village across the fields and the public footpaths . . . we retrace our way around the stone circle and arrive six hours later back at our van and drive off . . .

During the years that have gone by since this original initiation into Her mysteries, I have visited Avebury/Silbury many times at different seasons and various times of day and night. I have also slept within West Kennet Long Barrow, dreaming of the ancestors.

The first time I experienced the Goddess – had sensed Her powers within me – had been at the natural home birth of my second son in 1961. From then on I had felt that I was mystically in communication with, and guided in my painting by, ancient women, who perhaps in fact co-exist with us still, in a different dimension of reality.

I feel as if I receive the images in my paintings from ancient times . . . as though I am but a medium for an energy wanting to be expressed and given form. I feel that the British Isles were probably sacred islands of the north as Malta and Crete were in the south. Everywhere on these islands one comes across remains of ancient cultures and there is still great power that we can reach and be transformed by, embedded within the stones, the earth and the waters, in the sacred places. If one is present there – with the true openness and reverence – at certain times of the year when the spirit roams through the land and the moon is in Her appropriate phrase, then one is profoundly changed in one's psyche and awareness. This is as true today as it was in the past.

It is apt that during the 'trip' I had at Avebury, I should have seen three swans in the water-moat around Silbury Mound, since these are sacred birds of the Goddess. There are many tales of fairy-women transforming themselves into swans.

At Avebury I was helped by the sacred mushroom, psilocybin, to enter into Her reality, into another space and time. I feel that these tiny breast-shaped mushrooms that grow so abundantly all over these islands, are also the Mother's gift to us and one of the many ways in which She is now fighting for Her survival against the matricide planned by nuclear and genetic scientists. They have a way of reaching into the most hidden depths of our psyches and are capable of opening us up to intense communication with living and enspirited nature all around us. This experience of intense openness to all of organic and growing nature, feeling its breath and vibrating life, stayed with me for a long time. As a result the sea, stones, mountains and wells have appeared more and more in my images since then. Until that time my work had been mainly concerned with creating large, figurative paintings envisaging and bringing the Goddess into being in powerful women-figures.

As a result of my initiation to the Goddess at Silbury, I decided that I had to leave the city to live in the countryside and in 1980 I moved with my then lover, and my son, Leif, to a cottage near Fishguard in Pembrokeshire (now called Dyfed) in Wales. We lived there for a period of five years until the tragic death of my son.

Even there we found that we were only about eighteen miles from Brawdy which is the major US base for spying on and tracking Soviet nuclear submarines in the world. In nearby Trecwn there were rumours of missiles hidden within caves under the Preselau mountains. Many military nuclear missile installations are placed close to sacred sites. This is true of Greenham, Aldermaston and Burleigh, so near to both Stonehenge and Avebury. Brocken, which was the most sacred mountain of Germany where the people of the Craft gathered for Walpurgisnacht/Beltane May night celebrations, has been until recently a secret military East German zone.

It is a chilling thought that not only are many military installations placed near sacred sites – as if to drain their energies for malevolent purposes – but also that uranium is mined from under many Aboriginal Australian and Native American ancestral burial grounds and places of power. Perhaps the Aboriginal rainbow-serpent, that is multicoloured and dwells within the Earth, is the occult power of such substances as uranium. The Hopi people in the USA have prophecies that warn that if uranium is taken from out of the land, it will bring disaster upon us; but remaining in its natural place it might, in fact, have uncanny and benevolent powers. Who knows? The natural peoples are still the guardians of the sacred Mother Earth as were the women shamans of old. It is interesting in this context that pagan comes from the Latin word *paganus* which means land-dweller, and heathen means 'of the heath'.

With hindsight it now seems as if that fear and grief I experienced on Silbury that February day in 1978 was a foreboding both of my young son's death, and of what would happen at Greenham Common.

It so happens that it was on Silbury at Beltane full moon in 1985, that I first met Musawa, the American woman who I and my son, Leif, then fifteen years old, went to visit some months later in the South of France in August 1985. My son was killed there on a full moon. I had even written that the people recognised death as one of the sources of the first-fruit ceremonies and that Lammas was not only a time of birth, but also of sacrifice. My son was red (hair), black and white (mixed African and Swedish), the colours of the Goddess. There was a time after his death when I feared the Mother at Silbury . . . but since then I have made my peace with Her and have again experienced Her great love and grief. She is after all my son's Greater Mother and how can I presume to know better than Her?

I have always felt that the women at Greenham were somehow and in a mystical (dreamtime?) way inspired and empowered by the Goddess at Silbury in these dangerous times when She is fighting for Her survival and rising within us. She speaks to us through Her sacred places.

Dreaming the Sacred Land

My initiation at Silbury was a very personal experience. Now I write of another dream-journeying, this time across Salisbury Plain military land with a group of women from 30 April to 4 May 1985. This extremely powerful and empowering pilgrimage was magical and a highly political direct action which as far as I am concerned is a truly spiritual–political women's way.

We thought of ourselves as a tribe and moved as one body across the Plain.

I had set off from Pembrokeshire on 29 April 1985, hitching with Jill Smith and her baby Taliesin, born in the tipi village in the Black Mountains in Wales, in order to have some time to ourselves at Avebury before joining up with the Greenham women who had sent out a call for this walk. We found that two of the women from Galloway, whom I had got to know during actions at Greenham, had also arrived early. That night the five of us slept under the open sky on Silbury as it would have been unthinkable to put tent pegs in our Mother's belly. As a result, we experienced a cold and windy night during which, at one point, it felt as if we were watched over by a fairy presence.

In the early morning we went to greet Swallowhead, which is an opening looking like a vagina in a white chalk embankment from which the river Kennet emerges.

After meditating there, we carried on up to West Kennet Long Barrow. Time for breakfast in the friendly Ridgeway café and then on to Avebury to greet friends who were arriving. We joined a group of punk women from Greenham sitting within the stones. Police were also gathering by now, and when we were sitting later at the foot of Silbury having our lunch they approached us and warned us not to entertain any ideas of camping for the night anywhere in the vicinity. We all knew, however, that we would sleep on Silbury and by late afternoon we gathered up there.

This was the night of Beltane and we were here to celebrate the Mother. We made a Beltane-fire carefully so as not to damage the mound, and then gathered to discuss a possible ritual. By now, we had been joined by the American wise woman/witch, Starhawk.[4]

I shared with the women the vision I had had for so long of women reclaiming Silbury as our very own. (And for some years Silbury indeed became a place for a women's yearly unofficial festival at Lammas in August at full moon.) Starhawk, an experienced leader of ritual, suggested that we cast a circle, call in the elements, ground ourselves and dance the spiral dance. We danced and drummed and chanted in great joy. It was this night that I met Musawa and we got talking. Finally we slept, curled up close together around the mound like children on our Mother's belly or breast.

Next morning we were about a hundred women who set off along the Ridgeway, ambling through the green and lush countryside. It was a very long day and we finally arrived exhausted to set up camp in the area of the rubbish-dump on Redhorn Hill on the northern edge of Salisbury Plain and in view of the barbed-wire fences surrounding the Ministry of Defence land. The place was soon transformed into a comfortable women's space with tents, fires, cooking and women talking and singing in the gathering dusk.

Next morning, 2 May, we gathered around the fire to discuss what to do because the red flags, signifying firing in progress within the ranges, were up. Starhawk led a grounding meditation to centre ourselves and then we took the decision to walk through the fences irrespective of the firing. In the meantime, women were facing the barbed-wire fences whilst singing 'Earth is our Mother'. I had joined them for a while but was overwhelmed with tears and grief at the sight of those so-beautiful women and the thought of the patriarchal wasteland of destruction and barrenness that lay in front of us once we had entered the Plain.

I had joined a few women who performed a ritual burying of a Goddess figurine in the central firepit we had been using. When we went to find the other women, we found to our horror that there was no one there, and we were told that the women had breached the fence and had been rounded up and arrested. The feeling I had was that we were the only three women left on this Earth and that it was our responsibility to save Her. As we ran past the fences we saw to our relief that the women were there circling, dancing and singing while surrounded by police trying to contain them. We argued with the police who finally realised they would have to arrest every one of us women, or let us go on. Orders came through that the firing would cease for that day and that we could carry on.

We walked close together and at a slow pace because there were older women as well as mothers with young children. It was also safer. No way was it possible to stray off the ugly and bumpy 'road' that normally carried only trucks and military vehicles, as there were live shells and mines embedded in the land around us. There were no animals in sight, no birds sang and there were hardly any trees to give us shade from the sun.

It was eerie and dreary walking here, and hard going indeed.

That evening, we put up camp by the Bustard hotel which was still on military land, something I didn't realise until next morning when, yet again, we were surrounded by a large number of policemen who were attempting to barricade our path. This happened again and again on this last lap of the journey before reaching Stonehenge in the afternoon. The police seemed set on playing some kind of game of cat and mouse with us – except that we refused to be the mice. A number of times there were lines of police with army vehicles . . . they tried to drag women away but we linked arms and walked and circled many abreast and we would not allow any woman to be taken off. For some reason, the police were always called away at the very last moment. We saw both policemen and policewomen throwing their helmets on the ground in pure frustration at not being able to arrest us. It was strange indeed and we felt somehow protected. At last we left military land behind us and celebrated by picnicking, dancing, drumming and singing, all the while being watched by bewildered police. This was on Friday, the day of the great Scandinavian/Germanic goddess Freya.

We saw animals again in the fields but were struck dumb with anger and pain when we were met on the road by a herd of cows that looked utterly ill-used and maltreated. Some were barely able to walk because of the size of their udders and some had very bad legs, full of sores, that they were dragging painfully along bit by bit. To us, in our by now heightened state, this was yet another reminder of the fates of mothers – whether animal or human – in patriarchal societies. We had an argument with the young farmer who seemed unable to understand our point of view, profit being uppermost in his mind. Women were crying. It was terrible.

We had been told that we would not be allowed to camp by Stonehenge – but then a message came through that we could use the auxiliary car park right next to the toilets and the tea caravans. Tourists coming to visit the stones saw in amazement our banner saying, 'Salisbury Plain Women's Peace Camp', and notices explaining why we were there. By now we seemed like an invincible and unstoppable army of women/witches and felt magically empowered. Some women even cut holes in the razor-wire fences set up around the stones in preparation for the midsummer Stonehenge freak festival, and that night slept inside the monument.

I had, however, felt uneasy and declared my unease that the walk was to end at Stonehenge – a place which I experience as one of distorted and negative patriarchal energies that cannot be reclaimed or redeemed by women. We had many discussions about this and also disagreements. Nowhere else at the stone circles in Britain does one find deliberately shaped stones like the large sarsen stories forming the outer trilithon circle. Here I get a sense of heavy and brooding energies and the monument does not feel embedded in the maternal Earth but feels apart from Her.

On the other hand, the inner circle of blue stones feels more benevolent. These stones were brought from Carn Menyn in the Preselau mountains close to where I had lived during my five years in Pembrokeshire. Perhaps those stones once belonged to a more ancient moon temple of Cerridwen and represent Her womb or lunar crescent. (The function of the Aubrey holes, now filled with concrete, was to be a lunar eclipse calculator.)

Saturday, 4 May, was the night of a full moon total lunar eclipse, so this was perhaps after all the place to raise powerful Goddess energies. To the ancient peoples this appears to have been a time of extreme and powerful energies, perhaps a time of both fear and of magic.[5]

The Greenham women especially felt that Stonehenge,

imprisoned by the razor-wire and looking like Greenham itself, had to be liberated and reclaimed for the people.[6]

At 6 p.m. on 4 May, we cut holes through the fences and snaked our way into the stones across the field, all the while singing 'Return to the Mother' while police and tourists looked sheepishly on. Our number had by now increased since many women had come from London, Bristol and other nearby places to join us just for the weekend. Once within Stonehenge, we gave these ancient beings loving care and energies and danced for hours amongst and with the blue stones; we meditated, sang, lit candles and dreamed. The sky was cloudy most of the afternoon and evening but around 9 p.m. it cleared and, during a hushed silence, we could clearly watch the miraculously eclipsed moon. We stood there entranced on the grass outside the stones humming and singing softly while she went through her changes. Following the eclipse, a delicate sliver of silver radiance showed itself and slowly, slowly, she became visible again in her glorious radiant full moon roundness. This was true magic indeed.

Many women slept that night amongst the stones in the moonlight but there was trouble with the police. Some, who later tried to set up camp at a local farm, were arrested, but the majority had left for home because of the sudden bad weather.

We had been dreaming our land.

Many pagans and people of the Craft have a love for the land and a reverence for the Earth, but many too do not realise that this is not enough and that one must also take political direct action against those that ill-treat and exploit Her. It was this understanding that fired the women on our walk.

Our sense of having been magically empowered by the Earth Herself, the Goddess, stayed with each woman for a long time and we felt blessed.[7]

Journeys in the Celtic World

The experience at Avebury had inspired me to seek out other sacred places in Britain. Soon after, in 1978, I set off with some friends and children to travel down through Somerset and Devon to Kernow/Cornwall. We went through Dartmoor and Bodmin Moor and were amazed at the wealth of ancient remains everywhere around us: neolithic stone circles and cromlechs, standing stones and cairns, stone rows and hut circles; in areas now totally uninhabited and desolate. And not to forget the primordial tors, volcanic rock formations of immense power, inhabited by the fairy race.[8]

We visited a magnificent dolmen/cromlech ('cromlechau' means 'chamber of stone' and 'men' means 'stone' as in *menhir* in Welsh) called Spinster's Rock. It stands in a field on Dartmoor. Cromlechs consist of a number of vertical stones surmounted by a giant capstone. Some would have orginally been covered with mounds of earth and stone; they were never just burial places but places of power connected with the underground waters and star energies, and spirits of the dead.

It is said that this cromlech was built by a giant woman, Cailleach (the hag, crone or old woman), who moves mountains and carries the massive stones of the sacred circles and cairns in Her apron. She is the dark Mother of the Scottish highlands and islands. She was, perhaps, Danu/Anu, Goddess of the stone/megalith builder, tomb-Goddess of death and rebirth. There are innumerable remains of fires and feasting by the barrows.

There were few individual burials until the Bronze Age with its hierarchical and warlike society. Before then the Mother Goddess was the guardian of the seed hidden in the Earth. She was the guardian of the dead awaiting rebirth. The newly dead were seen to be particularly powerful and could be contacted during shamanistic trances within the darkness of the vulva-shaped cromlech or womb-shaped long barrows, when important healing and prophetic knowledge could be gained through them. The dead were thought to await rebirth inside the Earth womb. The cromlechs and barrows symbolised the entrance – the womb of death and rebirth – to the ancestral spirit-world, the otherworld, the dream-place of past and present, where psychic and physical realities merge. The ancient communal tomb was the source of power where energies meet and where one is closer to the sacred. Shamans in all ages have retreated into caves and rock-cut chambers to gain knowledge and to communicate with the spirit-world.

The megalithic stone monuments and the neolithic culture of Britain and Ireland, like that in Britanny, are thought to have been created by an ancient Iberian pre-Celtic people who were small, fine-featured and dark-skinned. They might have been related to the present-day Sami/Finno peoples of the far north. Their descendants still live on the fringes of the Celtic world. Their shamans would have been women who guarded the mysteries and led the rituals, communicating with the dead and the otherworld. They were peaceful, understood the calendar, knew the solstices and the lunar alignments. They also believed in reincarnation. The stone circles have been called lunar temples/observatories. A most important astrological function was to predict lunar eclipses and the tides of the seas.

Orgiastic rites would have been held in the light of the full moon, the giver of all creativity and fertility of mind, psyche and body. Any children born as a result of heterosexual rites would have been called 'virgin-born', mothered by the moon.

There appears to be a link between religious experience and women's sexuality. There are unique connections between the female forebrain and cerebellum that may account for the fact that some women experience orgasm so intensely that they enter altered states of consciousness similar to religious experience. Was this the reason why shamanism was originally a women's technique of ecstasy? Men, according to this theory, cannot reach these same transcendental heights because they lack the neurological capability to integrate pleasure into the neocortex or high brain centre, and so their sexual pleasure is mainly reflexive. This may account for the reason that, in all male-dominated religions of a God the father, sexuality is denied and devalued because true sexuality is about ecstatic union with the other as an equal in the mysteries of the Great Mother.

Women's sexual receptivity is not bound to the ovarian cycles, as amongst other mammals, and its primary function is not reproductive but for sexual joy and loving bonding. No such evolutionary changes have taken place in human males. Women have the neurobiological advantage of being able to integrate the conscious and unconscious mind.[9]

Only when women are free will humanity evolve as intended.

In the Goddess-religions, ecstatic sexual rites expressing all forms of sexuality are integral to Her worship, while male-centred religions practise denial of sexuality (particularly in women) and attempt to separate mind from body, spirit from matter, and enforce rigid male-controlled heterosexuality. In the Goddess-cultures men were initiated into the mysteries by women. This is still so in tantric writings and was so among the Celts.

The stones and the stone circles are always associated with water. They are encircled by underground waters and are placed above geodetic spirals of great magic and healing powers. They are placed by wells and rivers, by the sea or on sacred islands surrounded by water on all sides. The great oceans are the Mother of all life and the wells springing up from inside the earth were felt to be Her menstrual/lifegiving and healing blood. The stone 'circles' are never exact geometric circles but are organic and resemble wombs, caves and pots.

There are many stone circles near Land's End in Kernow/Cornwall and are called such names as 'Merry

Maidens', 'Nine Maidens'. The story goes that the stones had once been foolish young women who had been dancing and merrymaking on the sabbath and as a punishment were petrified by the vengeful, puritanical and joyless Jehovah. The local people obviously associate the stone circles with women, dancing and music – and defiance of the patriarchal male god!

Holed stones were widely believed to possess healing powers. We visited one such stone, called 'Men-an-Tol' on a bleak moor near Morvah. It was believed to have a fairy guardian who could work miraculous cures. Children suffering from rickets were passed through its hole nine times and barren women who passed through were thought to become fertile. Holed stones were usually positioned at the entrance of burial chambers and symbolised the birth passage of the mother in rites of initiation and rebirth.

We crawled through the Men-an-Tol in the mud and rain.

There is an extraordinary amount of quartz in the sacred stones everywhere. Quartz is a crystalline mineral and a carrier of electromagnetic currents. It is thought to have healing powers and is supposed to dispense wisdom and the power of divination (fortune-tellers use a crystal ball of quartz); it was (and still is) universally used in shamanistic rituals. Near where I lived in Wales there is a magnificent cromlech situated on the very beautiful coast and with the sea behind it. Half its upright stones are plain sandstone, while facing them are stones speckled with large chunks of quartz. The enormous capstone, weighing twenty-five tons, has a similar quartz content.

It has been found that certain standing stones associated with stone circles generate ultrasound when stimulated by elements in the electromagnetic spectrum radiated by the sun at dawn. It is interesting to see that within the Craft in the covens, the participants dance within a circle to build up a psychic power cone which can be directed towards a certain goal – to heal or to destroy. The ancients did this within the stone circles in the light of the moon.

It has been suggested that the ancient 'straight line' grid system of the leys was, in fact, an early attempt to contain female creative energies and for control, centralisation and kingship. The Earth spirit does not move in a straight line, however, but in constantly flowing serpentine and spiral movements.

One hears over and over again in early patriarchal accounts how the head of the serpent was staked by driving pegs into the ground and how the dragon/monster was in later myth slaughtered by the solar hero. Out of the dead body of the mother he then fashions the male universe.

Since that first initiation at Silbury, I have made innumerable journeys . . . to Carnac in Bretagne/Brittany, to the Callanish stone circle on the Isle of Lewis in the Outer Hebrides, to the Boyne Valley monuments not far from Dublin in Ireland and to many other places.

Whilst living in Cymru/Wales, I explored and became very familiar with many of the sacred sites of ancient and beautiful Pembrokeshire, her holy wells, magical trees, cromlechs and standing stones. She will always remain with me. Even though I was torn away from Wales because of the tragic circumstances of my young son's death and my oldest son's illness, in my dreams I still dwell there.

Several journeys to Ireland have made a very powerful impression on me, especially visits to the temples of the Goddess at Newgrange in the Boyne valley. This is what I wrote after my first pilgrimage there: 'Newgrange is a womb/tomb/temple of the mother of extraordinary power and beauty.' Here within Newgrange I felt, as I had done at Avebury/Silbury, a sense of recognition, of coming home, as if here is where I had once belonged. As an artist and a woman I perceived its space and form in a way that I felt sure had originated with ancient women, based on their female vision, power and wholeness, and coming from a time when motherhood was associated with creativity and high energies, but also with meditating stillness, from a time when the Goddess expressed gynandrous energies, yin and yang within Her. Here one senses woman-energies that patriarchal language simply has no expression for. I sensed within Newgrange – in Her living darkness – a maternal power, rounded in enormous stone spaces, that is both healing and fearful, dynamic and at rest. She is beyond all polarities; from Her emanate all energies.

Newgrange is a human-made earth mound that was probably originally covered in layers of organic material and faced with quartz, a ditch, ceremonial causeways, numerous small burial mounds, a sacred well, and a large henge of rough-hewn stones and single monoliths. It measures 700 feet in circumference and about forty to fifty feet in height. The earth mound is once again covered in quartz, which suggests the surface of a large egg which conceals the womb-like cave within. It also gives off a silvery lunar light.

Newgrange, which is contemporary with Avebury and the Goddess temples on Malta, is the cosmic egg, symbol of birth and creation and, as at West Kennet Long Barrow, one enters through a birth channel to emerge within the womb-shaped inner chambers. On the stone walls are carved spirals and zigzag shapes and wavy lines that, according to Marija Gimbutas, signify water.[10]

At the dawn of the midwinter solstice, the sun's dying rays enter the corbelled opening above the entrance to the mound and travel to the innermost chamber where they light up one of the sacred spiral designs. Here all could witness the death and the birth of the sun/son or daughter from the mother. Perhaps women were actually giving birth at the same moment in the large stone basins found in there. It seems that such hollowed-out stones were once used by women to ease childbirth. Perhaps they were filled with steam or vapour baths over which oracles made prophecies in trance-states for the coming year. The spiral, the labyrinth and the serpent are universal signs for the transformative powers of the Goddess, of death and rebirth. Every nineteenth year the lunar beam travels the same path into the womb of stone.

Martin Brennan, an American artist and writer,[11] has done much research at Newgrange, Knowth and Dowth. He thinks that the signs and repetition of the double and triple spirals carved on the gigantic entrance stones at Newgrange are charts which diagrammatically record the movements of the stars, sun and moon and that the ancients had developed a holistic mathematics and astrology not known to us. In ancient Ireland the sun was known as the Goddess Grainne or Granya and one derivation of Newgrange is 'The Cave of Granya'.[12] The Celts thought of the monument as the fairy palace, 'Brug na Boinne' of Queen Boann and her king Dagda, god of the Earth.

In Ireland I also came across the extraordinary stone-carved images of the Sheela-na-Gig, stark and giving the appearance of bone, showing just the skull-like face of the Goddess and Her hands holding wide open the genitals from which we come and to which we return. Sheela-na-Gigs like these are found all over the Celtic world: over the portals of churches (the people walking between Her legs to enter the sacred space), and by sacred wells. The later, prudish Christians saw Her as a monster or gargoyle and tried to hide Her away out of sight, and this is still true today. (There are still ten stonecut Sheela-na-Gigs gathering dust in the basement of the National Museum in Dublin which are not on public view.)

The Sheela-na-Gig became the symbol for an exhibition called, 'Woman Magic, Celebrating the Goddess Within Us' which travelled widely between 1979–87, first in England and then in Germany, Denmark, Sweden and Finland.

Children of the Living Stones

Don Robbins, a scientist involved in the Dragon Project at the Rollright Stones, has written a very interesting book called *The Secret Language of Stones*[13] in which he explores the inherent electronic or electromagnetic nature of stone. He calls the standing stones large 'macro-chips'. He explores the possibility that pressure waves of both touch and sound might interact with energy-cycles within the stone and that these may, in turn, interact with our human mind to form images. Robbins says that there is a 'shimmering web of electrons appearing and disappearing into the ghost world of crystal energy'; that these electrons running through the lattice structure of the stone remind one of the biological equivalent of ions carrying charges and messages through nerves – like the nerve impulses and the flow of blood through a living organism.

According to Robbins, the Stone Age might as well be called the Flint Age and he postulates a magical/transformative interaction between the crystalline structures of the flint and the human communities developing this ancient technology. Very delicate and precise work went into the making of incredibly fine and sharp flint slivers, used as scraping and skinning tools as well as arrowheads. With applied heat, magical changes were brought about in the stone. (Stone or flint was used not only for practical reasons but also for its magical qualities and there was an energy exchange between stone and the human community which contributed to, or even brought about, human evolution and consciousness.)

The archaeologist Margaret Ehrenberg points out in *Women in Prehistory*[14] that it can be argued that the crucial steps in human development were predominantly inspired by women. 'These include economic and technological innovations and the role of females as the social centre of the group.'[15] She says that a major difference between human development and that of other animals is the greater length of time during which infants need to be cared for and fed, and this would have led to food-sharing and long-term male–female bonding. Food sharing almost always takes place within the matrifocal group, between mothers and offspring and between grown male hunters and their mothers and sisters. Women would have preferred to mate with men who were willing to share, and this would have led to gradual evolutionary changes in favour of smaller and less aggressive males. This would have led to closer social bonds than in other species and the natural focus of such a group would have been the mother. Women are the guardians of hereditary qualities and choose their mate or mates, while in patriarchal societies men have chosen women who were physically weak, passive and limited in intelligence. Without the willingness to share and co-operate, human cultures would never have evolved.

In *The Great Cosmic Mother*,[16] Barbara Mor and I explored how early human cultures evolved around collectives of mothers for whom it was necessary to develop herbal healing skills, the use of fire, to be able to preserve food, the shaping of wood, rope and clay vessels to be able to carry water, babies and foods, etc. Women's knowledge of plants eventually brought about the neolithic agricultural revolution. If women in palaeolithic times skinned the animals and scraped the skins, they would almost certainly have made the flints that they used. And it was women who invented the digging sticks still used by hunter-gathering peoples, and who made the tools for grinding flour, weaving and other crafts.

In Sweden, the oldest remains found of a human being dating from the retreat of the Ice Age, about 7000 BC, was assumed to be male simply because it was buried with hunting tools and was powerfully built. Later investigation has revealed that the bones show this 'man' to have given birth to fourteen children! The women and men of the Sami people, Aboriginal shamanic peoples of the north, hunted side by side until recent times, and amongst them, as amongst most hunter-gatherers even now, there was great equality between women and men.

The great Mother spirit loves all Her children equally while the love of the father god is conditional on blind obedience, conformity and strict compliance with paternal orders. It is women who have to show that patriarchy is anti-evolutionary and based on a lie.

3

Explorations of Consciousness

The Goddess in Africa

In 1968 I painted *God Giving Birth*, showing the Goddess giving birth to cosmos from Her womb. At that time I was basing this image simply on my own experiences of the natural birth of my second son, Toivo, which felt like a very powerful initiation to the great Mother.

For the first time I had experienced the incredible power of my own body, as well as visions of great spaces of darkness and blinding light.

The Goddess in my painting is more African than white. I did not know then that Africa is the mother of humanity and that, in fact, the ancestor Goddess is black, although on another level, I must have known.

Africa is the womb and cradle of the human race and our common ancestress is a black woman. Western magic originates in the ancient stellar and lunar possession of cults of Africa.[1] 'Voodoo' comes from the Fon language of Dahomey (now Benin) and Togo and means 'protective spirit'. 'Black magic' is so called and slandered because it was originally the left-hand path of women's lunar and menstrual clairvoyance and magic.

When the Nile valley was still submerged in waters, there developed a thriving culture in the Sahara, then a fertile grassland. This began after about 10,000 BC and was at its height between 5500–2500 BC. Rock paintings portraying the horned Goddess have been found in what is now the Sahara desert. The python was a Goddess symbol of religion around the Sahara and far beyond, long before it became a symbol of Egypt. The Egyptian hieroglyph for 'Goddess' was an upraised cobra. Egypt's cultural origins lay in Africa. Its culture was not imported wholesale from the Near East as western historians, who used to deny the existence of any creative genius of black Africa, wanted to claim. Egypt is and always was, part of the great African continent.[2] It is in no way recognised to what extent cultures originating in Africa came to shape and influence western culture. It now seems likely, for example, that Libyans and Phoenicians emigrated to Crete and there, together with settlers from Anatolia (present-day Turkey), created the wonderful and joyous Goddess-centred Cretan culture which was the cradle of the later Greek mystery religions and thought. The religion of Isis, black Goddess of Egypt, had a major influence in Roman times and Her temples were to be found all over Europe. Her ritual was incorporated into that of the Virgin when Christianity subsumed the culture.

Buddhism and Women

When I painted *God Giving Birth*, I knew nothing about the skydancing Tibetan, Dakini, or of the ancient tantric path of India, and it is with delight and gratitude to Tsultrim Allione who wrote of Her in *Women of Wisdom*[3] that I have discovered another and ancient matriarchal strand still surviving in eastern religious thought. In this book, Tsultrim, an American who spent a number of years as an ordained Tibetan Buddhist nun in Nepal, wrote the life stories of great Tibetan women who achieved illumination and were the spiritual teachers of their people in the past and in the present. She writes that the ancient Tibetan indigenous Dzog Chen practice, derived from bon shamanism, is the oldest form of meditation and is taught in the twilight language of Dakini.[4]

The world is, indeed, not as solid as we think, and the more we open the gaps to other realities, the closer we are to the wisdom-play of the Dakinis who support the opening of awareness into pure being. The Dakini is the messenger of the state which is beyond the control and paranoia of the fixated ego; she is naked and dancing and always shifting.

Tsultrim's vision is to spin the Dakini mandala around the world, thereby creating a network of places where it is established, an energy network for the benefit of all beings which will help the transformation that is happening now in the world. She and others with her have had visions and signs – like the appearance of a cloud Dakini during one of their retreats – of the actuality of the Dakinis and their very real powers.

Tsultrim writes that the cosmos is fertile and that creation is a birth process. The world is not commanded into being.

The 'source of dharmas' is the cosmic cervix or the gate of all birth. She is the space or emptiness/void or matrix that gives birth to the phenomenal world.

In Hindu tantric teaching the active principle, or energy, is shakti the Goddess, and in Tibetan tantric Buddishm; one finds the active dakini/shakti and static 'yum' or cosmic Mother who is also prajna paranita: total wisdom or tara. Dakini is the 'skygoer' – one who moves in the sky – of many forms. She is naked, wrathful, dancing – sexual and spiritual, ecstatic and intelligent, wrathful and peaceful – and speaks also to our biological selves. In tantric teaching, the human body is seen as one of the primary mandalas and sexuality as a means of transformation.

Tsultrim says 'Dakini creates a different effect on the psyche than the sweetly smiling Madonna adoring Her own son' and 'in the patriarchy we are the underground daughters turned into frustrated furies because of the denial of our dreams, ecstasies and body-minds'.

The Dakini tradition teaches that luminosity and vision are already within us, the 'rainbow body of light' in women needs to be reawakened because women have a natural affinity for working directly with energy and vision. Women are the guardians of culture and also the source of change; we know that life is a thing of wonder and can guide humanity into a reconciliation of spirit and body. We call for social action, our woman-religions incorporate the dark and the light and hold both sacred as different aspects of the Mother.

Tsultrim Allione's life brings together intensive forms of religious practice – she was ordained as a Tibetan nun in Bodhgaya in 1970 – and is also the mother of three children (she had a child that died) and has lived and taught back in the USA. For nearly four years she lived as a nun, spending intensive periods in solitary retreats, studying the Tibetan language and meditation practices and making pilgrimages to India and Nepal. Tsultrim's teacher is Norbu Rinpoche who is based in northern Italy.

She is critical of Buddhism for its emphasis on suffering and for the suppression of emotions so often encouraged in its practices, as one is asked to separate from, and to observe, one's feelings rather than to participate in them.

Buddha saw all life as suffering and wanted to be rid of the dark and the painful. He wanted only to experience the light and blissful nirvana. Buddha, however, is only a guide and his followers are not required to achieve union with him.

Buddhist practice teaches women to give up ego or self; and these are women who have not even found their 'self' and have a very weak sense of ego. This leaves them wide open to use or abuse by male teachers who certainly feed their own egos and act as vampies on women's sexual and spiritual energies. To be 'generous and compassionate' in this setting and context can be just another form of repression and avoidance and may result in leaving oneself open to exploitation. It is often a refusal to look at women's very real and well-founded anger; a refusal to face up to actual political and economic patriarchal realities.

Buddha himself had said: 'I want to be freed from the impurities of women's bodies. I will acquire the beautiful and fresh body of man'; he further believed that women cannot reach enlightenment in a female body that bleeds and gives birth. Women were not meant to live a religious life outside the Hindu patriarchal family nor outside their caste – Buddha, after all, was of the princely caste and lived in patriarchal Hindu society – and Buddhist nuns alive in the sixth century BC, during Buddha's lifetime, had to bow down to and obey every monk however young or new, even though the nun was far senior in terms of years of service.[5] The Buddhist notion of Karma has in fact hindered social critique and reform.

There is also no concept in Buddhist thought of the sanctity of Earth as a living Motherbeing, nor of the life-process as inherently sacred.

Tsultrim Allione says: 'When the energy of the Earth is disturbed, the Dakini is disturbed and supported by devas and spirits. She causes diseases, famine and warfare. The dark Goddess is seen as an obnoxious upstart when the patriarchy rips apart and poisons Earth.'

Tsultrim writes that people go into meditation to solve their problems, but instead of this happening, they often merely become hidden and emerge in shadowy personality conflicts, power plays and sexual secrets. She now gives week-long 'Five Dakinis Retreats' for women in which she brings together Tibetan meditation practices with therapy, art, maskmaking and movement. What shocked her into starting with these retreats was the death from cancer of a close woman friend who had spent years in intensive meditation. When she stopped the meditations, she found herself ill as a result of the emotional issues that had never been dealt with during that time. Tsultrim works within the mandala of the five Dakinis – transmitted from the wisdom Dakini herself to the great yogini Ayu Khadro – with the transformation of blocked energies into wisdom. She works very closely with a young Native American woman called Sparky Shootingstar, who is part Cherokee and a carrier of the sacred pipe tradition.

As Tsultrim says, how can one bring the Tibetan Dakini teachings to the American soil without asking permission from, and honouring, the ancestor spirits of the indigenous peoples and of the land itself?

The sacred pipe ceremony was given to the Lakotas by White Buffalo Woman – known to the Plains Indians as Ta Tanka Wian Ska – who is Goddess as well as mythical ancestor and teacher to Her people. According to prophecy, She is now returning and is to be reborn in the west. Therefore, the original sacred pipe that has been guarded by one particular Lakota family, was ceremonially brought forth on full moon in June 1987. From the sacred pipe came the teachings of the sweatlodge, the vision quest and other rituals in native American tradition.

Turning the Wheel – American Women Creating the New Buddhism[6] is a book edited by Sandy Boucher who has travelled far and wide across the USA speaking with Buddhist women in the different traditions from Japanese Zen to Tibetan Dzog Chen. She describes how sometimes it happens that a woman in deep meditation during a long retreat may suddenly go into a state of trauma because of long-repressed memories, such as having been sexually abused as a child, which well up into the conscious mind, and simply having no way out or not being allowed to express or communicate what is happening to her. She is told by her male teacher only 'to sit, not to explore emotions.'

One of the chapters in the book is called 'Conspiracy of Silence: the Problem of the Male Teacher' which describes how many supposed 'gurus' are addicted to womanising, alcohol and abuse of power. In 1982 and 1983, 'Women and Buddhism' conferences were held in the USA for the first time and, as women came together, they began to compare notes and to exchange information concerning their various teachers or gurus and were shocked at what they were finding out.

Radical Buddhist women are now looking at their conditioning as daughters within the nuclear but still patriarchal family where women are always taught to defer to male authority, to yield, to give up self and always to feel guilty for whatever goes wrong. Even young girls who have been sexually abused by their fathers or male relatives are made to feel as if it is somehow their own fault that it happened, and this is reproduced in Buddhist centres where women think that perhaps they had somehow led the guru on or tempted him into 'sin'.

Biblical and Goddess Images

Renaissance artists, sponsored by the Catholic Church, the merchants and aristocracy, painted idealised madonnas while women were actually tortured, raped and burned at the stake in the town squares in front of churches for attempting to protect the Mother and Her nature; for having women's traditional knowledge of herbal healing, astrology, midwifery and for practising the pythonic or magical/psychic arts.

Today, millions of women and their children live abject lives and suffer miserable deaths from hunger in the Third World while white western New Agers are producing idealised 'beautiful' images of anorexic young women.

Today, the Virgin Mary gives birth to a deformed 'jelly baby' in the Pacific; She is a sexually mutilated girl child in an African Muslim country. She dies from a back-street abortion in a South American Catholic country or is burned alive by her parents-in-law and 'husband' in a dowry murder in India.

The awaited Messiah is black and in detention in a South African prison; has just been shot by Contras in Nicaragua, or has died from alcohol poisoning on a Native American reservation, or is an Aboriginal man who has been hanged or beaten to death in an Australian jail.

Or perhaps the Messiah is a She who died at birth in Ethiopia where there was no stable at all. All the relatives of Mary and Joseph died in the gas ovens in Europe.

Mary Condren writes in her brilliant book, *The Serpent*

and the Goddess – Women, Religion and Power in Celtic Ireland,[7] that Teilhard de Chardin, who has influenced much New Age thinking, welcomed the first test explosion of the atomic bomb in New Mexico and wrote that 'it disclosed to human existence a supreme purpose' and called the exploding of the atom – this ultimate violation of the Mother – 'supercreativeness'.

Mary Condren, who grew up as a Roman Catholic in Dublin, entered a cloister as a nun at an early age and then became the editor of a radical student Christian movement journal before studying under the radical feminist theologian, Mary Daly, in the USA. She has a great insight into the fundamental deathwish inherent in Christian teachings which, in fact, advocate the death of female nature. She writes that we are taught in school that the Christian religion brought mercy, enlightenment and justice to a world where people had lived in darkness and heathendom. The very opposite is, however, true, as Christianity, in Mary's words, 'created a barbaric culture such as the world had never seen before and plunged women into an abyss of serflike hopelessness and despair'.[8]

Mary Condren points out that nuclear war is 'not an accidental feature of an ideology that would otherwise promote the growth of the human spirit', rather that 'nuclear destruction is intrinsic to the spirituality and theology generated by western culture'. The explosions of nuclear bombs have indeed been perceived as the second coming in wrath.

Hebrew scholar Savina J. Teubal who lives in Los Angeles and is involved in the radical gay synagogue, wrote *Sarah the Priestess – the First Matriarch of Genesis*[9] in 1984. Her thorough research is from a feminist point of view, which means reading between the lines of Genesis in the Old Testament. This is important because the Hebrew Bible became God's revelation, and Genesis became the story of creation for the whole of the western world after the Christian canon had been established by the church fathers in the fourth century AD. Genesis has, ever since, been used against women and women have, after Eve, been blamed for every conceivable sin and ill, including death itself.

Savina Teubal came to the interesting conclusion that the matriarchs, Sarah, Rebekah, Rachel and Leah were the actual descendants, and held the religious tradition of, an ancient Mesopotamian priestesshood and were often in conflict with their menfolk and the emerging patriarchy in their newly adopted land in the Bronze Age. This would explain, amongst other things, the ritual 'barrenness' of the matriarchs.

It now seems clear that while the patriarchal prophets made their tyrannical edicts on monotheism and the maleness of Jahveh – and stirred up bloody and cruel wars against the Goddess-worshipping Canaanite people – the ordinary Jewish women and men hung on to their ancient Mother Goddess and baked cakes to the queen of heaven.[10]

Astarte/Anath was, in the Bronze Age, the Goddess of both Canaanites and Hebrews, whilst Asherah/Shekinah appears to have been a purely Hebrew Goddess and was co-creator with Jahveh and dwelled in the temple with him.[11]

The Hebrew prophets, however, insisted on a monotheism in which the male god is separate from his creation, and a morality and laws that come from 'on high' – a system in which women's life-giving creative powers are no longer an expression of the sacred, and Asherah is banished forever.

Charis was the name of the female Christ (anointed one) of the gnostics, whose natural blood of menstruation was held to redeem humanity, and it was said: 'Charis has descended upon you, open thy mouth and prophesy.' Wine symbolises Her blood.

The gnostics[12] questioned whether all suffering, labour and death derive from 'original sin' and thought that the world had been created by Samael who is a false, blind, cruel and jealous god. This demiurge, whom William

Blake also wrote about, was originally the creation of the Great Mother, but he has got out of hand and has usurped Her powers. He is like a distant but possessive landlord who loves only those that please him; he makes edicts like those of a schoolmaster and functions as the 'thought-police' of the sky.

Eva/Havah gives life to Adam (Adamha means 'Son of the red Mother Earth', Adamah, the ancient Hebrew Earth Mother) and instructs him. She was sent by Sophia – wisdom – Mother of all living, and is a woman of spirit who raises Adam from his merely material condition. The very first created woman was, however, Lilith who was also the serpent in the garden of Eden. She was originally a lunar Goddess of menstrual, sexual powers and was connected with Ninlil, the Sumerian lady of the air. She was also called 'the hand of Inanna'. To the patriarchs, however, she was a night demon and foul seducer of men, a slayer of men and children, mother of demons in the desert.

The gnostics distinguished between the popular image of God – as patriarch, lord, creator and judge – and the ultimate source of being, which to them is both mother and father and is invisible and incomprehensible. They felt that the demiurge made false claims to power and that this 'creator' was a lesser divine being who acted as a military commander. This lord-god, at the head of the divine hierarchy, then serves to legitimise the whole structure of authoritarian rule on Earth. The gnostics were a threat to Catholic clerical authority because their belief in gnosis, direct experience and realisation of the true source of divine power, offered the people a theological justification for disobeying bishops and priests. They claimed that the pope and bishops, ruling the community as 'god rules in heaven', represent this demiurge. They believed that Christ can be experienced in the present through spiritual vision, in trance, and in dreams and that we can receive resurrection while we still live.

Mary Magdalene represents, in the gnostic 'gospel of

Mary', their claim to experiencing Christ's continuing presence, and authority for themselves as co-equals. Because whosoever receives the spirit communicates directly with the divine, while the orthodox Christian teaching says that you must trust the teachings and the Church hierarchy more than your own experience. To the Church, fear of God the father is essential, and the belief that God is one and inseparable sanctions divine and human authority. Women are only allowed to participate when they assimilate male teaching; as mere women we are not worthy of life: witness the present Pope's stand on abortion, contraception and other issues that touch women's lives.

But, Mary Magdalene stood up to Peter, the apostle, and challenged him, and Jesus had spoken first to her when he returned after three days in the tomb. The gnostics did not believe in Jesus's bodily ascension to heaven, but saw the 'risen Christ' as a spirit being – a 'great angel of light' that shows itself in multiple forms – whom Jesus represented. Orthodox Christians were threatened by seeing gnostic women preaching, baptising, curing, as they did amongst the Cathars in the thirteenth century in Languedoc in the South of France. Gnostics were everywhere persecuted as heretics and the first crusade was undertaken against the Cathars.

The Patriarchal Occult Thinking of the New Age

The most frightening aspect of the New Age is its adoption, and perpetuation, of a mishmash of the reactionary, patriarchal occult traditions and thinking of both east and west, all of which have in common a hatred of the Earth, authoritarianism, racism and misogyny.

The New Age does not, on the whole, relate to the radical pagan tradition of the European peasantry with its love of the Earth, centred around the Goddess and women

– and also the horned god, Her son and lover who is not transcendent and abstract but firmly rooted in nature – and its ecological/political awareness.

From the time I discovered the ancient cultures of the Goddess, I felt I was a medium for ancient women and I experienced painting as a shamanistic act, entering into other realms and bringing back images evoking other times and possible female-oriented futures. I felt certain that only if we women rise and reclaim our powers and selfhood worldwide, is there any hope at all of Earth's survival; this vision haunted me and kept me going during many years of grassroots work in the Women's Liberation Movement in the 1970s. I was dreaming the past and the future in my images.

I have said, half-jokingly, that if I had painted God as a beautiful white woman, sexually pleasing to men, with long blonde hair, flowers in her hair and stars in her eyes, there would never have been any trouble. As it is, She is a non-white woman, gynandrous in appearance, stark, large and powerful.

Now, to my dismay, I find that the images of women and of the Goddess that are popular and acceptable in the New Age movement are the very sentimentalised and sickly sweet ones that I had rejected years ago as sexist, racist and heterosexist. As a rule, I find that what passes for 'art' and 'music' in the New Age is uninspired, lacking in honesty and passion and is primarily meant to soothe and please. What New Agers forget, as far as women are concerned, is that the assertive female guards the earth on behalf of us all. Instead they want docile and non-threatening Virgin Marys, sweetly smiling while the earth burns. They are busy discouraging women from reclaiming our powers. We are not encouraged to see ourselves as positive when assertive and angry on life's behalf. My paintings have often been called 'aggressive' because they portray powerful women.

William Irwin Thompson, who announced that the New Age began at midnight on 31 December 1967, wrote in

Passages about the Earth – an Exploration of the New Planetary Culture[13] that he was worried by the politics of mysticism and the anti-democratic attitudes of the flood of Indian gurus in the USA who almost all came from the brahaminic Indian upper class. Many Tibetan teachers also belong to the privileged class of Lamas. These gurus speak of some 'men' who are more highly evolved than others and Bhagwan Sri Rajneesh, a former professor of philosophy, even called himself a 'guru of the rich' and claimed to be without gender. Gopi Krishna was hoping for a new caste system for the future. The gurus are tolerant and merely condescending now because they have no political power, but even without power they show full evidence of human frailty and vanity and tend to think that their own yoga is bigger and better than the other gurus.

Thompson writes that mystics may not build factories but more often than not welcome the death of the Earth and the emergence of a 'cosmic man'. Even though he questions some of this, he appears to hope, as do Marilyn Ferguson and David Spangler, that multinational corporations are creating structures of planetisation that will accelerate the 'mystical transformation of mankind.'

Thompson, who wrote a book about the Goddess in the early 1980s,[14] founded the Lindisfarne Association on Long Island in 1973. Together with Sri Aurobindo's Auroville, the 'planetary city' in India,[15] Findhorn and Iona in Scotland, it is one of the so-called 'light centres' in a network of light whose 'strands of light, like the proto-neuronal pathways in the body, attract physical matter and energies to them so that light could be embodied in a new college for a new culture'. These would replace the dead and decaying centres, like New York or London, of those who cannot let go of the old.

There is a belief in the New Age that the planets also go through reincarnation, this being the earth's fourth and the first when She is completely physically materialised. Now the earth will return to its spiritual origins as a body of light in the age of Aquarius. The old etheric web of the previous world cycle is now unplugged from its cosmic source and is running out of energies.

It might be, though, that, far from humans being the pinnacle of Earth's achievement, or the global brain that New Agers arrogantly claim themselves to be, 'man' has become a sickness in Her great planetary mind.

Patriarchy in its onslaught on Nature has wiped out whole species of animals and other ancient beings, such as the forests, that make up Her consciousness, thereby tearing apart the great etheric web of life. Patriarchal societies have generated worldwide electrical pollution, as well as forming cities, which drain the energies of the land and are like festering cancerous growths on Her living body. Our minds are sickening as we are cut off from our dream-minds which sustain and keep us connected with the spirit-realms, the ancestors and spirits of nature. Instead of communicating with the spirits, we are now haunted by monsters produced by our own distorted minds.

4
Banishing Darkness: Findhorn's Plan of Light

A Flawed Garden of Eden

William Irwin Thompson spent some time at Findhorn and calls it a balance between American politics and eastern mysticism, bringing together animism (communication with nature, spirits, fairies or devas) and electronics. He wrote in *Passages About the Earth*[1] of Findhorn that it is a community where the leaders can talk to 'the little people, sprites, elves, devas, sons of God and God himself . . . a community which spoke of extraterrestrial links with space and intraterrestrial links with planets.' He describes it as a synthesis between humanity and the divinity within nature.

The community had its modest beginnings in a caravan park by the sea near Forres, Morayshire in Scotland not far from Inverness in 1962. It was founded by Eileen and Peter Caddy together with a Canadian, Dorothy McLean. Eileen is mediumistic, Dorothy communicated with the nature spirits, which made it possible for them to grow large vegetables on what was thought of as sandy and infertile soil, and Peter was the central administrator. Peter and Dorothy have since left the community.

By 1987 Findhorn had grown into a thriving spiritual community. Today it owns a number of large buildings, such as Cluny Hill hotel (now a college), and it has been granted custodianship of the Isle of Erraid off the west coast of Scotland. It is wealthy. It runs expensive courses and conferences. The majority of its members are white, middle class and well-off. Many come from north America.

I found it quite distressing to read Eileen Caddy's autobiography, *Flight to Freedom*.[2] She grew up in Egypt where her father was a director of Barclays Bank. She was married for a number of years to a British RAF officer stationed in Germany by whom she had five children.

Peter Caddy, also an RAF officer, was a friend of the family. He was interested in Theosophy and believed himself to be directed by 'secret masters' to join together with Eileen to help develop her psychic gifts, and that she was his other spiritual half. Eileen writes of years of suffering when she lost her children (she wasn't allowed to see them) and Peter used her and 'trained her' in ruthless ways. When pushed to the edge, she started to get a voice coming through which she interpreted as the 'voice of god' that, over many years, directed Eileen and Peter to start the Findhorn Community. It was only this, an inner voice of male presence (most likely that of her beloved father who died while she was still young), that was listened to. When she spoke as herself she was ignored. When the voice, after a number of years, refused to give more advice to the community or to Peter, who relied on it even for mundane practical details, she felt completely lost and Peter drifted away from her. She has for long periods lived like a hermit in her caravan at Findhorn whilst Peter, who left the community, has remarried several times since. Eileen admits to having a fear of 'elemental' forces. For her the emphasis on light and the voice of a father is surely therefore a flight away from the dark Mother (and Black Africa?) even though she admits to having had visions of the madonna and of Quan Yin, the Chinese mother of the world. Eileen thinks that she was the heart and mother while Peter was the head and light. Throughout her life she seems to have obeyed what men told her whether they were her husband or the voice in her head.

Daphne Francis, a friend of mine, lived at Findhorn for

two years from 1980 to 1982. In 1984 she wrote an article called 'Is New Age spirituality offering anything really new to women? Reflections of a New Age survivor.'[3]

She considers the time she lived at Findhorn the most depressing in her life. The attitude to women there was mediaeval and its ideas were formulated by a core group mainly of men. She says that although there supposedly is no 'New Age Bible', a great reverence is paid to the works of the occultist Alice Bailey, and the right-wing writings of the American David Spangler.

She found that there was a lack of shared childcare; living in nuclear families was encouraged and unsupported mothers were not made welcome. Daphne herself was thought of as a 'very negative person . . . stuck in her victim role . . . stuck in the form-level'. It was thought that she was preoccupied with material concerns when she raised feminist issues. Findhorn claims to be a centre of synthesis and to have absorbed feminism; by a strange logic it then follows that men can speak for women and even work out policies for us; if women object to this they are seen to be aggressive.

Daphne writes that another factor suppressing criticism from women is the stress on positive thinking and talking. To take a stand on an issue is interpreted as a sign that you are 'attached to your negative emotions' and that you are not 'spiritually advanced', whilst arrogant and cold intellectuality is not seen as a problem!

It follows that 'radical political ideas are denounced as irrelevant or, worse still, the distress of someone's "victim pattern"', and conservative ideology and practice is accepted with very little question'. After all, if you are a privileged white male, you are quite comfortable just to go along with the patriarchal status quo which appears to be perfectly 'natural' and 'normal'.

Daphne Francis considers overall that the supposedly spiritual positions taken by Findhorn and other New Age communities 'condone sufferings, stifle action and reveal huge arrogance in the face of the mystery of life and death, happiness and suffering'. The so-called 'non-attachment and non-involvement' taken from Buddhism, covers over a holier-than-thou mentality and élitism, and there is an implicit dualism which separates politics and spirituality.

She felt that there is a 'narrow selfish concern for the welfare of the community itself', for a privileged community that sets itself up as a light centre of global importance.

Sitting meditating for peace – very popular with the New Age – was considered a positive action, but backing it up 'with positive action with a peaceful inner orientation was not'.

Daphne Francis was particularly offended by the male light-oriented invocation used at full moon celebrations that is practised at Findhorn. The meditations take place on the full moon because the moon is then reflecting the light of the sun! (Sir John Sinclair explains in *The Alice Bailey Inheritance*[4] that what is taken advantage of, in this opportunity of the lunar cycle and tides, is the run of solar energy and the subtle beneficient forces that form part of it.)

Daphne writes that, significantly, the Dark Moon – never ignored by people of the Craft for fear of becoming ungrounded – was not observed by the Findhorn Community and the connection between the moon and women's menstrual cycles was ignored. Solar festivals were celebrated four times a year, however the four pagan lunar and five quarterday festivals of the Goddess were not only ignored but were even feared by some older members of the community.

As Daphne says, this is a dangerous way of practising magic, and, coupled with the fear of the dark, points to yet another solar cult. This makes it easy to see an uncanny connection between the countries mainly involved in the network of light and centres of white capitalist imperialism. In David Spangler's words, 'Findhorn is the training-ground . . . a reformed sanctuary and a homeland for the brotherhood from which our colonial ships may go forth again . . . to carry cargoes of new vision and the seeds of the new world.'

Daphne ends her article by saying that she was numb and depressed when she left Findhorn and hopes that New Age groups will recognise in time that they cannot regard themselves as free from the culture from which they stem and that they will come to question the philosophies they adopt. She grieves that 'they've even colonised the future in the name of the powers of light; no place for me, creature of darkness, of night, and lover of the moon'.

The New Age groups, like the Nazi world-changers before them, often work with sacred sites, sacred to the Goddess, but for their own ends, and seem to play at magic without any real understanding. They are afraid to welcome the Goddess who is maiden, mother and hag, the original trinity. Reinstating the wisdom of the witches, however, is really threatening to the status quo, for to embrace the Goddess fully means to acknowledge women's power and to work consciously to redress the patriarchal stranglehold on things material and spiritual. Whilst 'New Age' groups scapegoat women seeking to redress this balance, they are creating nothing really new and it will be up to women to redefine our own future.

The very common New Age notion that you 'create your own reality' is popular at Findhorn. It implies that if you are poor, ill or dying, it is of your own making, and if women are having a hard time, we should work on ourselves; patriarchy has nothing to do with it.

New Agers seem to think that being wealthy, white and healthy in this life is a result of deserved and earned good karma. By the same logic, if you are dying from hunger in the Third World you also made your own karma and you choose what you want to be born into as well as your parents.

Underlying much of New Age thinking is a sort of feudal mysticism, a male spiritualist imperialism that expresses itself in terms such as 'lord God on High' and 'king Jesus the saviour'. Much of the thinking and commonly held ideas of the New Age movement in fact originate with the Theosophists. It was the mediumship of Blavatsky, Steiner and Alice Bailey that introduced and popularised the legends of Atlantis and Lemuria and of the famed Shambhala and Agharti in the Gobi desert, the belief in angelic hierarchies and hierarchies of Secret Masters or World Wise men that direct the evolution of humanity and our destinies. It was belief in the inherent superiority of the white race that made these mediums emphasise the goodness of light, whiteness and of fire. Their real credo was 'My lord is a consuming fire', a lord battling the sacred earth and her lifegiving waters. This kind of thinking, that originated with patriarchal Indo-European invaders into Goddess lands in the mists of time, has led to the making of the nuclear bomb that threatens to truly engulf the earth in a burning and deathly fire. It always imagines the spiritual realms as profoundly patriarchal and undemocratic and a mirror image of this society as it now is. There are thought to be an infinite number of 'higher' and 'lower' devic and angelic 'kingdoms' and there is an unquestioned belief in the superior wisdom and benevolence towards humanity ('man'), of all male Secret Masters, mahatmas or brotherhoods.

Influences on Findhorn

From ancient Rome to present-day London, the philosophy of most magicians and occultists has been tinged with a dualism that sees spirit as good and male and matter as evil and female. 'Man' is an immortal spirit that is trapped in the 'world of flesh' or dense matter, ensnared in the world of 'illusion' or Maya, the Goddess.

Russian-born Helena Blavatsky (1831–91), an extraodinary woman of great mediumistic and clairvoyant powers, founded the Theosophist movement, together with the American, Colonel Olcott, and W Q Judge, in 1875. She has been called the founder of modern occultism and her most important writings were *Isis Unveiled* (1877) – a master-key to the mysteries of ancient and modern science and theology – and *The Secret Doctrine* (1888). Blavatsky, who had, at one point, been involved in spiritualism, was involved in many scandals and was accused of fraud; she was either abused or adored all her life. It seems, though, that she did have some unusual knowledge which she claimed to have received from the 'White Brotherhood' of the White Lodge which supposedly exists in the other realms, ('white magic', not racial colour) of Egyptian and Tibetan Secret Masters. Theosophy means 'divine knowledge' or 'knowledge about god' and sets out to teach the divine wisdom that underlies the universe, no less. Blavatsky claims to have experienced direct inspiration from Isis, the Egyptian universal moon Goddess.

Helen Blavatsky considered her 'negative mediumship' to have been a 'psycho-physical weakness' of which she needed to 'cleanse' herself. She was to take full control of her occult powers during extensive journeys from 1867 to 1870 to Egypt and Tibet where she was supposedly taught the secret occult knowledge by the 'Master Morya'.

Blavatsky and Olcott moved to India and set up the headquarters of the Theosophist movement in Bombay in 1878. They were, perhaps, the first westerners who went to India and respected and learned from Hindu and Buddhist teachers and they brought ancient vedic and yogic teachings to Europe. In this, they did the world a great service.

There was then the long story of the appearing and disappearing 'mahatma letters'[5] that Blavatsky claimed 'materialised' and were written by the Master, Koot-Hoomi (KH). Some think that Blavatsky did indeed have access to secret Tibetan teachings, and that she was an 'adept'. For instance, W I Thomspon wrote in 1973[6] that the present-day Dalai Lama co-operates with Theosophical groups.

The Secret Doctrine[7] was, according to Blavatsky, written as a commentary to an otherwise unknown manuscript called 'The Stanzas of Dzyan'. According to one account they were revealed to Blavatsky in a trance whilst communicated telepathically by the mahatmas KH and Morya from Tibet. 'The Stanzas' are thought by some to be a fragmentary extract from the *Mani Kombourm*, sacred writings and magical secrets attributed to the Dzugarians, a long-vanished people who once lived in the mountains of northern Tibet and who communicated with the 'Sons of Light'. There are many confusing accounts of their origin.

The Secret Doctrine claims, no less, to reach the essence of all religions. The book sets out to give a truly grandiose perspective of cosmic events and human evolution, at times quite breathtaking and poetic. 'The Eternal Parent [space] wrapped in Her invisible robes, had slumbered again for seven eternities' . . . She, 'the Seven-skinned Eternal Mother-Father' . . . 'Time was not for it lay asleep in the infinite bosom of duration' . . .

According to Blavatsky, human entities originated hundreds of millions of years ago and were destined to evolve through seven 'root races'. The first root race was purely spiritual and lived in an 'imperishable land', whilst the second were the Hyperboreans who were without bodies and lived at the North Pole that was then a tropical region. It was only the third root race, living 18 million years ago, which descended to the physical plane because some wanted to experience physical existence. They started to procreate and develop gender and were born of a mother. This entrance into a physical body was, to the anti-sexual Blavatsky, the real fall. According to her, our ancestors are the *pitris* (the fathers) who are lunar deities, and who created us as physical beings while the seven kumaras or mystic sages are solar deities, the fire masters from Venus led by Sanat Kumar, who created the 'inner man'. The *pitris* were 'the progenitors of men' who created 'the first human Adams out of their sides, as astral shadows.'[8] According to Blavatsky, the lunar Fathers are lower angels or Nature Spirits, while the male 'living Fire' is needed to create self-consciousness.[9]

There is a great emphasis on fire as a mystical and divine element . . . The vital electric principle resides in the male Sun/Fire, while the Moon/Mother is cold and radiant. There is an 'eternal struggle on the physical and psychic planes, between spirit and matter', and spirit seeks to slay the 'purely material form'.[10]

According to Blavatsky, this sixty-foot-tall giant third root race lived in Lemuria in the Pacific which was destroyed by internal volcanic fires and sank into the ocean. The statues on Easter Island were theirs and their remains are in the Andes and in Australia. The fourth root race were the Atlanteans. They were also giants and built the pyramids and other cyclopic structures, and knew about electricity and flight. Some say they also developed nuclear power and that it was this which brought disaster upon Atlantis. The Atlanteans misused their powers and became 'black magicians'. From them descended the Sami, Eskimos, Native Americans and Chinese. Their civilisation was destroyed by flood. But, apparently, the elect, the divine instructors, left before this happened and had gone to the sacred island of Shambhala in the Gobi desert or Altai mountains 'from whence the last saviour will come'. So it appears that two-thirds of that race were ruled by dynasties of 'lower, material spirits of earth' while one-third 'remained faithful and joined the nascent fifth root race and are the divine incarnates'. Thus, according to Blavatsky, did the 'Aryan fifth root race' evolve in North Asia where the Atlanteans had taken refuge in the caverns of the high mountains about a million years before. These, in time, became the 'sons of light and fire', as the Indo-European warriors called themselves, as they pillaged, enslaved, killed and raped the 'daugters and sons of the Dark Mother'. They included the vedic Indians, the Arabs and Persians, the Celtic and Germanic peoples. Everywhere they introduced caste systems based on colour of skin and military might. The fact that we, their descendants, are smaller in stature is a sign of degeneracy and we are the most solid and entrapped race so far. The sixth root race is, however, already beginning to take form and it is in America that this transformation into a more ethereal race – that will grow out of its bonds of matter and flesh – will take place . . . to be at last overtaken by the seventh that will again be disembodied and non-sexual spirit beings on a higher plane. Lemuria will reappear out of the sea. They will live on a continent that does not yet exist.

There is hardly a self-respecting New Ager who doesn't talk knowledgeably about Lemuria and Atlantis as if they are historic and self-evident facts. Some think that they themselves are reincarnated Atlantean priests. The New Age is eagerly awaiting the non-physical, demateralised and 'spiritualised' beings of a transformed earth in the age of Aquarius.

Blavatsky wrote that we will die off after cataclysms, that 'we will be degenerate and die out like the native peoples today who were once mighty races'.

This is where Blavatsky showed her true reactionary and imperialist self. Underlying many of her theories and grand vistas is a vicious and dangerous dogma of Darwinian 'survival of the fittest'. She talked of 'sub-races' being dropped and 'higher races' being begotten. Apparently so-called 'civilised peoples' are the perfection of evolution; those who built cities were helped by divine intelligences, whilst nomadic peoples have 'bad karma', and karma also worked its force of destruction on 'savages', who are the 'failures of nature'. The Aboriginal Australians and other indigenous peoples like the dark Dravidians of India, the Native Americans etc., are the descendants of those who, instead of vivifying the spark dripped into them by the flames (the soul of things), extinguished it by 'long generations of bestiality'.[11] They are the last descendants of the last remnants of the third root race[12] and must make way for new and more highly evolved races. So, when the Tasmanians were murdered and hunted to death like animals by the white settlers in the 1860s, both Darwin and Blavatsky were in complete agreement over how fine and inevitable this was and rejoiced in that 'as the Tasmanians are now completely extinct and the Australians rapidly dying out, so will the other races soon follow'.[13] Their extermination was seen as the inevitable consequence of their inferiority.

Annie Besant became involved in the Theosophist movement after initial hesitation, and became its president when Blavatsky died in 1891. She was British, born into a devout Christian family in 1847.[14] She suffered many losses in her youth and went through a disastrous marriage to a cruel and dictatorial man of the Church from whom she got divorced and thereby lost her two children. She became involved in the free-thinking movement together with Charles Bradlaugh, who was imprisoned in 1877 for distributing the Knowlton pamphlet which advocated contraception for women along neo-Malthusian lines. She was an early feminist and a socialist and worked for both the trade unions and the Fabians. She was involved with the matchgirls' strike (1889) until she met Blavatsky, who persuaded her to give up her political activities. Blavatsky advised her that it was more important to study the 'laws of karma' than to work for social reform!

Besant lived to a great old age at the headquarters in India where, still being something of a radical, she worked for self-rule for India and was even for a while president of the Indian National Congress. Apparently she saw the caste system as karmic justice and did not oppose it. It was Besant and her co-worker, C W Leadbeater, another leading Theosophist, who adopted Krishnamurti and his brother on behalf of the movement, with the intention of grooming Krishnamurti into becoming the new world teacher or awaited messiah of the New Age. It was hoped that Krishnamurti would build his earthly paradise in 'Happy Valley' on the west coast of the USA. In 1929, however, Krishnamurti dramatically refused to take on this imposed role and publicly announced his resignation from the Theosophist Movement at a great meeting in Holland. He said that truth cannot be found in organised religion but can only come from one's inner being and in freedom from outer pressures and he had a great aversion to all talk of 'Secret Masters'. Besant never recovered from this blow and she and Leadbeater died within a year of each other in the early 1930s. The Theosophist movement subsequently declined.

It was Blavatsky's teachings on the root races that fired the imaginations of the German Nazis as they were setting out to make the way for a Nordic sixth root super-race composed of, in Blavatsky's words, 'glorious adepts' – a hierarchy of the elect. Hitler's final solution, like the American manifest destiny and European witchhunts, involved the genocide of yet more peoples, this time the Jews, the gypsies and all other alleged 'subhumans'.

Blavatsky had stated that the Jews were 'an abnormal and unnatural link between the fourth and fifth root races'. Studies of the Aryan race were perfectly respectable before the Second World War and anti-Semitism was rife. By the 1920s, racist books were pouring from the presses.

The Aryans, or Indo-Europeans, who invaded India some 4000 years ago had set up a racial aristocracy based on colour.[15] The word 'varna' that came to mean caste, means 'two colours', that of the white conquerors and that of the dark Dravidians. Purdha for women was introduced in the name of 'racial purity' to prevent the Aryan women of the ruling caste from mixing with the 'inferior' Dravidians of the lower caste. There is already evidence of racial discrimination in the Vedas, the sacred poetry of the Hindus, composed about 1500 BC.

The legend of Shambhala and Agharti is found right through Europe and Asia. To the Theosophists and to the Nazis this was the great Aryan magical civilisation located somewhere in the Gobi desert from which, after a catastrophe, peoples emigrated to Europe and the Caucasus. It was a great city of light that passed into higher dimensions in a former time. The Nazis, who wanted to connect the origin of the Aryan root race with Nordic lore, believed that these people were led by the wise initiates, Odin and Thor.

The World Wise Masters, in the meantime, went underground in the Himalayas and from there in a fabled Shambhala, they rule our destinies by occult means. It was thought that the Secret Masters of Shambhala practised 'white' (right-hand) magic, whilst those at Agharti practised 'black' (left-hand) magic. One of these Masters called Koot Hoomi (KH), who was 'channelled' through Blavatsky in 1881, said that the guardians who obey the king of the world and head of the hierarchy will re-emerge and will invite 'mankind' to co-operate in creating the 'New Age' and the super-race – our planet being a field of operation for magicians. Of course to the Nazis these elect would be none other than the SS, the Nazi aristocracy, faithful servants of their master.

There all kinds of rumours of Tibetan lamas being the contacts for the Thule society to which Hitler and many prominent Nazis belonged and where *The Secret Doctrine* was avidly studied. The Tibetans were contacted through the Buddhist adept Haushofer and the Swedish explorer, Sven Hedin, who spent many years in Tibet and was friendly with many lamas in Tibetan monasteries. Hedin's 'mission' was to prepare the way for the coming of the unknown higher being from Tibet, a then feudal society ruled over by hierarchies of lamas. The members of the Thule society made connections between Blavatsky's occult history, as expounded in *The Secret Doctrine*, and ancient Germanic legends. They set out to create an Aryan Theosophy. The mystical anti-Semites, Hess and Rosenberg, who took from the Theosophists the idea that the Aryan race had originated in Atlantis and were the occult theoreticians of the Nazi party, both belonged to the Thule society. They claimed, as did Blavatsky and MacGregor Mathers of the British occult order of the Golden Dawn, they were mediums for legendary secret chiefs in Tibet, who were the descendants of the Atlantean survivors living within the remote Himalayas.

These Mahatmas or Secret Masters of the White Lodge are supposedly ruled over by the King of Fear who will one day return to rule after a global war. Hitler believed that he was this very Manu or king of the world, reincarnated, and saw it as his mission to bring about the return of this Master. The war the Nazis were carrying on was as much on a magical, psychic plane as it was on a physical one. They studied astrology, developed their psychic powers through meditations, worked with leyline energies and with rune magic and they placed their strongholds on geomantically powerful places.

The Nazis claimed that 'creation is not yet completed' and that we are now waiting the coming of the 'sons of god/the lord of cosmos'. This sounds uncannily like pronouncements made by many New Age gurus today.

Morning of the Magicians was written in 1961 by Louis Pauwel and Jacques Bergier.[16] I was amazed and shocked by this book that talked of the Nazis as 'magic plus tanks' and of a terrible esoteric knowledge, the secret of energy and matter, that was kept safe by the alchemists of old but that has now fallen into the hands of men such as nuclear scientists who are technicians of destruction instead of the sacred; men who do not respect life and are hurtling us fast into a sterile oblivion where nothing will grow and nothing will live. I was surprised to find that Louis Pauwel is now involved in the French new right movement.

Nigel Pennick, author of *Hitler's Secret Sciences*, writes that the SS was consciously modelled on the Jesuit order, the command structure of initiates who were the religious wing of the Spanish empire, founded by Ignatius Loyola (1491–1566). The Jesuits were the driving force behind the Spanish Inquisition. They were very knowledgeable about sacred geomancy, astrology and the occult, and took over the sacred sites of the pagans everywhere for the sake of spiritual and psychic conquest of the peoples both in Europe and the Americas.

Hitler himself was born a Catholic while Himmler was

the son of a devout Catholic schoolmaster. Hitler reassured the Church that he would do nothing more to the Jewish people than what the Church had already done during centuries of pogroms encouraged by the Christians of Europe. Christians have always blamed the Jewish people for the death of their saviour, forgetting of course that Jesus himself was a Jew and that it was in fact the Romans who were ultimately responsible for his death.

Himmler set out, as the leader of the SS, to create a new Aryan warrior caste to rule a world returned to feudalism, a new order created by the Nordic race possessed of special mystic and psychic powers. Nigel Pennick points out that one in four members of the SS possessed the degree of doctor. Intellectuals, students, professors, land owners, the upper-classes and industrialists eagerly flocked to join this new élite.

The SS also modelled themselves on the mystical knights of Arthurian legend and on the Teutonic knights of mediaeval Germany who terrorised the Slavic people with the sign of the cross. They were *Männerbunde*, male separatist brotherhoods like the Catholic priesthood, who were above the law and aimed to rule society.[17]

This New Man was to become the perfectly logical man who had abandoned all passions and all illusions and who had achieved immortality. The state was the overlord and father of the legal order and had the absolute right to kill.

The nulear scientist or Pentagon general who discusses in matter-of-fact terms the possibility of megadeaths and the expendability of entire human populations is hardly less fascist than were Hitler and the Nazis.

Fascism is endemic in all patriarchal societies throughout history as they subjugate the female half of the human race. As long as the New Age movement persists in adhering to patriarchal religious thinking and philosophies, it will be part of the problem and not the solution.

Alice Bailey (1880–1949) has had a major influence on the thinking of Findhorn. She came from a well-off and puritanical Christian family in Britain, and had like Annie

Besant, been a battered wife and mother.[18] She became involved in the Theosophist movement in the USA and then broke away in the 1930s to found a school of her own. For thirty years or so she was the 'channel' for innumerable books dictated to her, telepathically and through automatic writing from a Secret Master known as Djwhal Khul (DK) supposedly a discarnate Tibetan. He was one of the Rishis or 'high adepts' who, according to Alice Bailey, are planning to walk on the earth again and offer their assistance in nurturing and governing the planet. Alice Bailey wrote *The Great Invocation* (of light) which has become the mantra or hymn of the New Age and is totally patriarchal. She saw it as her life task to work for the reappearance of Christ, whom she described as the 'head of the hierarchy' and as one with the 'father or cosmic source' and for the materialised 'kingdom of god on earth'.

She envisaged that this would be brought about through a network of organised light-centres such as Findhorn invoking 'the presence', the second coming of the male messiah or saviour, around the Earth. Christ, who is the Maitreya Buddha and Buddha are the heads of the hierarchical lodge of love, and together they are the lords of light and love, according to Alice Bailey.

Here are the words of Alice Bailey's *The Great Invocation* which is intoned as a New Age hymn at many gatherings to meditate on 'world healing' in Britain and the USA:

From the point of light within the mind of God
Let light stream forth into the minds of men
Let light descend on Earth.

From the point of love within the heart of God
Let love stream forth into the hearts of men
May Christ return to Earth.

From the centre where the will of God is known
Let purpose which the masters know and serve

> From the centre which we call the race of men
> Let the plan of love and light work out
> And may it seal the door where evil dwells.
>
> Let light and love and power restore the
> Plan on Earth.

The racist preoccupation with whiter than white has had disastrous consequences for the Earth and for ourselves. In our attempts at eternally whitening our clothes and our surroundings, we have been turning Earth itself into a poisoned sewage pit, its waters full of chemicals from bleaches and cleaning/washing powders. We are also poisoning our own bodies by eating white bread and white sugar from which all nourishment has been deleted and we use bleached paper products that transmit the highly toxic dioxin into our blood streams through certain tampons, sanitary towels, baby nappies, milk cartons, tea bags and coffee filters. The only purpose is for these products to appear 'white and pure'. To the ancient pre-Indo-European Goddess peoples, however, black was the colour of life and fertility. It is the colour of damp, protective caves and rich soil, of the womb of the Goddess where life germinates and begins. White was the colour of death, as in white hair, snow, ashes, ghosts and bones.

The Goddess is both dark and light, both of this and of the otherworld of the spirits.

Alice Bailey was obsessed with fire and light and solar energies and must have feared darkness, deep earth energies and lunar water powers. One of her influential books 'dictated' by master DK is significantly called *Treatise on Cosmic Fire*.[19] In it she explains that there are three esoteric aspects of fire: fire by friction, solar fire and cosmic fire, which is the fire dormant within the energy of the atom.

At the heart of every atom is a blinding point of light and the sun itself is a nuclear furnace. At the sun's core, hydrogen nuclei fuse to make helium nuclei. The energy liberated is sunshine. The Master DK proclaimed in the

1930s that the release of atomic energy would be a great discovery that would revolutionise the world, bringing about a super-consciousness and a global civilisation. Like the Christian mystic Teilhard de Chardin, DK welcomed the explosion of the first atomic bomb in 1945 as a great 'spiritual event', and as being the first step taken towards harnessing cosmic energy and 'consciousness'.

He revealed that the hierarchy of Secret Masters have in fact encouraged the emergence of the multinationals and the manufacture of the machine which was meant to be an instrument of release.[20] Energy, the 'soul-force within the atom' is to be liberated from matter. 'This is for matter itself a great and potent initiation, paralleling those initiations which liberate or release the souls of men.'[21] The Lord is indeed a consuming fire.

The first nuclear experiment at Los Alamos in the USA was known as Project Trinity and the result of the fusion was code-named Baby Jesus. In the Second World War the US government, comprised of men whose only culture is power, led the universities in research into weapons and behavioural science. The nuclear bomb was produced and used *after* the Germans were defeated.

A course was run in the summer of 1988 on 'Nuclear Energy, New Clear Energy' at Findhorn during the course of which it was planned to visit a nuclear power station. It says in the prospectus advertising that year's residential courses:

> '. . . [We] seek a creative response to the use and function of the atomic and nuclear domain . . . The forces released out of the atom are as much in the atmosphere of our inner world as the atmosphere of this young planet . . . to examine the nature of the energy as it is known to exist at the atomic level; how it separates into masculine force and feminine power when the atom is split; how we may find parallels with these aspects of energy in ourselves and in the heavens.'

No doubt nuclear waste and what has happened to the indigenous peoples of the Pacific, Australia and Namibia were never mentioned. To discuss this would, after all, be a sign of being 'negative'.

Gender Bending in the Development of Science

I now explore gender thinking in the development of science and for this I am entirely indebted to Brian Easlea, a former physicist who has written some very important books on science and gender thinking.[22]

Some male historians have claimed that the 'witchhunts' that lasted for three centuries and were nowhere more virulent than in Germany (something like 80 per cent of the 'witches' who were murdered were women), were the end result of the struggle between the new enlightened male thinking on the one hand and women's ignorance and 'superstition' on the other hand. The wise women supposedly stood in the way of 'progress' and the final flowering of individualistic male consciousness. But it was women's early and wise scientific/magical/rational thinking about our fertility and healing, our organic and magical relationship to the Earth and all that lives, which was wiped out. We have long been suffering the consequences of this 'death of nature'.[23]

Brian Easlea writes of how the new philosophers in the seventeenth century, led by Francis Bacon in Britain, advocated the 'male birth of time' and 'male philosophy'.[24] Bacon promised that nature, the Mother of us all, would finally be under male control. He would 'lead to you nature with all her children to bind her to your services and make her your slave'. The new philosophers declared that women possessed no creative powers in the production of life and that living creatures, themselves included, were in no way the immanent product of the Earth Mother but the created product of god the father.

The natural philosophers would demonstrate their virility by the scientific and technological appropriation of a mechanical Earth and by the scientific penetration into the dark 'womb' of female nature. From men's ancient incestuous son/lover relationship with Mother Earth, She was denigrated to lifeless machine and mere matter in motion. Nature was barren, lifeless but still female, and life itself was banished from the universe. We were to live in an unmothered world. This control was in the interest of the rising capitalist classes in post-seventeenth-century Europe.

The so-called Enlightenment and social progress consisted of men imposing their value systems on women in a homocentric, patriarchal, imperial culture. 'Reason' was born from man's urge to dominate Matter/Mater/Mother. The mechanical philosophers, led by Descartes (1596–1650), who had lost his mother at birth, declared that Earth is barren and sterile, inert matter that is incapable of creating life. Nature was stripped of mysterious female creative powers and rendered totally barren. This is our legacy.

Nobel-prize-winning molecular biologists Jacques Monod and François Jacobs claim that 'Evolution is not the property of living beings', that life is a mistake. There is, according to them, no Mother Nature and the 'universe was not pregnant with life nor the biosphere with man'. The Earth has no conscious mind and chance alone explains evolution and innovation. Descartes said: 'There exists no occult forces in stones and plants' and that animals have no souls but are simply automatons without feelings. Vivisection is justified by this thinking. The philosphers attempt to explain organic processes by mechanism and we have inherited a throughly irrational science which is based on male uterus-envy, the myth of male fecundity and an aggressive phallic psychology that wants to tear apart the dark womb as well as the dark centre of the atom.

The scientists Oppenheimer and Lawrence beheld

'heavy water' in 1945 and enthused that here was something that existed on Earth in gaseous form some billion years ago, long before there was any water of life and with the power to return Earth to its 'lifeless state'. Through atomic disintegration in matter, scientists are now able to revert Earth back to chaos. Marie Curie, the great woman scientist, identified and isolated radioactive X-rays – the blue glow of the future – in 1896 and the uranium atom was first split in December 1938, the very month and year I was born. Marie Curie had thought that her discovery, achieved at the cost of her health and life, would be a tool for the good and for healing.

Rutherford, called 'father of atomic physics', wanted to pierce the darkness of the atom and 'attacked the atomic nucleus' to deprive atoms of their secrets. Scientists are set upon unravelling life's most intimate and hidden secrets whether in 'atom smashers' or playing around with genes and DNA. There is also an insane momentum towards war as an end in itself, scientists thrilling at doing the impossible, however dangerous for life and survival, as seen in the Gulf war, an electronic armageddon. The release of monstrous and destructive forces in the nuclear bombs were represented as the birth of 'sons' and as 'fathered' by Oppenheimer and Teller.

Easlea speaks of the 'pregnant phallus' and of patriarchy's deadly self-knowledge. The scientific research leading to nuclear weapons and the explicit sexual imagery and metaphors used by scientists in their work, are intimately connected. Before the Second World War scientists were discussing the interior of the sun. They have, since then, unlocked the very power that the sun god commands.

Uranium was discovered in 1789 by a German chemist and was given its name from the nearly discovered planet named Uranus in 1781. An original Greek word for heavens is 'Ouranos'. The god Uranus was at first the consort of Urania, the queen of heaven. He then usurped her powers, became sole heavenly ruler and the lover of Gaia, the Earth, who legends tell is also his Mother.[25]

The discovery of Uranus coincided with revolutionary change in France and America and with the beginning of the industrial revolution, and has therefore astrologically come to symbolise rebellion, genius and change, with flashing insights, with electrical energies in brain and nervous system, with prana, a subtle energy associated with breath or spirit. Some hopefuls even believe that mutations from radioactive fallout might help evolution. Outer space flight is now 'sexy', space shuttles are virility symbols, rockets images of space rape. Easlea says that, 'Nuclear missiles with their sleek phallic forms, are the ultimate symbol of male intelligence divorced from religious impulse and feminine cherishing.'

American laboratories have been racing with each other to oblivion, producing and inventing every conceivable fission and fusion weapon. With the discovery of nuclear fission and the breakthrough in electronics, physicists became, almost overnight, the most important military resource that a nation/state could call on. They lost their 'innocence' and from then on became civilian soldiers. Release of nuclear energy is necessary for space flight so that the 'spirit of man' can be set 'free' to dominate cosmos through genetic modification of his physical body and the elimination of women. War negates women and creativity. Ecstasy, joy or love is not part of this plan.

The USA emerged from the Second World War as the strongest industrial nation on earth. While some 300,000 US troops were lost, the Russians lost 20 million people and Russia lay in ruins. The USA initiated the nuclear arms race which extended to the USSR and other countries around the world. It is dependent upon a permanent war economy which has been in operation since the Second World War. The survival of capitalism depends on ever-increasing arms expenditure – the largest industry in the USA is that of arms production – arms are continually destroyed and need continual replacement. A major enemy is always needed; with the ending of the 'cold war' the USA has turned its attention to the Middle East and to creating the New World Order.

The Electric Shock Book is by Michael Shallis,[26] who is something of an electro-sensitive as well as a scientist interested in the effects modern technology has on society. He is also a student of parapsychology and the occult.

His thesis is that there might be extrasensory perception between people and computers and that there might be spiritual entities being created by electronic circuits.

There is a connection between electricity, allergies and the psychic dimension. We are now living in a technological society in which there is a total and polluting overload of electromagnetic energies. We are being ensnared all around the globe. We are literally being 'wired up'. In this situation, people begin to feel physically and emotionally drained and some feel as if their will and being gets taken over by an alien force.

Earth is like a giant magnet with powerful electromagnetic fields, and light is a propagation of such changing fields: matter is therefore primarily electrical and so is light. There is an interdependence of the electrical fields of living things with that of the magnetic Earth. The atmosphere shields us from life-threatening, high-energy radiation from the sun and from lethal cosmic rays. Without the ozone layer, we would not be here. The electromagnetic properties of the sun and its light affects the Earth and all of Her creatures including us and so does the eleven-year sunspot cycle. All material is both electrical and magnetic and acquires its different forms and structures from what Shallis calls 'life-fields'. He thinks that these electromagnetic fields, which are manifestations of energy, shape the biological patterns that hold our forms. Kirlian photography traces our 'electrical body'[27] as flaming and multi-coloured auras are made visible at last. Electrical fields and currents flow in our nervous systems and in our brains. Many psychics can see these auras.

We are naturally electrical beings in a by-now totally

unnatural electrical world and the interference with our subtle biological electrical fields by an imposed gross electrical environment is damaging the sensitivity in us all and is making us ill. Natural electromagnetism is a good and life-creating power of light and healing and joins our physical realm with the world of the spirits. Electromagnetism is the physical manifestation of a more subtle energy that the Chinese call Chi and the Hindus Prana. And water and blood are symbols of the flow of the life-giving spirit.

Shallis says that there is an electrical interaction between the physical and the psychic realms, and supposedly shamans of all times were/are particularly sensitive to Earth's electromagnetic field. Stone circles work with these energies. Shallis believes that modern electronics technology is a perversion of these subtle energies and has become as he says the 'dark side of the force'. Further, that alien and malevolent entities are being summoned into being through the finely tuned electronic circuits of computers that are akin to our own nervous systems. Our nervous systems relate on an electrical level to the fields around computer circuits ('electronic brains'), and our minds get caught up within them. We become a part of the machine.

At the end of the 1940s, the US government poured vast sums of money into electronic firms because it considered that the new electronics would be important for its defence programme. In fact, in the Gulf war electronics were used not in defence but in attack on a Third World country. The Gulf war was played by US generals and aircraft personnel as though it were a video game.

At the end of the 1960s the silicon chip came into being and by 1980 a million components could be etched on a minute wafer of silicon. IBM became a multi-national corporation and now electronics permeate every aspect of modern society. Computers can be connected up right across the globe. They are instruments of power as they enable governments, police and security intelligence to monitor and keep total control over more and more people. Electronic communications have been spread for political and military reasons and for commercial information exchange, while it has been sold to us as an extended form of human exchange, the so-called Global Village. We are fed more and more information about less and less, just as we are given more and more 'choice' in buying artificial and useless products. Robots and computers take over at the workplace because they do not go on strike or become ill. We can now communicate via telephones, television etc. without any human touch. Computers are autonomous, self-regulating, information-processors. Anything that can be tuned into an electrical signal can be fed into a computer. Robot weapons such as cruise missiles can make their own decisions about their trajectory and even which target to strike. In other words, it is left up to a machine to decide over life or death and killing, and star wars nuclear weapons in space would rely on such automated decisions by computers.

Shallis says that the cult of the computer has given rise to a diminished view of human beings. There is a desire to replace and reduce the role of humans. There are psychologists already talking of human beings as 'biological information processors'. Computer technology emerges from a reductionist scientific philosophy that sees everything as physical, chemical and electrical processes and where nothing has meaning. This is the heritage from the mechanistic philosophy developed by Descartes who perceived the Earth as a clockwork mechanism devoid of life-creating powers or spirit. It is a patriarchal, necrophilic and nihilistic view of creation, and the computer embodies this philosophy to the hilt. Shallis says that computers were designed by groups of male scientists to whom quality, wisdom and knowledge were unimportant – only information-processing mattered. The computer reduces complexities and subtleties. Computers were designed to improve military efficiency and targeting. Then they were used to develop hydrogen bombs and today they are used for business efficiency. Computers were also designed to enhance the power of those who possess them.

Shallis, like Brian Easlea, considers that scientists are unaware of the forces they might be invoking. He sees nuclear physicists as 'black alchemists' producing poison and death instead of spiritual understanding. Plutonium is the most toxic element known. No coincidence that Pluto was the Roman god of death and the underworld, and with the atomic and hydrogen bombs he has materialised in a physical force of terror.

The alienated left-brain thinking of patriarchal men results in monstrosities. The so-called Enlightenment and 'rational' thought of modern scientific reductionism has created nuclear bombs and computer brains. Shallis calls this the incarnation of Ahriman, the Persian god of darkness, who is a calculating, unemotional, detached, cold, objective and intelligent god who reduces everything to measure, weight and numbers. He is all head and no heart. Shallis says that these are precisely the characteristics that develop in those working with and obsessed with computers and he describes the utterly alienated and artificial environment in which advanced computer programmers work. Rooms without windows or natural light, everywhere synthetic, arid and sterile materials, and the glowing screen of the computer with its electronic hum. People become addicted – using a computer is like a fix. It is as if the computer feeds on people, and apparently a feeling of coldness over the chest, disorientation and nausea is not uncommon. Humans are seen to be a stage in the evolution of robots who are supposed to succeed us. The ultimate computer room is the space station and the ultimate aim is to conquer nature, the Mother, and to deny any links to our living, ecstatic, watery, sexual body organisms and to Earth itself. Disembodied brains plugged into the machine, a man/machine symbiosis and total subjugation of will to the electronic command is what is envisaged.

Already in the USA, psychiatrists are worried about a

whole generation of teenagers who have grown up addicted to watching television and playing computer games. These children seem to have no heart, no sense of human justice, emotions or compassion, and they only come alive when in front of an electronic screen. Computer games are violent and often involve killing and even rape. 'Heavy metal' music, plugged into the machine, calls up the demonic and advocates violence and rape. Shallis fears that computer programmers are acting as agents for a cold, dark, unnatural world and that the unnatural electrical fields around computers interacting subliminally with human electric life fields spell disaster. But of course our electrical matrix (the Goddess) is ignored by scientists. Shallis's point is that, in the outer spirit realms, there might well be entities such as Ahriman who feed on negative emotions and naked unbalanced electrical energies, and for whom the electronic brain of the computer is the ideal medium to enter fully into this world. There are already reports of spirit entities using computers to materialise, and of electronic poltergeists. The devil is the curse of those who have abandoned the Goddess and partriarchal societies have truly created monsters from the Id.

Robert Monroe, author of *Journeys Out of the Body* and *Far Journeys*,[28] has some interesting ideas concerning the Secret Masters. He has travelled in his second/astral body out into astral realms for many years and suggests that an organised group of entities/people, who were able to achieve this at will, could indeed control the destiny of humankind. Human beings operating in the 'second body' can affect people mentally and through dreams, and the wilful misuse of this power is potentially so great that other means are helpless against it. Monroe suggests that there might have been some kind of conspiracy afoot to stop human beings from exploring our psychic powers and from journeying out into other realms, and he feels that such entities/masters would certainly wield the power to bring this about.

The Church did, indeed, set out to undermine and to

destroy the ESP potential that exists in us all to a certain degree throughout centuries of witchhunts and the hunting down of heretics and shamans amongst many peoples. The ability to enter into dreamtime, and the shamanistic powers to communicate with spirits and to shapeshift, was always seen as a threat by the men of the Church who set out to imperialise our minds and to prod into our dreams. We have since been left with an anti-mystical church and the derision of scientists who deny the non-material world and the invisible realms of the spirits with which women are the primary communicators. Our abilities to 'see the unseen' have been vastly diminished.

Monroe writes that the 'voices' that so many so-called psychotics hear, may indeed be real, and that many of those labelled mentally ill or even physically ill, might suffer, in fact, from some disturbance of the second or astral body. What we now term the unconscious (made unconscious because repressed and denied) is aware of, and is familiar with, the other realms that we often enter in lucid dreams. Our actions in those realms while we are dreaming, and what we learn there, have a strong effect on our daily lives, although consciously we no longer remember. Many shamanic tribal peoples set great store on the prophetic importance of dreams. Considering that we spend half our lives in the dreamstate, this seems an eminently sensible thing to do.

I have found another explanation for the predominance of male spirit guides and Secret Masters in *The Nature of the Psyche* by the American poet, Jane Roberts.[29] She was a channel for the wise and witty spirit-entity, Seth, and her books are dictated by 'him'. Seth says that in the thought or astral realms, where everything takes place through thought and visualisations, spirit beings have no gender but can adopt whatever role or gender that is projected upon them from our world. In partriarchal societies such as ours, it is the male gender that is assumed to represent universality and even women mediums feel more comfortable identifying with and projecting male spirits.

Seth also says that bisexuality is the natural state and that it is the rigid gender roles imposed by our society that so thoroughly block out our awareness and knowledge of former lives, of reincarnation. In former lives sometimes we were female and sometimes male but in no way would a patriarch admit to ever having lived in a woman's body with a woman's consciousness! Seth is the only spirit guide I have come across who is quite so radical and unbiased, and this is to a large extent due to Jane Roberts's own intelligence.

Seth also says that our bodies are aware of both birth and death and that the dreams of those who are about to die often involve dream-structures that will prepare them for future experience in other states. I know this is true because every time my son Sean, who suffered from cancer, was close to death he had the most vivid and magical dreams of fantastic landscapes. He also had visions in the waking state that left him in a state of awe and wonder.

Lawrence Le Shan writes[30] that our western, supposedly common-sense, view of time as one-way and irrevocably linear is, in fact, peculiar to our culture. It is not accepted today by modern physics neither was it accepted by the ancient world. This linear sense of history and time is Christian and dates from the birth of Christ, a unique event.

The older religions did not have unique events; the great events were cyclic and seasonal, the people lived and experienced the sacred dramas of the Goddess and the death and rebirth of Her young son/lover each year with the lunar and solar changes and the waxing and waning of Earth's energies. Jesus replaced all the sons and lovers of the eternal Mother.

The Hebrews had prepared the way for this new concept of linear time, with Jehovah handing down the tablets from Mount Sinai and a Messiah who was to appear but once, but it was Christianity that spread the message throughout the world. Christians preached that there was one god who made the world and everything in it, and this belief is echoed in those of Catholics, Protestants, Jews and Muslims alike. One set of laws, so-called 'natural laws' covered everything and god, himself, was bound in this web of single definition and 'rationality'.

But, Le Shan points out, it is important to ask in what realms we observe such phenomena as telepathy; whether it is in the realm of everyday sensory experience or in the realm where concepts such as time and space do not exist. There are different metaphysical systems with their different 'logics', but common sense,'that collection of prejudices accumulated by the age of 18' as Einstein said, boggles at truths from other dimensions. There are two kinds of time: ordinary 'linear' time and dreamtime/great time/ sacred time of the all-at-once. The ancients journeyed at ease in and out of these realms, as some indigenous peoples still do, while with us the 'doors of perception' were truly locked after the burning times during which even women's dreams were investigated and declared taboo. We were burned for knowing starlore and divination.

Native American elder Chief Seattle, speaking out of the dreamtime consciousness said: 'The earth does not belong to man; man belongs to the earth . . . [man] did not weave the web of life; he is merely a strand in it. Whatever he does to the web, he does to himself.'[31]

Some modern physicists, like Fritiof Capra who wrote *The Tao of Physics*, are now coming back full circle to the ancient understanding of the interconnected weave and pace of life. This was the world of thought, of Spider Woman of the Americas and of the Scandinavian Norns who spun, wove and cut the threads of our lives and of all creation. A Polynesian woman will only become pregnant when the spirit of the unborn is welcomed by her; the Bambara of West Indian Sudan believe that the correct balance of the entire cosmos depends on their speaking good words because speech carries part of the vital energy present in matter. So too, the Kahunas of Hawaii had extraordinary insights into clairvoyant realities and other selves.

In that world there were the same love and empathy between the humans and earth/cosmos as between a child and its mother. The Christian Church has much to answer for in this our severance from oneness with cosmos and communications with the otherworld realms. Mircea Eliade, speaking of shamanism, writes that in ancient times there was a bridge between Earth and heaven and there was not yet death. Once this link was broken, people could only cross the bridge in death or in ecstasy.

New Age Patriarchy

In Findhorn, according to Daphne Francis, politics is separated from spirituality. The American David Spangler's work is recommended reading for new members and guests, and his books are published and distributed by the community. He had a profound influence on Peter Caddy, his writings were treated as 'holy writ' and his book *Revelation: The Birth of a New Age*[32] was used to define New Age energies and laws for this 'Centre of Light'.

David Spangler is, like Eileen Caddy, somewhat of a psychic – although he has also studied biochemistry and genetics in Arizona, which I find significant. Like her, he had a guide, Master Rakoczi (Master R), also supposedly from the inner court of the brotherhood or hierarchy of Masters, who claimed to be the voice and force of light and discipline. He was born in 1945 and appears, like Eileen Caddy, to have spent his childhood in north Africa. When he arrived at Findhorn from the USA in 1970, the community was only an extended family of about fifteen members. Spangler stayed there for three years. While there he set in motion the educational programme which developed into the University of Light. His books are deeply influenced by Alice Bailey's right-wing thinking and are dedicated to the 'network of world servers', a 'spiritual Freemasonry' which works behind the scenes worldwide for the 'Forces of Light' and the Christforce. Like Alice Bailey, Spangler thought that nuclear holocaust would be a revelation from the Masters and that the élite would be untouched by it.

Spangler advocates cold intellectualism and New Age élitism, as well as a belief in the superiority of the white 'Aryan' races in his books *Towards A Planetary Vision* and *Explorations: Emerging Aspects of the New Cultures*.[33] According to him, Findhorn was attempting to develop a 'theocratic democracy', and 'a centre like Findhorn exists because a planetary birth is taking place'.[34] He suggests, as did William Irwin Thompson, that we should begin 'seeing corporations [multinationals] as ways of serving the planet-strategies for establishing planetary consciousness.'[35] Government, according to Spangler, 'did not originate with humanity; it originated with beings who were the original teachers of humanity.'[36] Like Rudolf Steiner before him, Spangler advocates that humanity must now leave behind the 'instinctive group attunement' and that we must graduate from 'the experiences that earth has to offer'. We have to be weaned from the Earth and the function of industrial society is to remove from us 'the natural clairvoyance and the awareness of the inner realm of nature and life.'[37] We are to be asked to 'step free from Earth into the immensity of cosmic experience, and the voice of nature as we know it will no longer be present.'[38] The point of entry for this new energy is 'through a being who is known as the Lord of the World. This being is also the king or the head of the Hierarchy' and 'a new Christhood is coming into being'.[39]

Alice Bailey's 'The Great Invocation' is promoted by the World Goodwill organisation, which is an organ for the World Servers, founded by Alice Bailey and her Master DK as a service activity of the Lucis Trust. It would seem that both David Spangler and Peter Caddy are involved in this organisation which has its headquarters in London, and branches in New York and Geneva, and close connections with the United Nations. World Goodwill published a pamphlet called *Money – The Medium of Loving Distribution*, compiled from Alice Bailey's writings. Master DK states that the World Servers will need money in large quantities and recommends money to be visualised as a great stream of flowing golden substance that is transferred to the 'Forces of Light' and away from the forces of materialism. To Master DK, money is but a manifestation of energy and is a neutral force. Need, love and magnetic power are the three things which attract money. The World Servers are to plan each week their 'financial co-operation with the Hierarchy'.[40] This kind of thinking is prevalent in the white and privileged New Age movement; at least DK made it clear that one has no right to draw money to oneself for purely selfish reasons, which is something which has not been heeded by some New Agers, such as the Rebirthers.

These global family and Earth stewardship networks seem to have very much a western focus. The Findhorn-inspired journal *Link Up* speaks naïvely of a European union of nations that will benefit all, with no apparent awareness that the west is responsible for disharmony and poverty in other parts of the world, that our economies thrive from arms sales to the Third World, and that the EC countries are partners in building a fortress against the Third World. Everything becomes even more grotesque now when one considers the recent war in the Gulf conducted by the USA and its European allies, and sanctioned by the United Nations.

David Spangler and the World Servers make it clear that the ancient powerlines of the Earth – the ancient sacred sites dedicated to the Goddess – have to be sealed so that their new Christ energy will be able to take over and the 'King of the World' and the 'Hierarchy' will walk again on this earth. As put by DK and Alice Bailey, 'From the centre which we call the race of men let the plan of love and light work out. And may it seal the door where evil dwells.'

This is a meditation to be presented every Sunday morning to Christ and his 'Hierarchy' by the World Servers.[41]

In a Findhorn discussion paper called *The Plan of Light*, power points, the etheric web and the significance of ancient sacred places, originally of the Goddess, such as the island of Iona and of Glastonbury, are discussed. It explains how the etheric body of the earth is a field of energy and radiation, an aura that gives vitality to our planet's physical planes. It is the source of the primal creative energy from which physical forms are built and sustained. All human beings have an etheric body that interacts with it. Earth possesses terrestrial magnetic currents that are multi-dimensional and that flow along Earth's grid and pressure/fault plates. There are natural windows which open to other dimensions – something well known to the Earth Mysteries movement. Lunar and solar influences produce large fluctuations in Earth's magnetic field. This field is criss-crossed with lines of power flow, an etheric web of power (or perhaps the radiant fibres spun by Spider Woman), that are linked together by power-points. In the human body these are called the chakras. There are different kinds of centres attuned to different kinds of consciousness and energies. A power centre is where the energies of several dimensions meet and where gateways between different realities are thin.

The paper claims that the ancients harnessed these energy flows to human purposes in the leyline system and the stones. Human consciousness can raise the level of the flow for good or for evil. Also 'dark centres of evil power came into being' and the original neutral spiritual force was 'sundered by human consciousness into twin aspects of light and dark'. According to the plan of light, energy tapped from the cosmos was also stored at certain power centres to be released in the future.

It says that in the New Age new energy requires new channels of release, and a cleansing of the etheric body of the Earth is happening now that more powerful new forces are entering the planet. There is a formation of new centres to receive the soul energies of the planet such as Findhorn, withdrawal of some and the cleansing of others. A new etheric body of the Earth, of a higher vibratory expression, is now being formed, a new world is being born as the old one disintegrates and is transmuted. This is so for many ancient sacred power centres where the 'old gods' sleep still, their time passed.

Many New Age centres need to tap into the powers of ancient centres because they themselves are of the existing etheric web. Glastonbury and Iona are two such main planetary centres, key points on the old web and used by Atlantean adepts, that were consecrated to Christ and 'became points of focus for the distribution of the Christ life through Britain and, indeed, all of the world'. Certain centres were charged by Christ to hold their energies until this time for 'the New Age represents a time when the majority of humanity will pass the first initiation and experience the birth of Christ within . . . it is in his name and the name of Christ consciousness within humanity that these ancient centres are being re-awakened and re-consecrated, that all might know that the Son of Man again walks the earth and the sons of men know that they are one with him.'

The Plan of Light discusses the significance of Iona, the sacred island off the coast of western Scotland which is claimed to be a major centre of planetary power 'attuned to the Christ'. According to the Findhorn philosophers, its energies 'were anchored there in Atlantean times by priests of the Sun who, in anticipation of our time, invoked the energies of the Solar God and beamed them westwards to the new worlds beyond the sea and east to the cradle-lands of Europe'. It was later the headquarters of St Columba and his monks who 'carried the lights of Celtic Christianity' during the Dark Ages after the fall of the Roman Empire. It is now a centre for 'the release of New Age energies' and, in 1972, the Findhorn Community were given a sanctuary and centre on the island.[42]

The conclusion I draw from all this is that pagans and

Goddess lovers are seen in relation to the ancient powers that are to fade away in the New Age to give way to messengers of solar male consciousness. The sacred sites from Avebury/Silbury to Callanish (on the outer Hebrides) are presumably places of dark pagan powers because they are not touched or manipulated by Christianity and, like the Tasmanians, we Goddesswomen are supposed to die off so as not to stand in the way of 'New Age man'.

However, with the increasing damage done to the ozone layer and the deadly ultra violet rays of the sun entering unhindered because the Earth's own immune system is being destroyed, perhaps we will all soon know the destructive powers of the solar god.

As years have gone by, changes have of course come about at Findhorn. Carol Riddel, who has lived there many years now, has recently brought out a book called *The Findhorn Community – Creating a Human Identity for the Twenty-First Century*[43] in which she discusses its present evolution. Carol, a former radical feminist, has become a Sai Baba devotee, however, and writes throughout the book of 'God' and 'he'.

The Goddess Re-emerging

The ancient tantric teachings of India state that the Goddess is light itself and transcendent and that rays of light emanate from Her body. It is by and through Her that all things moving and motionless shine. It is by the Light of this Devi that all things become manifest.[44]

My experience and that of innumerable other women is that the sacred places of the Goddess are reawakening and instructing us in this late hour when the Earth Herself, the great planetary Spirit Being, is fighting for Her survival against patriarchal destruction and insanity. We are only conscious because She is conscious and sacred. If Her immune system breaks down, we also sicken.

Increasingly, women and many men seek out the sacred sites and find that if they are approached with reverence, love and respect, they speak to us and teach and heal us. Many have life-transformative experiences in this way and gain a far greater awareness of the sacredness of our Earth Mother and an expanded psychic sensitivity. The ancient Goddess sites are trance-inducing; there, spirits speak to us in dreams and visions.

5
Reclaiming the Dark Mother

Light and Dark in the Realms of the Goddess

In women's mysteries the gynandrous (that is, both female and male) Great Mother always has a dark side which has both 'positive' and 'negative' aspects, both birth-bringing and death-dealing, and women were the guardians of both.[1] The Goddess contains within Herself all energies and is the centre from where they emanate. She can live with paradoxes and mystery and Her message to us is: 'As I dying live, so you dying will live again.' In the natural world, light and dark are interwoven without contradiction and disharmony.

Women were always the traditional guardians of fire; the tribal fire harmonised with the light of the moon Mother in the night and kept wild animals at bay, while people gathered around to share dreams, wisdom, tribal lore and teachings. There are innumerable lunar creation myths and the moon was thought to give healing, wisdom, fertility and the powers of the mind.

The primal mysteries of all religions emerged from women's direct biological and psychic experiences in planting the seed, in growing the child, in making a pot. Water, like fire, was sacred to the moon Mother. Women were the ancient makers and keepers of fires. Blood is the physical counterpart of the mystical life force circling throughout the cosmos, nourishing the universe, sustaining its breath and manifesting itself.

Women first discovered how to use and produce fire

and, with the use of water, brought about the transmutation of clay into another substance; they were the ancient potters and pots were conceived of as the 'womb of the Goddess.' Women transformed wheat into bread and through the use of fire they found ways of drying, cooking and preserving foods. Women were constantly bringing about transmutations; with blood, with water, and with fire.[2] Women's internal menstrual and sexual fires create life within the watery caverns of our bodies.

Celtic Brigid was not only the Goddess of fire and water, but also the Goddess of poetry and of smithcraft. She was the lover of the waters as maiden of springs and she was the indwelling spirit of the healing wells. It was women's discoveries of directed heat and their invention of ovens for making bread and other foods, as well as kilns for firing pots, that led to the making of furnaces within which fire could reach temperatures high enough to melt metals. The oven and kiln were perceived as a transformative fiery womb.

The pineal gland – seat of the third eye and the soul – is triggered by the light of the moon. Perhaps our right-side brain, the visionary dream mind, developed under the polarising light of the moon or perhaps it was women's menstrual cycle that created human mind and intelligence. The fact remains that the ancients' words, in most cultures, for mind and wisdom – and also for time-reckoning – were derived from words for moon. Sanskrit, Greek, Latin and Polynesian words for spirit and mind (manas, menos, mens, mana) are connected with Indo-European word-roots for moon and month (menstrual words like mas, men and mensis). Looking at these root-words, one can certainly draw the conclusion, as suggested in *The Great Cosmic Mother*, written by myself and Barbara Mor, that women's menstrual cycle was the great evolutionary force in the creation of human consciousness.

Many people worshipped the sun as the Goddess, life giver and life sustainer who loves us into life with her warmth and sustenance. Allat was the Great Mother of

Arabia, known as the sun that gives life to the day; on Malta she was known as Ma Lata; Arunta is the sun woman of Australian Aborigines; she is Amatesura of Japan and sun sister to the Inuit; Arinna was the sun of the Hattians of Anatolia in Turkey; Celtic Epona carries the sun disc in her arms as she travels on the shamanic white horse, and in Scandinavia ancient Nerthus brought the sun and spring and peace to the villages as she journeyed on the solar wagon at the vernal equinox.[3] After the long northern, dark winter months, the return of the spring and the warmth of the sun is truly ecstatic and the sun is experienced as an all-embracing mother.

Women's knowledge of herbs made them natural healers. Some herbs could also be used for inducing hypnotic states and producing trances and visions in religious rites. The hilltop fire rituals and torch-light processions, the mysteries of the wells and the menstrual life-giving waters, the birth of the sun child in the womb/cauldron of Cerridwen, the lunar Mother as the giver and creatrix of all life and mental powers, these were the mysteries of transmutation brought about through the dragon/Goddess powers in women. Women were the mediators of the Goddess and the creators of early culture.

The Celts, who never developed centralised states, measured time by the nights and kept their reverence and love of the Goddess. In the Celtic and Roman worlds, sacred priestesshoods, like the vestal virgins and the priestesses of Brigid, still tended the sacred flame. The Roman Goddess, Hestia, was the fire of the central domestic hearth which was also the entrance to the fiery and transformative furnace/womb of the underworld, the internal fires of Earth that created life. The core of the Earth is red-hot magma – blood as primal lava – and gestation takes place in the furnace of Earth's uterus.

Immortality lies in seeing death as an integral part of the cycle of life and its secrets are to be found in the cauldron, the secret that opens the door to the otherworld. The ancients believed that the moon is blood and that she menstruates. She pulls the tides of the oceans in which life was born – blood and sea-water are close in composition – and both represent elemental life fluids.

The Milky Way is the girdle of Ishtar or the milk from the udders of the heavenly cow Goddess. She lays the cosmic egg which is the moon and seed of the world, Earth is Her twin sister and child. The light of the moon and Her magnetic force bring fertility, movement and growth. The sun has been seen as the Mother, and the moon as Her eternally dying and reincarnating daughter. She also sends the fertilising rain.

There are many fiery volcanic mountains that are revered as the living abodes of the Goddess; lava is lifegiving and creates islands. Such sacred mountains are Mahuea on New Zealand/Aotearoa, Mount Fuijiama where the Goddess Fuji dwells, and Pélé of Hawaii.[4]

The ancient shaman women were midwives/healers and also astrologers. Moon is the great midwife, and who but the midwife knows the exact time and under what starsign a child is born? The neolithic stone circles are lunar temples and star observatories as well as being magical, psychic centres of entrance into other realms.

The moon is a symbol of connectedness between polarities and of continual transition. This lunar ability to live within the moment is the aim of many spiritual practices because it liberates us from the constrictions of the mind. Lindsay River and Sally Gillespie write in *The Knot of Time – Astrology and Female Experience*: 'It is unfortunate that many astrologers have reduced the importance of the moon to its moody, changeable nature, failing to see the wisdom of ancient teachings.' The authors reclaim astrology as ancient women's wisdom from its present-day patriarchal bias and they say that our experience of the moon has indeed been integral to human consciousness as biological processes in the brain are induced by light which affects psychic behaviour. With the banning of the Goddess and women's wisdom has gone the legitimacy of half the human psyche because with the Isis/moon side of the brain we perceive deep inner realities. We now suffer from alienation, cancers and a cosmic home-sickness. Our technologies push beyond the limits of biological safety. We now face possible irreversible pollution and an ecological crisis, both of which are the consequence of belief systems that exploit and violate nature. Disturbed rhythms create disturbed people and what has most of all been denied in patriarchal solar cultures are the lunar rhythms.

There are many legends which tell how the Goddess was born of a star. Sirius (Sept) was regarded as the sacred star of Isis (Au Sept); it is called the 'grandmother' by the Bush (wo)men and it is of great and sacred importance to the Dogon people of Mali. The Semites of Mesopotamia believed that Ishtar and her holy women had descended from Venus. Astarte of Canaan was said to have descended as a fiery falling star or meteorite, landing in a lake near Byblos in Lebanon, or at the sacred shrine of Aphaca, near the site of the most ancient Natufian culture of 9000 BC. The Goddess is associated with many meteorites: sacred stones of Diana of Euphesus and of Cybele, who called up the dead, the 'black stone of Kaaba' at Mecca which originally belonged to Al Uzza and is serviced by priests who to this day are called 'sons of the old woman' or moon. Many legends tell of a sacred relationship between holy lakes and stars, original creation occurring on flaming islands in a lake, of the first Mother/divine star ancestress. Deep in caves of the mighty volcano, the Goddess of Oceania keeps half of our spirit soul while we are alive, the other half returns when we die. Venus is a morning and evening star. The Virgin Mary is *stella maris*, star of the sea, and she is Almah or Moon-Maiden, who gives birth to the 'Healing Moon Man' (Christos Jasus of the Essenes). She was originally Ishtar-Mari-Mare-Sea, bride/Mother disguised as Venus, the evening star, who presided over the death of the sun/son Jasus, Tammuz, Adonis, Dionysus, all Middle-Eastern saviour gods. As Morning Star she gives birth to them anew.

Merlin Stone, in *Ancient Mirrors of Womanhood*, says that

Nammu, the Mother who gave birth to heaven and earth, is probably the oldest recorded name of a universe-creating deity so far discovered anywhere.

'MA' is the basic mother syllable of Indo-European languages and the most fundamental name of the Goddess, writes Barbara Walker in *The Women's Encyclopedia of Myths and Legends*[5] and there is no equivalent syllable for father. The blood-bond of the matrilinear clan was called Mamata (mine-ness) in the Far East. MA is the spark of life (Bindu) in the Great Yoni (cunt), the mystic essence uniting all souls. Those who share the same blood from a common mother cannot injure each other and hence there is peace between them. The Russian word *mir* means mother, peace, village-commune and the world. MA is the intelligence, the maternal force which bound the elements together in the beginning. Maat of Egypt was the 'all-seeing eye' of truth and justice and her laws were benevolent. Sanskrit Mati means 'thought, intention'. Mawu is the African great Goddess. Ma-Nu is the primal deep symbolised by three cauldrons; tantric Mamaki is the fertilising waters. Am-Am is eater of the souls, Ama or Amu is the Sumerian name for mother, the primaeval Ocean, and Mater Matuta is the morning boat of the sun.

Lunar Consciousness

The ancients knew there was a source of psychic sacred energy in the universe which must also be renewed as it is drawn upon, that there is an interdependence between all things and a transmutation of one substance into another. They believed that the trees and stones absorb psychic energy from human emotion – we know that plants also do this – and human rituals activate the stone circles, and they are invested with sacred power through the force of human worship. They also invest us with sacred powers.

Francis Hitchings tells in *Earth Magic*[6] of visions that the Yorkshire artist, Monica English, has had within stone circles. She says that there was dancing and feasting within them for three days at each of the four major festivals of the year with processional movements, sacred fires, chants and music during which human emotion was poured out, making the circles powerful. She says that the high point was the entrance of the Goddess queen into the circle and the enormous reverence given Her. The circle protected Her and also allowed the life force to enter Her. All the rituals led up to the great moment when She was possessed and made Her oracular announcements concerning healing, the safety of cattle and humans, future and past events. This was the original and natural 'witchcraft'.

I think that ancient women had developed spiritual technology and science that was both life- and death-enhancing and which existed within multiple realities. I also think that ancient women (and men) had a lunar consciousness (right side of the brain, 'Isis' side of the brain according to the Egyptians), which was very much more open and alive and in no way dominated by the left (analytical, linear, intellectual) side of the brain which has a tendency to become rigid and overly abstract if allowed to dominate. It is with the psychic, trance-inducing powers of the lunar mind that we are able to sense and absorb the spiral energies of the stones and waters. The ancients believed that mind and mental powers were the gift of the lunar Mother, and that should She disappear all mental activities would cease. Mental powers and menstrual powers were seen as interrelated.

It is only women who are capable of the heightened and intense emotional and sexual energies needed to activate the magnetic energies of the stones. Throughout all ages it tended to be the women who were mediums, oracles and psychics.

I believe that ancient women and men were bisexual. In patriarchies, vast amounts of energy are taken up with suppressing half of what we are, and infinite amounts of energy go into acting out heterosexual gender roles. The ancient peoples were able to let their energies flow freely and were therefore able to gain great knowledge and psychic powers.[7] Their knowledge was never gained at the cost of violating the Earth or themselves, and was therefore life-enhancing.

There is much speculation concerning the magical and practical results of the power of the stones and the waters, and of the human communities interacting with each other. There is an old folk belief that if anybody places an object on the capstone of a cromlech and walks three times round it on the night of the full moon, it disappears. Psychics have felt the stones moving and dancing about in a circular direction, perhaps picking up the energies still remaining in the stones from the ecstatic circular dances that were once performed there. Perhaps levitation was possible along the energy lines and in this way the enormous stones could be teletransported vast distances. It seems that so-called UFOs have been sighted mainly along these energy paths, just as the dragons and fairies of old.

We live on a unique double planet. The moon has had a profound effect on the Earth's evolution and may have been necessary for life to occur here. Without it, we could have ended up frozen like Mars or in a 'greenhouse' like Venus. Why, if the Sun is such a singular life-creator, are the planets that encircle it not teeming with life? The moon caused the Earth's core, its red blood-magma, to become abnormally heated, enhanced its magnetic field and radiation shield which brought about the creation of the ozone layer which protects us from the deadly radiations of the sun. The magma is a molten mineral core endowed with the will to become living. Thanks to technology and science, this ozone layer is now being slowly thinned out and destroyed.

The pineal gland – the third eye, or Ajna centre – attributed with spiritual visionary powers, our cosmic receptor, transmits biological messages of its light-reception to the pituitary gland which stimulates growth hormones.[8] We are in fact a kind of human plant.

All of life was born in the womb-like environment of the planetary ocean and moon-tide-blood-waters are in our brains. The lunar-tidal rhythms were transferred into the female body. Our menstrual cycle and sexuality is an evolutionary force strongly connected with the moon's cycles. During our menstrual period, dreaming becomes power.

Patriarchal societies suppress these spiritual-sexual-psychic powers in us all. We are meant to live cosmically and biologically by the natural light of the moon in her phases. We are now finding that not only does an electrified environment upset women's understanding and attunement to our body–mind cycles, but it also causes all sorts of distress and illness in both women and men. We are deprived of darkness – and moonlight – in modern electrified cities.

James E Lovelock writes that a series of regulatory systems maintain constant levels of oxygen, carbon dioxide, nitrogen and other gases in the atmosphere and regulate the surface temperatures of the planet.[9] Einstein discovered that matter is dynamic and active energy. Quantum physics sees existence as a web of dynamically interrelating quanta – the smallest particles yet isolated – in an intricate dance. Gaia, the Earth Mother, is a gigantic, living cosmic being with a self-regulatory system and the air and moisture surrounding us in the atmosphere is Her in-and-out breath. The tropical forests, now being cut down for short-term economic profits, are the lungs of the Earth and wells are the menstrual flow from Her underground blood-water arteries. Why have we forgotten this?

Why has patriarchy attempted to cut us off from the radiant fibres that connect us to Her psychic/etherial web, since our parasenses (extra sensory perception) are there for the purpose of gaining and maintaining knowledge of the universe? Refusing to recognise the very real connections that tie us to the cosmos does not make them go away.

It is by feeling and intuition that we experience her creation as alive, unpredictable and spontaneous. Humans and nature, mind and matter, are intimately and subtly interlinked – 'I think, therefore matter also thinks' is what Descartes should have said. 'Keep the hole on the top of your head open' say the Hopis. Humans and animals make use of clairvoyance to enable us to make responses necessary for life.

The mind/matter dualism of Descartes has limited western thought for nearly four centuries. The brain might be a receiver of, a sensitive filter for, as yet unknown physical/psychic processes. Holograms have shown us that there is no 'here' and 'there', that the part also contains the whole. There is no distance in super-space, we exist in multiple universes and realities simultaneously.

It has even been postulated that ESP is a vestigial function, just a regression of the unconscious to an archaic form of communication that 'man' has outgrown during 'his' evolution. That it is about delusions and infantile fantasies of still childlike human beings in interdependence with the Mother that adult male individual minds must abandon to be able to conquer nature. Since these powers break through in crises and in mental illness, they have been defined as pathological and not conforming to the consensus delusion of Freud's 'reality principle'. But time is a function of consciousness, linear time is but one possibility. In clairvoyant reality, time is undivided and whole – all is always here – which is the reason that precognition about the future is possible and is perfectly natural.

Our biological survival may well now depend on us redeveloping our extrasensory faculties so we can hear the Earth speaking. Matter has memory and there is a relationship between electrical field forces and ESP that has an evolutionary function. Even particles in the sub-atomic world are influenced by the very act of observation. There is no 'objective reality'.

Human beings evolved in a dark and light world and we have developed a genetic response to the moon. Light triggers ovulation[10] and tribal communities of women ovulated on the full moon – time of conception and of births – when orgiastic festivals to the Goddess were held. The moon also triggers sexual desire: when women menstruated at the dark of the moon, it was a time of powerful sexual, mysterious and deep experiences. The Balinese believed that walking on the moon is a serious violation of its sanctity, an attack on our collective spiritual health. Most ancient peoples have thought of the moon as the land where the souls await rebirth. It seems that the US astronauts who landed on the moon in the 1960s and 1970s, came back profoundly spiritually changed.

The Earth affects our minds through dreams, visions and voices. The oracle at Delphi prophesied after breathing in the fumes from the underworld. The Goddess is also the dark Earth within which things rot, the great underground vessel. The patriarchs interpreted Her redhot belly as being the fires of hell. Hel, the Scandinavian-Germanic queen of the underworld, was also the magical fairy-queen of Summerland. She was Helena of the sacred pathways and wells. Words like whole, healing, holy derive from Her.

The ancients knew that life and death are merely facets of the same creative power and process. Spirits of the dead are close to the waters of knowledge and the generative, fertilising fires within the bowels of the Earth; they can therefore give healing and prophetic powers. The ancestors were always thought to be accessible if invoked with the right rituals, to give help and advice.

Initiation is an active choice to enter into darkness, the deeper parts of one's being. In Greece, at the oracle cave, the seekers or initiates had to lower themselves into a cave through a hole similar to a birth canal and there they had to stay for three nights and days, after which they were helped out by therapeutes/helpers. If we avoid this experience of descent because of fear of our deeper selves, we block ourselves from powerful, transformative processes. This has been the shamans' way in all ages. Initiations always took place in caves, within mounds, in underground chambers like the Hopi Kivas, reproducing the dark womb and involving death and rebirth experiences. The temple is a late development of the cave and is a symbol of the Goddess as house and shelter. The temple-gate is the yoni or entrance into Her womb.

The initiates that took part in the Eleusian mysteries, originally women's mysteries of Demeter and Persephone/Kore, were promised a better afterlife. Demeter, who took into her womb both the dead and the seed, could provide them both with rebirth. She makes children grow in the womb and seeds germinate within the dark Earth. She is mistress of the tomb, the great underground vessel or cauldron into which the souls enter and from which they are reborn. Grain was stored in subterranean Pithoi jars, in which the dead were also buried in the foetal position at Eleusis, on Crete and in the Near East. The vernal symbolism of vegetation rising from the Earth jar in the spring – personified as Kore, Adonis, Osiris – compares with seed-grain being taken from the Pithoi or 'underworld jars'. Kore the maiden was the personification of the seed of corn who descends into the underworld every autumn to reappear in the spring and bring the spark of life in the darkness. She is the source of physical and spiritual rebirth and illumination. The mysteries were performed in darkness and the night. 'The lover of nocturnal journeys, I light torches to the Great Mother'[11] sang the initiates. On Crete these rites of the Goddess had been celebrated by the whole population and were not secret or exclusive. The corn Mother, Demeter and her daughter, Persephone, who in the underworld becomes the dark queen of the underworld and is reborn in spring as Kore, were one and the same and personified the seasons, the growth and death of vegetation and the cycles of the moon. The Goddess unites opposite elements, brings light to darkness and understands the necessity of death for rebirth. The male initiate of the mysteries believed that at death he would be allowed to enter Persephone's bridal chamber.

In the beginning, Persephone had voluntarily descended into the underworld at winter, but in emerging patriarchies a new myth developed that she was abducted by force and raped by the Lord Pluto, king of the dead, who made her his queen for six months of the year. Demeter grieved over this separation from the daughter and, as a result, the Earth, her body, grows barren until Kore returns.

But now with continuing patriarchies and rape of the Earth Mother, the daughter is never able to return at all and we live with the industrial wastelands of the death of natures.

We now have Persephone-like souls, women trapped in our mental hospitals, forever cut off from the Mother. But some of Her daughters are now returning; we are hearing Her call.

Healing Water and Hidden Wells

The moon lives in the innermost watery recesses and caverns of our own bodies. To Australian Aborigines, Spirals represent sacred springs from which spirits can travel to and from the underworld. Their sacred Chirunga stones were thought to contain the spirits of their ancestors. Native Americans treasured and were recharged by their sacred medicine stones. Holy wells were seen to heal and prolong life. Natural crevices, caverns and caves – the vulva and womb of the Goddess – were powerful spirit realms and givers of immortality, healing and rebirth.

Nigel Pennick writes of an old mediaeval romance, *The Elucidation*,[12] in which there is an account called 'The Destruction of the Land of Logres'. The story goes that once there lived at certain puis or holy wells or mounds, maidens who refreshed travellers with food or drink which would be brought out in a bowl. But, one day, one of these maidens was raped by a king who also stole her bowl. The puis at once became deserted and the whole country went to waste. King Arthur's knights set out to find the wells or springs to protect their guardian priestesses and they prayed to God to put things right again, but to no avail. The land stayed waste and nothing would grow. The only way that the puis could be reactivated was to find the Holy Grail, the stone or cauldron, that can channel cosmic and electromagnetic energies into the disrupted system.

This is clearly an account of what has happened to the Earth and to women during patriarchal times. The search for the Holy Grail is the search for the Goddess and a desire to return to Her and for Her to return. The Grail is Her transformative and magical womb, the cauldron of Cerridwen, and without it everything remains a wasteland. No amount of praying to a patriarchal father god will make an iota of difference.

In our own times, the holy wells, clearly seen in this legend as crucial for the health, on all levels, of the land and of the human community, have not only been left unattended and neglected, but, what is worse, in many places the wells have been entirely forgotten, built over, destroyed and now polluted.

In recent years there has been a movement amongst pagan and Goddess/Earth lovers to seek out yet again the sacred wells, to clean them and give them love and care. The wells were never wholly forgotten in the Celtic world and there are still many venerated and miracle-working holy wells in these isles. The words for well-being and healing in the English language are clearly the same as those used for the water-source; and in the Scandinavian languages the words for origins and the beginnings/source of things are the same as those for wells. The sacred wells were seen as lifegiving and maternal. They are also trance-inducing and function as scrying mirrors for prophesying and in ancient times priestesshoods of the Goddess surely dwelled by these wells, healing and acting as oracles for the people.

The cult of the sacred waters was not easily defeated and the early church fought well-worshippers and forbade divination by trees and stones. The Second Council of Arles stated in 452 AD: '... if in the territory of the Bishop, infidels light torches, or venerate trees, fountains or stones, and he neglects to abolish this usage, he must know that he is guilty of sacrilege'. In 640 it was decreed:

> 'Let no Christian place lights at the temples, or the stones, or at fountains, or at trees, or enclosures, or at places where three ways meet ... Let no one presume to make lustrations, or to enchant herbs, or to make flocks pass through a hollow tree or an aperture in the earth; for by doing so they seem to consecrate themselves to the Devil.'

But when such beliefs could not be defeated or destroyed, there was placed an image of the Virgin – our blessed Mother – or of some saint, in a sacred tree or grove, over a holy well or fountain, on the shore of a lake or a river. The Church slowly got the people accustomed to praying to the saints at the sacred water places, instead of to the spirits residing there, and this is the reason for all the statues of saints placed in niches at so many wells and fountains. The people had believed that it was by passing under the waters of a well that the Sidh – the abode of the Spirits in the tumuli or hills – was reached. There were circular well shrines in Sardinia in neolithic times where circular stone structures enclosed the well waters below.

Just as the cult of the fountains and wells was absorbed by Christianity, so was the worship of the sacred trees, such as 'Our Lady of the Oak' at Anjou. Sometimes a whole tree would be enshrined in the wall of a chapel in the same way that standing stones and whole cromlechs were included in some churches. There are haunting images of the Virgin – often shown standing on a lunar crescent – deep within grottos, as at Lourdes where there is also a wonder-working well.

During the summers in olden times, when all the water from rivers and lakes was lukewarm to drink, it was only the clear and cold water from the wells that was refreshing and exhilarating – it made you feel high and heady. I remember as a child my own delight when coming across and being able to drink the water from some cool, clear well deep in a Swedish forest on a hot summer afternoon.

A holy well is one that is powerfully and miraculously healing at some certain time in the seasonal year. Usually this special time (when the lifegiving, healing and magnetic dragon/Earth spirit travels and moves underground) coincides with one of the eight festivals of the year.

I found that in Denmark there were no fewer than 200 wells dedicated to St John the Baptist (St Hans in Danish) and, up until the end of the last century, people would gather, at Mid summer, by the thousands to sleep by the wells overnight and then to drink their waters at a certain time and in a reverential and hushed silence. These wells are now all but forgotten.

In the Celtic world, the many Bride's wells would have been particularly sacred and holy/healing took place at Imbolc or on Brigid's Day, first days of the waxing moon in February. Ancient peoples would have noticed that animals came to the wells to be healed and that the grass was greener and the Earth more fertile in their vicinity.

To be entirely effective as a cure the sick were advised to revisit the well nine days later and then again nine days after that. One should wash oneself in utter silence. If you drank from the waters of a holy well on Midsummer's Eve together with your beloved, you would soon be married to each other.

It was thought that droughts were caused by badly kept wells and that when a well was cleared it would rain. Catholics dip their holy cross in a well to bring rain. The farmers in Scandinavia and until quite recently in the

Celtic world continued the tradition of honouring the dead at the seasonal festivals and making sure that the peace of the dead/fairies was preserved and protected within the mounds. On the festival nights, a bowl of porridge or an offering of milk was brought to the burial mound that shared the name with the farm nearby. The milk was for the serpents who represented the spirits of the dead and were totem animals not to be harmed. It was thought that, without the milk, the serpents would not successfully shed their skin to renew themselves.

The dead and the serpents are of the nature of the Dark Mother of the winding underground waters, the sacred stones and mounds. As the serpent sheds its skin and is reborn anew, so the moon eternally waxes and wanes but never dies and women shed our womb lining in our monthly menstrual flow. We bleed, but we live and we miraculously create life.

As Marija Gimbutas has pointed out in *The Language of the Goddess*, symbols for water and fertile moisture are everywhere carved on the neolithic images of the Goddess – and there are many images of Her as water bird and as serpent – and on the megalithic monuments and sacred stones. This symbolism forms a kind of very early universal and sacred written 'language' understood by all and was spread far and wide on women's pots.

Water from the Earth's depths contains miraculously healing and often radioactive qualities. Paul Deveraux suggests in *Earth Mind*[13] that water is Earth's receptive sense organ which is open like an ear to the cosmos, in the same way the forests are Her lungs. It is suggested that water has memory, agitated water 'remembers' even the faintest traces of substances it contains; that water is sensitive to very slight variations in electric and magnetic fluids. The waters of the sacred wells might remember the crystals, ores, minerals and rocks of the Earth's fiery womb, and carry the voices of the ancestors from the Underworld. Waters, lakes and wells have magical properties and are dwelling places of supernatural beings and were believed to be the entrances to the otherworld or fairy realm. The women oracles at Delphi drank great amounts of water before prophesying, and shaman-priestesses dwelt by the trance-inducing wells, healing and teaching. Thermal springs, such as those at Bath, were always associated with healing, prophecy, the creation of life, death and the otherworld of the spirits. Water might be the conduit for the Earth Spirit energies.

In divisive patriarchal thought, waters are associated with (female) emotions and fire with (male) mind and spirit. But to the ancient Celts, for example, their great Goddess Brigid/Bride embodied the ever-living sacred fire as well as the serpentine spirit of the waters, and She taught smithcraft, was the giver of inspiration, prophetic and poetic utterance.

Since 1977, when active hydrothermal vents were discovered at 3800 metres depth along the Galapagos rift system west of Ecuador, it is known that these submarine hot springs or geysers which gush forth water at 350° C nourish a biological community. The vents, which are formed as the plates of the Earth's crust which make up the sea floor, pull apart. They are the hottest yet found in the oceans and are loaded with sulphurous minerals. Ordinary sea water descends here most of the way to the earth's magma chamber before returning to the sea floor, and under extreme heat and pressure the sulphate in the sea water converts to hydrogen sulphide, which is then metabolised by bacteria and multiplied. The hydrothermal water has a different composition from sea water; it is highly acidic and contains abnormal amounts of certain radioactive isotopes. These hot springs deep in the dark ocean emit a flamelike eerie light, and an abundant community of animals, such as giant tube worms three metres long, thrives here. Here in the total darkness of the abyss, an energy source other than sunlight triggers a chain of life by a process called chemosynthesis, and animals form a food chain based on energy from within the Earth Herself. No one knows how many such vents exist along the giant system of oceanic rifts. It has been found that they help sea water to offset the disruption caused when rivers deposit material from the land into the oceans.[14] The ancients might indeed have been right in thinking that Earth is the parthenogenetically life-creating Mother, that spirits arise from the underworld[15] and that the oceans are truly the womb and original source. Dumping nuclear and chemical and sewage waste into Her womb is matricide indeed.

Shaman priestesses prophesied while breathing in the vapours from the waters of the Gap[16] of Bath in England. At Delphi in Greece, the priestesses, possessed by the pythonic spirit of the chthonic Mother (Gaia), entered into trances whilst breathing in hot steam from the underworld and the spirits of the dead spoke through them.

The Catholic church has since taken the credit for the healing powers of the wells. The Gothic Cathedrals of Our Lady are often built over oracular wells. Chartres cathedral stands on an ancient neolithic mound within which was a grotto with a sacred well. This was a place for pilgrimage for the whole of the Celtic world. There was, within this grotto, an image of the dark Mother, one of the oldest wooden sculptures of the Goddess to be found in Europe. It was carved in the hollowed-out trunk of a pear tree and showed Her giving birth ('Virgin Paritura about to give forth'). She was the black Goddess of the underground waters, of death and rebirth, also venerated by the Christians who, after hearing mass in the cathedral, went to sing psalms to pay honour to Our Lady under the Earth. The pilgrims went from the mound by a passage leading to a crypt, to visit a grotto where the black Virgin was to be seen; there they made their devotions and were sprinkled with holy water from a well. During the French Revolution, this sculpture was hauled out and ceremonially burnt.[17]

There are many other wonder-working images, probably pre-Christian and portraying black Isis of Egypt, whose shrines were to be found all over Europe in Roman times. Ean Begg writes in *The Cult of the Black Virgin*[18] that there are 302 such in France alone. In folk tales the black madonnas possess miraculous and healing powers and their shrines are often to be found in underground grottos close to water sources and wells. One such place is Lourdes, another is Montserrat in Catalonia. This beautiful white mountain where rare herbs and plants grow, is the home of La Vierga Negra, a wood-carved black image of the Goddess that, according to legend, was found by some shepherds in a cave. Probably She was hidden there after the great Moorish civilisation of Spain was defeated by the barbaric and intolerant Christians. Up there on the sacred Montserrat mountain, amongst its strange rock formations and pinnacles, there are now no fewer than nineteen monasteries. It has become the domain of monks but the power of La Vierga Negra is great and the cathedral where She is housed is an important place of pilgrimage.

The Black Madonna still has a cult following, especially in the South of France where she was venerated by the heretical gnostics and Cathars in mediaeval times. She was to them Maria Magdalena who, according to legend, arrived in the Camargue by the sea, pregnant with Jesus's child when fleeing from the Roman persecution in Palestine. She came with Mary, the mother of Jesus, Salome, Mary and Sara the Egyptian, and here by the sea in the Camargue is the little town, actually called Les-Saintes-Maries-de-la-Mer, where, according to legend, they landed. In this place gypsies, both Romany and Gitano, gather once a year in May to worship their black Sara-la-Kali who dwells in a small, dark and mysterious cryptlike church.

Without the wells there is no mystical vision and people perish or become dangerously alienated from the source of Being.

The Radiant Darkness

Peter Redgrove, in his book *The Black Goddess and the Sixth Sense*,[19] writes that darkness is light not recognised; and depression is withheld knowledge. In patriarchal societies, the fear of our own body-organism cuts us off from experiencing our true and real connectedness with nature and cosmos.

Science has favoured abstractions and sublimations. So-called rational thought is thought that has been deliberately limited. The supposedly rational Greeks passed on knowledge they received from other cultures (such as sacred geometry from the megalith builders) but they left out the greater maternal wisdom, which is now called intuition.[20] Presiding over the transition from unconscious to conscious experience is the powerful presence of the black Goddess in the form of the sphinx, winged moon Goddess of Thebes, in the illuminated darkness. The image of this sphinx haunted me since the early 1960s for many years before I knew who She was and is. The Theban sphinx was, indeed for me, the messenger and guardian spirit between the realms of understanding. Her message is the shamanistic knowledge of death and rebirth and of invisible things, according to Redgrove, and this seems prophetic to me now, so many years later. Like Lilith, if rejected, She becomes the source of plagues, but when accepted, She is the 'soul of every living thing and of prophecy.' The unconscious mind is, in Redgrove's words, a 'living, breathing, sensing, perfumed, luminous sphinx'. And our non-visual dark senses are organs of womb-knowledge.

We have cut ourselves off from the rest of creation and from the animal world not as part of organic revolution, but as an act of violation. In shamanism, animal powers and spirits give us knowledge; the Native Americans say: 'If all the animals were gone, man would die from loneliness of spirit, for whatever happens to the beast, also happens to man.' Animals are telepathic and respond to

Earth energies and underground waters and 'live by voices we shall never hear'.

All of nature is full of chemical 'moods' and of invisible colours; what we call light is only a narrow band of electro-magnetic radiation from the sun. The sun, moon, planets and stars are sources of direct and reflected radiation. It has been held in Europe since Newton that only visible light is involved in the generation of light, but to those animals who can see in the infra-red spectrum the night is brilliantly lit by the moon.

Living things fluoresce visibly. According to Redgrove, night time as well as day time are primarily infra-red environments and both are important to our bodies and all living things. The moon sheds natural and visible light *and* invisible and biologically active 'natural radiation' (infra-red). This we have feared and avoided, although it is the radiation that affects us most strongly.

The night landscape is bathed in infra-red and if we could see in it a field of corn it would look like a vast array of fluorescent colours in the moonlight, and in the sunshine of the day we would see beautiful psychedelic auras. We ourselves are everywhere surrounded by radiant matter and our bodies are a living fire of warm-blooded infra-red emission or heat.

There are similarities between Redgrove's descriptions of seeing in the infra-red and the accounts I have read, transmitted in automatic writing through mediums, of life in the 'world unseen' and also the likeness to the vibrant, transparent colours and matter transformed into multi-coloured light-bands or waves during acid or mushroom trips. Spirits of the so-called dead have been filmed and photographed in infra-red light and so have ectoplasm materialisations. A short while back, I had a dream, after a particularly powerful meditation, of walking through a dark night-landscape that suddenly lit up as from inside itself and was transformed into the most radiant, breath-taking, fluorescent colours.

Nature's moods are presided over by the dragon-force

Chi, of the Chinese, which resembles the sphinx, whose composite body was an astronomical calendar-picture of the Theban year: lion for the waxing and serpent for the waning. Chi is cosmic breath and nature's energy. The Hindus call this subtle creative energy 'Prana', while Wilhelm Reich called it 'orgone energy'.

The Black Goddess is that part of the Mother serpent Goddess of the oracles that we do not see but that haunts us all our lives. The rhythms of Her menstrual processes are those of cosmic processes, the lunar pulse. We are womb-creatures, even after birth. Peter Redgrove writes that She is before light and beyond it. She, Wisdom-Shakti, was always there and he who sins against Her does wrong to his own soul. He also goes in great detail into the effect that weather – the atmosphere and negative and positive ions – has on us. He says that, because weather cannot be controlled, there was a move, in the eighteenth century, towards containment: society moved indoors; nature was landscaped. Since then, human populations have been controlled in the artificial environment of factories and cities. Women in particular are sensitive to the weather and suffer allergies and reactions to the unnatural electromagnetic environment.

There is a wonderful web of electromagnetic forces that seems to regulate all living processes on Earth. It is like a great collective mind that we call unconscious for the reason that we are for the most part unconscious of it. Our body-field 'wobbles' with the Earth-field and the travelling Earth-currents. We probably have localised sense-organs for magnetism that fluctuate rhythmically with the daily changes in Earth's geomagnetic field and with the monthly lunar changes. Life has come into being and has evolved in the presence of this field. There is high sensitivity to it in the water/blood molecule. Water is a physical manifestation of the flowing, life-creating force. The body is surrounded by a 'glowing egg' as Carlos Casteneda says.

Humans have changed the electromagnetism of the Earth to a greater degree than we have changed any other natural feature and to magnitudes and frequencies never before present. Cancers, suicides and depressions follow the pattern of high-tension overland wiring. The human being is like a radio receiver, our body crystals vibrating to cosmic sources and interacting with Earth's electromagnetic field. It may be that invisible human electrical pollution is responsible for the rarity of visionary experience in the modern world and for the predominance of the removed, over-analytical 'onlooker' intelligence that has taken its place. If this is so, such an intelligence has produced conditions favouring its own evolution and survival. Our birthright, to think, to dream, to feel, is being tampered with.

The attempts to deny and suppress our Black Goddess, who is also the holy spirit or Ruach, stem from the sixth century when Isis was demonised as 'Black Isis'. It was then said that She 'will continue to come back until the Messiah comes and drives out the unclean spirits from the land'. Yet Redgrove writes there is a persistent rumour that She Herself is the Messiah come to redeem the divided souls of women and to unite the known senses with the unknown, higher and lower, by virtue of Her ability to circuit the sky and traverse the depths of the abyss. We all come from Her womb/web resonating with light.

Nuit of Egypt said that Her colour is black to the blind but blue and gold to the seeing. She is, in Redgrove's words, the Goddess of the night sky, black light of radiance-pulsating evolutionary energy that we cannot see, and She is infinite space.

Peter Redgrove thinks that Isis might have been an extra-terrestrial responsible for the mutations of the pre-human primates that led to the development of the human race. The evidence for this could be the sacred black stones or meteorites associated with many Goddess sculptures and temples. She is star maiden and gateway – birth canal and yoni – to other worlds. The 'dark holes' in space might be entrances, like birth-channels, to other universes.

Redgrove says that the geomagnetic field traced out by the dark magnetic core of the Earth resembles a great hooded, winged angel: Gaia wearing a robe of magnetism embroidered with sun, moon and stars.

Kundalini – our sexual electromagnetic energy – is the black she-serpent of invisible fire which, when raised to the top of the head, brings illumination. We are created in the dark furnace of our mother's womb – paradoxically, the divine light within which we are born.

6
The Lord is a Consuming Fire

Light Versus Dark –
The Emergence of Patriarchal Thinking

I now turn to where many patriarchal notions originated in the ancient world, that is, to the Indo-Iranian 'Aryans'.

After the defeat of the ancient women-led Goddess cultures, and the rise of hierarchies and warrior castes in the Bronze and Iron Ages, there were hundreds of years of barbarism, constant war between tribes and truly Dark Ages of the spirit in many parts of the world.

The 'darkness' that patriarchs throughout the ages, and present-day New Agers, rage against, are the mysteries of the black and shining Mother who brings lucid dreams, creativity, rules madness, gives life, death and rebirth. She is the dark underworld *and* the radiant white light of the astral realm.

Heinz Mode and Subodh Chandra write in *Indian Folk Art*[1] that in Mohenjo Daro, the great neolithic culture in the Indus valley there have been found no signs of temples or organised priesthoods, or princely rulers, but everywhere terracottas of women (women were the ancient potters and artists with clay), the Goddess and of animals. They say that the statuettes are extraordinarily alive and have surfaces treated to suggest the motion of inhalation and exhalation, a pulsating life of the skin, seeming almost capable of motion and often having a circular opening in the head. Even now in Hindu temples, the Holy of Holies is called Gharba or Womb. This Indus valley culture was destroyed by the middle of the second millennium BC by warlike pastoral tribes.

Even today, Indian lower-caste women carry on ancient traditions, their wall paintings, textiles and wonderful embroidery showing a relation to ancient rock paintings and archaic vessels.

Reading between the lines, it would seem that the Hindu Goddess triad was originally the one Great Mother in Her different aspects.

According to patriarchal myth, She was created by Brahma, Vishnu and Shiva who, with their combined energies, summoned up a female form so brilliant that it illuminated all the heavens and was coloured red, white and black.[2] Since all the male gods desired Her, She divided Herself into three forms which represented past, present and future. They were white Sarasvati, the red Lakshmi and black Parvati or Kali/Durga – the most ancient triple Goddess of the moon.

Mahadevi or Devi was the complex and powerful great Goddess of pre-Aryan times. She later became Shiva's Shakti, or his female energy, while as Kali She subdues him and as Mayavati She was called the 'deceiver'. Shiva, Her consort, was the inexorable destroyer of Time who, like Kali, dances the world into creation and destruction.

The free and boundless Aditi, Mother of the gods, was the limitless heavens and ruler of the world and the twelve Adityas were the eternal forces behind the celestial bodies. As Aditi, She was the mother of the Dityas who were the enemies of sacrifice.

The mythology of the struggle of the forces of light against those of darkness has its origins far back in the history of the Indo-European peoples. After wave upon wave of invasions, from around 2000 BC, the ancient matrilinear cultures of India and Europe, including those of Crete and northern Italy, were devastated.

According to Merlin Stone, light and dark first became associated with good and evil in Sanskrit.[3] The Sanskrit word for nature is *prakriti* which, like Shakti, is of female gender and means power and energy, signifying the supreme female creative power of the universe.[4] But another word, *prakrit*, means common, insignificant and natural, and represents the upper-class Brahminical view of the language of India's common people. By association, therefore, nature/*prakriti* is devalued as a term.[5]

The Indo-Europeans worshipped a fiery godfather who dwelled on volcanoes and high mountains and produced storms, lightning and thunder. Being pastoral and warlike, they did not connect with the soil and its spirits. They called themselves the 'sons of light' and the peaceful, agricultural peoples of the Goddess which they conquered and utterly despised they called 'the peoples of the darkness and the serpent'.[6] These heroic 'sons of light', who Marija Gimbutas calls Kurgan warriors, delighted in their shining metallic weapons and worshipped the fires that smelted the iron ore ripped out of the Earth Mother's womb, and their bright and fiery shining gods were formed in their own brutal image as they set about to conquer and enslave the dark peoples of Earth.[7]

Much of the Christian notion of salvation came from Persian eschatology.[8] Mithras was the sun's light and spirit of fire, later adopted by Semitic eremites and sun-cultists such as the Essenes. The Persians passed on to the Jewish Essenes the prediction that 'the Son of Man would come in a cloud with power and great glory'.

Mithras, the Persian saviour god, was born in a cave (womb of the ancient Mother) on 25 December, birthday of the 'unconquered sun', and in the fourth century AD this was proclaimed to be the date when Jesus was born. Mithras became the God of the Roman soldiers and mercenaries. He was the self-created Bull from whose blood creatures were born. Mithras/Jesus's blood was worshipped, while women, the actual creators of life, were to hide theirs in shame; his priests were celibate and misogynist men. The ancient Persian as well as Hebrew religions were male fertility cults.

In the Mithraic worldview, there was a cosmic battle

happening between forces of light and of darkness. The Mithraic teaching was to join the light to be saved. The Roman soldiers adopted this religion and became soldiers for Mithras/Christ who was the light of the world, Helios, or sun of righteousness. The Mithraic high priest, Pater Patrum became Papa or Pope, the 'Holy Father' of the Catholic church.

Earth was the sewer of the devil to the Christians and woman's body a latrine, because she gives life and by doing so binds the male spirit into the bondage and snares of the flesh; men wanted to put away the 'filth of the flesh'. In patriarchal societies, heterosexual love-making becomes rape because of a man's obsession with defeating a woman and conquering the dark and secret spaces within her body. The ancients had always known and respected the intelligence of our organism, the body-mind, but patriarchal men envy women's natural capacity to create life and are unable to recognise the Earth as a deity because only She, a female body, can produce life without mediation.

Because the deity was now exclusively male, and Earth is obviously not his body, She was to be his handmaiden and do his bidding.

Because women and not men create and sustain life, women were to be demeaned; our most ancient female rights of decision over our own fertility, under the guardianship of the wise women/midwife/healers, were to be taken from us. Instead of women welcoming the spirits of the unborn willingly and in joy and in our chosen time, we were forced to adhere to a male god's edict, and that of his celibate male priesthood to multiply in sorrow and in pain. This is the reason, in my opinion, for human overpopulation. It can never have been nature's intention that we should multiply to the extent that we have, killing off all the Goddess' other creatures and polluting the Earth.

The princes of the Roman Catholic Church, speaking, preaching and writing in Latin – the language of the conquerors – set out to defeat the European peasantry and their spiritual leaders, the shaman women and men of the Craft (the 'witches') in the name of Christ. The Church became one of the world's greatest money-making organisations, and that in spite of Jesus's poverty and humility.

The patriarchs set out to divorce spirituality, love and devotion from sexuality, thereby making sexuality profane, while love and devotion were to be centred on the male god, his priesthood, Church and state. Christians are supposed to love their 'fellow man' – an abstract concept not grounded in any actual experience of love, as Christians set out to break up tribes and extended families which are the true source of love. The Inquisition was primarily invented to force public acceptance through terror of a Church that the people did not want. Priests, who were pretending to give Christ's body to the people for their salvation, were often whoring and money-grabbing, while people were forced to honour them. The men of the Church were above the law and not accountable to anyone but their own bishops. Inquisitors were ordered to persecute those who believed that Jesus was a poor man who held no property.[9]

The cathedrals of Our Lady were built in the twelfth century to placate the common people who longed for the Goddess. But, none the less, almost every natural impulse was viewed as an anti-Christian perversity. No wonder that the wretched, unhappy and poverty-stricken populations of Europe succumbed to all sorts of plagues and madness. The Church made its fortune from grabbing the properties confiscated from heretics persecuted by the Inquisition. For over five centuries there were persecutions, tortures, burnings of gnostics, heretics and witches. Sadistic sexual perversion and the inflamed and hateful minds of celibate monks and priests were the driving forces behind the witch-hunts.[10] And a woman could be put to death for having had a miscarriage, even if it were known that the cause was a brutal husband's beating.

The Inquisition remained active until 1834 in Central and South America where it persecuted the shamans of the indigenous peoples. Hitler's SS merely copied the organisation and tactics of the Catholic Inquisition.

Were the mass burnings of women during the witch-hunts in every city square in Europe for hundreds of years, fire sacrifices to the god of fire and light? In Hindu India in 1987 alone at least 900 young brides were murdered and burned alive in dowry disputes, and suttee – widow immolations – is on the increase.[11]

In ancient Scandinavia, the tribes defeated by Odin's warriors were hanged in great numbers on sacred trees by his temple in Old Uppsala in Sweden. Jahweh commanded that the matrilinear Canaanites, men, women and children, should be mercilesly slayed and their cities burned to the ground. Much later Hitler and the Nazis, also sun-god worshippers, instigated the holocaust of the Jewish peoples and of all other 'undesirables' or 'sub races'.

The torturer of mediaeval times today works as a vivisectionist, while the Inquisitor is an interrogating officer in a black ghetto. We are now threatened by nuclear death at the hands of a contemporary solar priesthood, the nuclear physicists, who want to finally defeat the Earth and turn Her into a nuclear furnace like the sun itself. What an utter disaster for a world religion to be centred upon a male saviour god who refuses to be reborn from the Great Mother.

Sacrifices – Fire and Soma

The sun god is the warrior who battles eternally with the 'serpent of darkness' and overcomes Her with his phallic metal sword. The male 'hero' murders the dragon/serpent who is the Mother Goddess Tiamat of Babylon, Tehom of Israel or Delphyne of Greece. He also steals Her treasures and wealth in the caves and underground caverns. Remember the sagas of the dragon who guards the treasure in the cave and who is slaughtered and robbed? The dragon is the Earth spirit and Her treasures are the minerals, ores and magnetic and healing underground waters.

These myths or songs are not simply stories about the destruction of the Goddess temples and the capture and rape of Her priestesses by patriarchal men; they are also accounts of the actual rape of the Earth. The ancient women shamans had been the custodians of the healing waters, springs and wells of the Earth, and had believed that minerals corresponded intimately with the planets that surround us. The dragon/serpent was as grey as the mud; she is matter/mater/mother, golden as the sun and multicoloured like the rainbow. She produces fire from her breath, causes storms, winds and rain; she is the Milky Way and below her chin she carries the lunar pearl. She gives magic powers to those who are in tune with her nature, and those who have accidentally tasted of her blood can understand the language of birds and animals; she is the living waters within our bodies and, as Kundalini, she slumbers at the base of our spines. When called upon, she travels through the centres of our bodies and gives illumination, magic powers and enlightenment. She is at one with our menstrual nature. She is the astral light.

In alchemy, the dragon represents the 'flame of spirit', and the dragon's 'fiery breath' signifies transmutation of matter through intense heat. John Mitchell writes that the oldest branch of alchemy 'was concerned with bringing about the earthly paradise through the fruitful union of cosmic and terrestrial forces'.[12] Alchemy, astrology and geomancy were originally united in a system that recognised correspondences between planetary influences and the dragon spirit of the Earth's minerals, crystals and ores. Women had been the custodians of this ancient science and occult knowledge of magic transformations, both in nature and in our psyches. The new patriarchal solar myth justified the rape of the Earth Mother by patriarchal men in search of raw materials for the growing war and metal technologies.

Indo-European warrior peoples had very early on learnt to smelt iron-ore from which they were able to make tools and weapons much more durable and hard than the ones of bronze.[13] Iron weapons were much less costly to produce and sources of iron ore are plentiful. One can say that the discovery of how to smelt iron ore 'democratised' warfare.

Only with warfare and metal technology did men become 'real men' – anti-Mother, sexually and economically dominant, and set on the conquest and destruction of nature/She. Without the incessant mining and smelting, especially of iron, men would not have been able to create imperialistic centralised and warlike city-states. With iron weapons and iron tools such as ploughs to rip the Earth open for agriculture on a large scale and axes for cutting down the vast forests, patriarchal men could finally take over and impose their own anti-life values based on left-brain linear thinking. The belief that the sky/sun-father was the real creator of life and the passive Earth/Mother reduced to being simply his vessel to act upon, gave men, who had now broken out of tribal communistic shared living, the political and ideological justification for their acts. I believe that from the very beginnings of patriarchy (rule by the fathers), the logic was created that has now culminated in the death of nature and a devastated Earth. The treasures of the Earth were tainted with the blood of the dragon and what is taken from Her by force backfires on the violator and leads only to ruin. Even patriarchal men cannot actually live without their Mother, the Earth – and there is *no* heavenly father to escape to.

With patriarchal societies, fire (of the furnace, of war, of volcanoes, of the scorching sun) takes on a different symbolic meaning from that which it had in the Goddess cultures where it had been creative, transformative, protective, maternal. The fire-sacrifice now became all-important. The dead were now to be cremated, instead of returning their bones to the womb of the Earth Mother, to 'free the soul from its bodily prison' and to offer the flaming spirit to the sun god. The ancient Mother 'dragon of darkness' is now to be subdued by dragon-slaying solar 'heroes', archangels or gods such as St Michael, St George,

Perseus, Hercules, Egyptian Ra and Babylonian Marduk. Marduk slays his mother Tiamat and with her mutilated body he then creates the new male-ordered universe and 'law and order' as perceived by despotic patriarchs.

These male 'heroes' in emerging patriarchal times attempt to stake, control and fix the journeying, electromagnetic dragon/Earth spirit of the lunar currents and waters. Tiamat was the Babylonian cosmic dragon creator-Goddess whose two opposite serpent coils encompass the universe and reach to the highest heaven as well as deep into the primordial darkness from which all light emanates. She lives in our very cells and Her sacred laws have been benevolent. The Egyptians in the twelfth dynasty cried that Ma'at (wisdom and law) was cast out, and that iniquity was in the midst of the council hall. War/Amazon Goddesses fought back as ferociously as a lioness protecting her cubs – but to no avail. This is the lament for Ningil, great lady of the moon, at the destruction of her temple at Ur in Sumeria, about 2000 BC:

> Your city has been made into ruins, you are no longer its mistress;
> Your righteous house has been given over to the pickaxe,
> You no longer inhabit it;
> Your people have been led to slaughter, You are no longer their queen
> Your city weeps before you as its mother.[14]

By military edict the sun god now becomes supreme creator who gives life to the seed with his phallic solar beams. The dark maternal soil was now thought to have no inherent creative powers. The sun was seen as the greatest warrior of all, the victor in the eternally renewed battle with the 'serpent of darkness'. As a celestial warrior-king, the Sun travels through the sky in his war chariot while at night he fights the devouring womb/serpent of the underworld. Even the Egyptians forgot that Isis/Hathor, the Celestial Cow, bore the sun disc between her horns because she was Mother of the Sun.

The introduction of the male-centred solar religion and calendar reflected the interests of an emerging male, property-holding, ruling élite. It was introduced by military force and priestly rule in Egypt, Sumeria, India and pre-Columbus America. The solar cult was invariably imposed from above and never arose spontaneously from the people, who everywhere persisted in their love of the Great Mother and of moon gods such as Osiris. The ancient priestesshoods of the Goddess resisted the emerging patriarchal economic interests and increasing exploitation of the Earth's resources. They therefore had to be defeated.

With the new patriarchal belief in the sun god as a sky-father and husband of a passive Earth Mother, it was no longer possible to conceive of him as a child born of the womb of the Mother. This god was never born of a woman and, like the sun, he never died. He was all-powerful and a law unto himself. What the Mother in the past had freely given out of Her own volition and love, the son now tries to wrench from Her by force. The sun now begets his own mother.

With the destruction of the ancient Goddess cultures, elaborate theories were developed in India about the afterlife. The dead at first passed through the moon to become soma or food for the gods. Stars were the souls of the dead or of women who had died in childbirth. Yama, king of the dead, had discovered the 'path of the fathers' which led to heaven. This path of the Pitris of Manes was resided over by the fire god, Agni, who carried aloft the skin and limbs of the created dead who were born on the winds to the ancestors' magical homeland. Agni, who might have been of Iranian/Persian origin, was said to have been the son of the pre-Aryan Mother Goddess Prithiyi and her son/lover Dyans/Vritri of matriarchal India. Significantly he consumes his own parents and it was the members of his priesthood who were the originators of sacrificial rights. It was believed that the gods derived much of their strength from these fire sacrifices. Sacrificial fires and funeral pyres guaranteed an entrance to the path to heaven, the realm of light. Yama's kingdom was at a later stage transformed into a hell full of tortures and Yama himself became a figure of terror. Kali became a bloody and insatiable sacrifice-demanding Goddess, her temples slaughterhouses.

The Brahmins, the priestly caste, had sole monopoly of the fire sacrifice and were thought to possess power over the very gods by offering or withholding soma – the hallucinogenic liquor that was the 'remover of death'. Practising austerities and offering fire and soma sacrifices – cults still widespread in India today – were the source of great powers. There was even a notion held during the Brahminic period, that sages or yogis (Shiva in one aspect is a yogi), could acquire powers superior to those of the gods and would be absorbed, even before death, into the universal world spirit beyond the gods, because of their austerities and great knowledge. (Are these the Secret Masters?)

The doctrine of dharma or karma was a Brahminic innovation and very useful politically since it taught that righteousness and justice are embodied in social and caste obligations. The Aryans originally had no concept of reincarnation; it is not mentioned in the Vedas.

Fire sacrifices were also of the greatest importance to the ancient, dualistic Persian religion of Zarathustra or Zoroaster[15] who was born in about 588 BC. The sacred books of the Zoroastrians were the Avestas and from early times the religion became extremely dogmatic and preoccupied with ritual impurities.

Although the Iranians were closely related to the Indian Aryans, and had probably originally worshipped the same pantheon of gods, their beliefs soon changed. To the Iranians, the only true god was Ahura Mazdah (the divine light) or Ohrmazd who was locked in an eternal battle against Ahriman, the destructive spirit of darkness.

Zarathustra preached an 'Aryan' religion that mirrored in the heavens the struggle on Earth between the Aryan light-skinned peoples and the older, matrilinear, dark-skinned peoples.

Ahriman, like Ohrmazd, is a pure spirit, but he is the creator of evil, of death and darkness, which in the world of the patriarchs cannot possibly originate with their godfather who is always and only light. They now represent two universal forces seen in opposition to each other.

Zoroastrians have to identify with Ohrmazd and cooperate with nature to multiply and make the Earth fruitful so that they will have the strength to be able to withstand Ahriman's onslaught. To be virtuous was to be fruitful, while sterility and celibacy were vices. They did not see the material world as inherently evil in the way Christians did later.

At the end of time Zoroastrians believe we will be resurrected in the final body, and that this will be brought about by a saviour, Mithras, who will then appear and will bring about the reign of eternal beatitude.

A Zoroastrian must go three times a day to the fire temple to pay homage to the fire which derives its brilliance from the endless light of Ohrmazd, and this will bring him worldly wealth and holiness.

Ohrmazd created the bull, white and shining like the moon, and Gayonart, the first man, who shone like the sun. The souls of men were created in the unseen world, while Earth was their physical mother; men's seed or semen had its origin in fire and not in water. The universe itself is nothing but a vast sacrificial fire to the followers of Zarathustra.[16]

Ahriman created the demon whore queen sent to defile women who were held in very slight esteem, their sole function being to produce sons who would take part in defeating the evil one. Ohrmazd complained that 'I did not find a vessel from which blessed man might proceed except woman whose adversary is the whore'.[17]

The 'whore queen' was the first woman and, like Lilith,

she had fled the first man Gayonart/Adam and had gone to dwell with Ahriman/Samael. It is the devil's kiss that causes menstruation in women, a condition abhorred by the Zoroastrians as being the highest possible degree of impurity or pollution. Through her all men are defiled until the final resurrection when both the sexes will be called to share in the universal bliss. But no women could enter heaven except those submissive to control, those who had considered their husbands as lords, and woman will forever remain subject to man who cannot reproduce himself without her.

Both Ohrmazd and Ahriman had been born from the womb of Zurvan, but Ahriman had made the 'wrong sacrifices' and had turned into the great serpent.

The Zoroastrians influenced the Hebrews from the time of the exile and much of this thinking was incorporated into the laws of Jahweh. Presumably Mithras was the saviour who, like Christ, was to appear at the end of time and bring about the millennium.

Long before the teachings of Buddha and Confucius, Zarathustra was to be adopted by the west. His doctrines reached Greece some four centuries before those of the Christians and Zoroaster became his Greek name. He was the great magus and the Mesopotamian mystical lore of magic and astrology were put under his authority.

Zoroaster has been seen by some historians as a kind of Mongol shaman-sorcerer intoxicating himself with hemp fumes. He has also been called the 'first theologian', using abstract notions that recall those of the gnostics and neo-Platonists. Zoroaster, however, was a priest by profession, a man of rank and family. He was a prosperous prophet who wanted society to progress in a traditional framework with 'social harmony; between husbandman and warrior under the sway of priest and prince. His own patron had been Prince Vistaspa of eastern Iran. His was a pastoral society not yet settled on the land, a people to whom a good deed was to defend and care for cattle.

Zoroaster was the prophet of the patriarchal lord who

preached the coming of the 'city of god' which is not of this world. His teachings were of 'righteousness' and his justice was of the eye-for-an-eye variety. But, unlike in Christian theology, suffering has no essential place in his scheme, and there is no room for the pessimistic notion that the whole universe, including the god that made it, is evil. To Zoroaster there was no 'fall' but there is a 'choice'. We are, however, all victims of the evil spirit, Ahriman, whose unhappy choice had disturbed the universe.

The 'righteous and wise lord' was worshipped with fire-sacrifices, creating a mystic bond between 'man and god', but he forbade the ancient matriarchal blood-sacrifice of the bull or ox that had created a mystic bond between the people and the Mother Goddess. Zoroastrians must have known, though, in their heart of hearts that they had done evil when they destroyed the first, advanced cultures of the Earth and sensed that they had to do more and more sacrifices to atone for this, the matricide of the Great Mother. Much tortuous thinking would have gone into creating religions and philosophies that would divinely justify and condone the realities of rape, conquest, murder, looting, taking land belonging to others and the most heinous crime of matricide.[18]

To Zoroastrians, Earth is 'devotion'. She is the daughter of Good Mind whose 'father' is the wise lord. She is to dominion of Good Mind as obedience is to rule. She is the diligent zeal that ensures the execution of the good commands – as women are supposed to be obedient daughters of fathers and of the lord.

With the development of sun/light/fire cults, there is inevitably a split in the human spirit; life becomes a mistake and the human body a prison of the soul. The male spirit has to overcome the Mother who bore him.

The universe itself was seen as a vast, sacrificial fire and fire was, to the Indo-Iranians since time immemorial, a means of participating in the cosmos. To them there is a fundamental identity between fire and cosmic law. There is an analogy between Agni – who we saw started out by consuming his own parents – lightning and the stars.

Soma, the vital fluid or blood in all beings, was a fermented milky drink integral to the vedic sacrifices and drunk by the priests. It is the watery nectar of the moon's light that sustains vegetable life and on which all creatures feed. It was churned from the milky ocean from which the moon arises; the gods derived their strength from its nectar and it heals all diseases. Shiva wore the crescent moon on his forehead to honour it. Soma was produced by Vach, Goddess of waters and called 'the melodious cow who milked forth sustenance and water'.[19] It was believed that Brahma committed incest with his daughter while intoxicated on soma.

Indra, the Aryan sky god, who was murderous, violent and who betrayed other male gods, had an insatiable thirst for soma. He, who had murdered the peacefully sleeping Mother Goddess of the Dravidians, the cow and serpent Prithiyi of the Earth and Her son/lover Vritri, the bull-calf with his phallic thunderbolt, lived on the sacred Mount Meru. The Goddess and Her son – cow and calf – were called 'demons' by the invaders. Indra had stolen and drunk the ambrosia from the three cauldrons/wombs of Kali's trinity. The ambrosia/soma signified the lunar cyclic recurrence and was the wise blood of immortality, magic and female menstrual manna.

Emanations

It would seem that the solar gods are fed, thrive on and are materialised by sacrifices and terror. The Mexican Aztecs would prolong the sacrifice of the victims to the sun god to build up the astral emanations of the victim and of the excited and terrified audience. By these means they fused the collective unconscious of the mass of people into the forms of the priestly caste. The interference with the life fields of those sacrificed and the emotions released become imprinted in the electromagnetic fields of the local surroundings as an emotional memory.

Violent death, as well as orgasm, can be turned into techniques for building up psychic emanations. The ancient esoteric astral technique of sexuality was the way of the Goddess who thrives on all expressions of love, ecstasy and joy. This was also the way of Taoism, of tantra and Tibetan shamanism. Its opposite and negative is the path of mass death, pain, rape and sacrifice and is the way of the patriarchs.

Monstrous male gods, projections from the alienated male Id, demand more and more sacrifice. The Devas and Asuras would seem to feed off the astral emanations of collective human thought and stir up wars and passions. Who are these entities? Are they simply projected thought-forms or do they actually materialise and take on powers on the astral plane, the 'thought world'? Matter is a form of thought and thought-forms interact with the physical universe. The Tibetans believe that the phenomenal world, as we see it, is a fantastic mirage, a materialisation of the forms we conceive. They consider that what happens in a dream, for example committing a sin, is as real or serious as to commit the same act in the waking state. One must not work evil while asleep and intention is equivalent to actual deed. According to Tibetan mystics, there is a dual origin of deities. They are born of the mental concentration of the masses of believers and then temporarily created by the thought of him/her who acts like a magnet attracting these already existing occult forces or entities. The subjective nature of the deities does *not* make them into negligible phantoms.[20]

Alexandra David-Neel described, with a great deal of humour, in her book *Magic and Mystery in Tibet*, first published in 1931, how she succeeded in creating a phantom monk or *tulpa* after some months of concentration on thought and performing certain rites.[21] She wrote that his form grew gradually fixed and lifelike, and he became a kind of guest living in her apartment. When she went on a journey, she found that the 'monk' had joined the party and had indeed taken on a life of his own and could be seen by others. 'He' then escaped her control and started taking on a malignant look and became troublesome and bold. It turned into a walking nightmare and she decided to dissolve him. This took her six months of hard struggle. She said that her mind-creature was tenacious of life and warns that the practice is full of dangers for anyone who has not reached a high mental and spiritual level and is not fully aware of the psychic forces at work in the process.

Dione Fortune has similar tales to tell in her *Psychic Self-Defence*,[22] and talks of the formulation of evil intelligences and the nature of the forces that are at work below the surface of everyday life. The universe is permeated by a psychic ether called *akasa* and this etheric fluid/astral light is thought to be a semi-material substance that has the quality of plasticity. It is part of the akashic records, a natural archive, a psychic library, that surrounds the Earth, and in which is imprinted every event, thought, action that has taken place since the creation of this planet. According to occult tradition, this information can be drawn on at will by some psychics and it can be manipulated to form entity images or 'artificial elementals' who are thought-formed creatures that are ensouled, have individual identity and can exist forever within the space-time continuum.

It is suggested that such astral entities increase in power and vitality in direct proportion to the amount of mental energy concentrated upon them and that finally they can develop self-motivated action.

The horrendous monsters, the great old ones of the Cthulhu Mythos, created by H P Lovecraft's imagination in his gothic horror science-fiction novels[23] written in New England in the 1920s and 1930s, show clearly his fear of sexuality, of the natural world and of women. To Lovecraft, the ocean is evil and populated by slimy and scaly monsters, the forest is evil, engulfing and predatory. The world was indeed demonic to those brought up with the hidden ancestral guilt for having murdered the indigenous peoples of the USA, devastated Africa with slavery and burned at the stake the wise women and men of Europe who still communicated with nature and conceived of Earth's forces as benevolent and sacred. The fact remains, though, that such distorted and paranoid male guilt-ridden imagination can also feed and create entities on the astral planes that take on lethal realities.

What monstrous thought-entities have been given 'life' over thousands of years of life-denying patriarchal cultures, and how do we counteract this if we want to survive on our beautiful Earth?

Sonia Johnson, the former Mormon housewife who became an inspired feminist, writes in her brilliant and exhilarating book, *Going out of our Minds: the Metaphysics of Liberation*[24] that it is imperative that groups of women, and also men, come together to project and visualise and meditate on a future feminist world if the Earth is to survive. And what she means by feminist is a world built on life-affirming ways of being, and living together. She suggests that what happens on this Earthplane reverberates throughout all other planes of existence, since the past, the present and the future are with us now. There might, indeed, be struggles in other realms, not between forces of darkness and forces of light, but between life-affirming and life-denying spiritual value systems. Perhaps we are indeed watched over by the ancestors who want to come back into this world as new born spirits into a more benevolent and maternal-based life on this planet. In the web of Spider Woman whatever happens in one part of the web reverberates and ripples throughout every one of its parts throughout all existence.

We must think new thoughts and imagine possible Goddess futures.

Aquarian Consciousness and the Second Coming

There is an utter lack of, and concern for, feminist values or recognition of the Goddess in the New Age movement – a movement which claims to be so aware of how our thoughts create realities. What kind of world does the New Age want to bring into being, and what sort of entities on other planes does it actually work with?

A New Age guru, Sir George Trevelyan, an elderly gentleman in his eighties, sets out to do battle against the Mother dragon of the night and moon like a latter-day Saint George. He ran courses on the 'Spiritual Nature of Man' at Altringham College where he was the principal from 1948 to 1971 and was a founder of the Wrekin Trust. He has always been closely connected with the Findhorn Community, has been awarded an alternative 'Nobel Prize' for 'right livelihood' and is a very messianic and popular public speaker with white, middle-class audiences. Amongst his influential books are *Operation Redemption* and *A Vision of the Aquarian Age*.[25]

I recently listened to Sir George speaking at a day of so-called 'world-healing meditation' in Bristol, which was a follow-up to the 'Harmonic Convergence' in Glastonbury in August 1987 at which he had been one of the key speakers. I found what he had to say full of contradictions. One thing he said, which of course I agree with, was that with the suppression of the right-side of the mind in us the spiritworld has retreated because it is the feminine, poetic and sensitive mind with which we can comprehend the spiritual whole.

He talked lovingly and movingly about the beauty of the living Earth, our Mother, and how we must live in ways that serve Her, that by destroying Her nature we are building for ourselves a vast cosmic debt. Gaia, the Goddess of Earth, will simply shrug parasite man off Her shoulders. (The repressed, now raging, Mother might just do this since She does not need us.) Planet Earth is a living, integral creature of which we are the organs of thought, all of matter is energy and we are a part of intelligent, living, breathing nature.

However, he then went on to say that 'the human kingdom' is the point 'where nature has evolved to intelligence' and we should be the 'stewards of the planet'. For all the talk in the New Age movement of 'healing the Earth', this is not very helpful as long as there is no recognition of the self-creating, and self-aware consciousness of Earth, the great spiritual being who is our Mother.

Sir George Trevelyan does, indeed, believe, like the Freemasons do, that Earth is designed by a heavenly architect and that it is for Her to carry out his plan. Trevelyan thereby denies Earth any actual autonomous creative powers as for him they are ultimately male-derived and not inherent in nature and in matter (matter-mater-Mother). This male transcendant god is, of course, all light and he is the craftsman of form. Earth was, however, according to Trevelyan in the speech he gave in Bristol, a gamble for God since it is prone to being taken over by the fallen angels or dark powers. We are beings of thought in a universe of living thought, we are droplets from God the father. Spirit descends into the sphere of heavy matter; the body slows the spirit down and without it we can astral-travel anywhere at the speed of thought. God descended into the holy of holies within the temple so as not to be 'contaminated with matter' and a 'son' is to be born to humanity. According to Sir George, the power of the awaited universal love and life – cosmic Christ power, our higher self – is now flooding into the planet and lifting souls into a higher vision. A great world teacher is anticipated – Sai Baba, in southern India, is believed by many to be this awaited avatar. Trevelyan envisages cosmic battlegrounds in which the forces of darkness are trying to bind us down and are fighting the forces of light. This battle also rages on Earth and we participate in it; the dark forces will ultimately be destroyed. In typical New Age speak, the 'chosen', those who have realised 'Christ consciousness' and have tuned into the light, will not be touched by coming disasters – not even from radiation from a nuclear war.

All through the talk, Trevelyan used very patriarchal language: man, mankind, cosmic man, god, he, etc. This tends to be the norm at virtually every New Age gathering or talk (and even in books written by women; I have never as yet heard a woman objecting publicly to being made invisible and silenced in this way).

Additionally, Sir George cracked a joke about silly feminists trying to change the language we use. He thereby managed to diminish every woman in the audience. As he is very aware of the power of thoughts (he said, for example, that if you think thoughts of illness and disaster or accident you are likely to draw precisely what you fear to you) I wonder if he has considered what this verbal denial of women's very existence does to us, much less his insistence on the maleness of spirit, spirit beings and 'masters'.

Sir George Trevelyan is a follower of Rudolf Steiner, the great mediumistic occultist and Christian mystic, who believed that nature is an enchanted grave of the divine and that 'cosmic man is crucified on the cross of matter'.

Knowing something of Steiner's cosmology makes it easier to understand some of the ideas of the New Age movement.

Rudolf Steiner had been a speaker at the socialist workers' high school in Berlin in the 1880s. He was very influenced by Goethe's theories of colour and esoteric insights. At the age of twenty-two he became the editor of Goethe's scientific writings. In 1902, he became the secretary-general of the German section of the Theosophical Society, with the approval of Annie Besant. Because of his increasing belief in the mystical Christ – who according to Steiner came to Earth to fight the 'Lucifer and Ahrimanic spirit' – he had disagreements with the Theosophists and in 1913 he broke away and formed the Anthroposophical movement. In the same year, Steiner and his followers started building the Goetheanum in Switzerland at Dornach. It was to be constructed according to cosmic principles and to stage Steiner's mystery-dramas. He was a talented artist and sculptor who influenced artists such as Klee and Kandinsky. His wife, Marie von Sieverts, developed the esoteric dance, Eurythmy. The Geotheanum burned down in 1922, most likely sabotaged by the Nazis who saw Steiner, who used 'white magic' in a battle on the occult plane, as an arch-enemy because he preached against patriotism and nationalism. Biodynamic farming was also among their projects, as was herbal healing and homeopathy.

Reading Colin Wilson's biography, *Rudolf Steiner: the Man and his Vision*,[26] I get the impression of a man of great artistic and mediumistic powers – a complex personality. His was a strange mixture of occult pagan knowledge combined with an insistence on Christianity as the central event of human history and this is what has been picked up by the New Age movement with its emphasis on Christ-consciousness. Steiner had advanced ideas on education, as witnessed by the Waldorf schools, the first of which was founded in 1919; he introduced biodynamic organic farming which is, in fact, based on ancient women's planting and reaping by the lunar cycles. Much of the holistic health movement has been initiated by pupils of Steiner, who wanted to disprove scientific materialism once and for all, and to re-establish nature as 'God's living garment' and to prove that Earth is alive with meaning. At the same time Steiner proclaimed that nature is the enemy of 'man's inner life'.

Colin Wilson writes that Steiner was often confusing and self-contradictory, that his occult vision was frequently misled by his imagination – and I would add, as with all these gurus, by patriarchal prejudices – which he shared with the majority of men of his time and of ours, unfortunately.

Steiner, like Blavatsky, claimed to be able to read the Akashic records (the cosmic memory). However, he also claimed that Blavatsky could only do so in a trance when the 'hidden masters' spoke through her. It followed, therefore, that what she recorded was only partly true. As *he* was able to perceive the spiritworld while fully conscious he insisted that his own revelations of the remote past ages were somehow more accurate. Steiner developed some different notions of the spiritual evolution of our planet and human beings, but he, too, referred to Lemuria and Atlantis as past realities. According to him, fear, illness, death and 'rebellion' came into the world thanks to the Luciferic and Ahrimanic spirits which had rebelled against the 'hierarchy', and he claimed there is a primal satanic force in the universe. Lucifer, a hot spirit, who tempts 'man' with pride and egoism, destroyed Lemuria, while Ahriman, who predominates in our time, tries to push 'man' to advance much faster than he should. In Atlantis, Ahriman pushed for merely scientific achievement and even the initiates became corrupt. 'Man became slave to matter' and the Atlantean civilisation vanished ten thousand years ago, having unleashed destructive natural forces working in air and water. This is now being repeated. Christ (the sun), the chief opponent of Lucifer/Ahriman in the hierarchy, descended and came to Earth to set a new stage of evolution in which 'man' finally established a conscious ego, an 'I' that can make its own choices and whose evolution would be purely in his own hands. Christ is the highest of the sun spirits and 'he' has been there from the beginning and is active on behalf of evolving humanity. The hierarchies, of whom Christ is a great master, were in charge of the evolutionary process and they interacted with the natural forces to create physical organs and the material world.

The spirit-entity Christ descended on to Jesus, the initiate and physical man, in the form of a dove (Ruach or holy spirit, originally female and of the Goddess) when he was being baptised by John. According to Steiner, Christ was a divine being who had been preparing for incarnation since the beginning of human evolution and his purpose was to turn the tide of battle against the forces of materialism – the dark forces of Lucifer and Ahriman – that would otherwise have overwhelmed humankind.

Colin Wilson writes that Steiner dismissed spiritualism and considered spiritualists to be materialists. This, though he himself had communications with the spirit-world in controlled hypnogogic[27] states, in the twilight realm between waking and sleeping.

It seems that at first Steiner had thought that Christianity was an excuse for indulging in day dreams of salvation, but after a vision of the mystery of Golgotha he became convinced that 'Christ's descent into history was to ensure man's ultimate salvation'. To bring out this message became the purpose of his life. Steiner felt that he had been chosen to usher in the New Age with his new mystery knowledge, that he was part of the world historical process. He started to repudiate the 'orientalism' of the Theosophists and made public his own cosmological teachings which led to Annie Besant breaking with him in 1907.

In 1913, the German branch of the Theosophical Society became the Anthroposophic society and Steiner was widely accused of simply forwarding his own ambitions. Steiner proclaimed that 'to grasp the idea of freedom without the idea of salvation by Christ, ought not to be found possible by mankind'. The archangel Michael, the dragon/Mother Goddess slayer, figured large in his thoughts as a solar spirit-being fighting 'evil elemental beings' or solar, chivalrous, victorious day, fighting against lunar, watery and reptilian night as Peter Lamborn Wilson puts it in *Angels*.

It seems that some Nazis like Rudolf Hess were interested in both Anthroposophy and Theosophy. To Steiner, Hitler was a personification of Ahriman come to spread hatred, destruction, darkness and chaos . . . and of course in this Steiner might have been perfectly right and the 'king of the world' that the Nazis supposedly communicated with might indeed have been a manifestation of this Ahriman spirit. Anthroposophists, however, regard Steiner as the greatest man of the twentieth century.

Sir George Trevelyan wrote an introduction, together with W I Thompson, to David Spangler's *Revelation – the Birth of a New Age* in 1975. In it he recognises that culture springs from the deep powers of the Earth and our 'unconscious', as well as from 'visitations from the gods' who release 'higher energies' on our Earth.

Trevelyan says that Spangler's is the new mediumship for our time and emphasises how it is achieved in 'full consciousness' and that in this way 'light-filled beings' work with us in mental communion, very much in Rudolf Steiner's style. These beings are mediators coming from our own thinking and intuition and involve intellectual understanding of 'higher worlds', the emphasis being on the conscious and intellectual understanding of non-participatory and detached onlooker-consciousness fostered in patriarchal societies, as opposed to ecstatic mediumistic women shamans' communications with Goddess/nature and Her spirit realms.

W I Thompson, in the same introduction, implies that the ancient ecstatic trance-state of the shaman during which she or he lost their everyday consciousness, meant that they were 'swamped by the unconscious'. I think that it is precisely because men and women like Spangler, Trevelyan, Alice Bailey and Eileen Caddy fear to go into the deep and the luminous darkness, where the Goddess is encountered in ecstatic visions and dreams, that the 'channellings' and voices they come up with are but the creations of their own patriarchally conditioned and limited minds.

Another guru of the New Age is Peter Russell whose influential book *The Earth Awakening – the Global Brain* also seems to assume that spirit and consciousness are not properties of Earth Herself, but are somehow passed on to Her by a male and transcendant spirit mind. The assumption is that human consciousness is the awakening self-awareness of the planet; 'we' (in this case the male mind) are the global brain. Russell does admit though that the global brain is onesidedly left-brain and male-dominated in present times and that this has led to the emphasis in modern societies on science – a science not concerned with things essential and holistic – and technology, to the exclusion of the 'feminine principles' (I would say Goddess-consciousness) that symbolises the energy of the living Earth, the creation and sustenance of life, the ecological principle of living in harmony with the planet.

Russell speaks of how people meditating in syncronicity around the globe are setting up resonating electromagnetic waves around the Earth: how we are all part of one great mind which is accelerating in awareness. But instead of recognising that we are intelligent, conscious and aware because She creates us so, and that this great mind is Hers, Russell keeps speaking of Gaia as slumbering and unaware and as if our Space and electronic technology is supplying Her with a nervous system She didn't have before.

He assumes that Gaia is finding out about other planets and Her own position in the universe with the help of men's deadly space-technology that cannot exist without nuclear energy and that is turning the cosmos into a wastebin for human refuse. It is as if planetary beings do not have far more subtle and clairvoyant means of communication through time and space, like in/out of the body journeying.

I sense in many New Age men an insufferably paternalistic and condescending attitude not only towards women but towards the very Earth who gave us all life and mind.

Women Experiencing the Goddess

Participating intuition was the ancient women's way and is characteristically human and evolutionary; it is the way in which we partake in Earth's dreaming mind. Ancient shaman women's creative gifts had been the inspiration of lucid frenzy and, as Peter Redgrove says, we have to redefine 'hysteria' as prophetic speech. Inspired artists have always known that one has to arrive at the unknown by the disordering of the senses and shamans believe their powers derive from the powers of animals, plants and celestial bodies, not mentally produced by us but existing in nature.

Ecstasy and non-dualistic wisdom always belong to the Goddess. It is women's untamable and ancient menstrual lunar powers that are feared by the 'nice' and obedient daughters of the 'godfathers', and even more so by their men.

Many visions of the madonna or virgin have appeared in many places, and to many people during this century, and women everywhere are now drawn to and experience the Goddess at Her sacred places, in dreams, visions and meditations.

Women now have to fiercely resist the present day solar priesthood and nuclear military complexes as they attempt to implement matricide and the death of nature. There is a growing worldwide ecofeminist movement with women and men returning to the sacred places of the Goddess where the voices of the ancestors are heard yet again.[28]

7
From the Rebirthing Movement to Biological Engineering

The Death of My Son

Only two months after Leif's death, my oldest son, Sean, was diagnosed as having far-advanced cancer. He had been ill for a long time but his homeopathic doctor had failed to examine him properly and had not recognised the classic symptoms.

Sean came to live with me in the cottage in Wales to give me support in my grief for the death of my youngest son. His body swelled up so that he was barely able to walk or breathe and he was taken to Cardiff University hospital where he was diagnosed as having acute Hodgkins' disease and immediately began chemotherapy treatment.

Within four days he was reduced to skin and bone and was very weak. It was from Cardiff, after a month or so, that we arrived back in Bristol so that Sean could attend the Bristol Cancer Help Centre as well as continue with the chemotherapy treatment at Southmead hospital.

The Bristol Cancer Help Centre is much inspired by the work and research of Carl and Stephanie Simonton in the USA.[1] Their emphasis is on techniques for learning positive attitudes and thinking, relaxation, visualisation, goal-setting, handling pain, exercise and emotional support in fighting cancer. The Simontons have come to the conclusion through their research that there is a 'cancer-prone personality', a person with a history of basic rejection and negative life patterns. For them, cancer patients often appear to have had unhappy, emotionally deprived childhoods which create negative, suicidal and despairing attitudes that encourage malignant growths. Grief and bereavement, as well as psychological conflicts, are a very common trigger of cancer. It is almost as if some have chosen to feel the inherent sadness in the universe and have legitimised this sadness by becoming terminally ill.

As a result of their findings, the Simontons developed a programme of meditation and visualisation aimed at enhancing the body's protective mechanism.

Sean was a gentle giant who was potentially a very fine artist. He was restless and streetwise, having had very little formal education and with a wayward sense of humour. He was always a loner and had felt rejected when his father and I split up and he was parted from his beloved brother. We make so many mistakes in our lives – but by the time they start manifesting in the form of illnesses as they did in Sean's case, it is too often too late.[2]

Sean had always been a vegetarian and was interested in yoga. It was not difficult for him, therefore, to accept the Cancer Help Centre's regime of raw carrot-juice, vitamin therapy and a very pure diet consisting of mainly organic vegetables. He constantly had to defend this to the NHS doctors and to his consultant who ridiculed any treatment that did not involve chemical drugs, and who undermined Sean's confidence in his powers to cure himself.

Sean experienced much pain, nausea and discomfort from the chemotherapy which destroys white blood cells and breaks down the immune system so that any minor cold or infection can become fatal. Chemotherapy may also cause the loss of body hair. It upset Sean, who was an animal lover and vegetarian, that the drug had been tested on animals in vivisection laboratories.

Sean and I lived a strange existence together in an in-between twilight world, he so close to death much of the time and I grieving for my young son, his brother, already gone before us.

We became involved in the holistic health movement to seek to make our damaged lives whole, healthy and loving. Sean and I read vast numbers of books on allopathic and alternative medicine, on health, diet, allergies and about the food and drug industries.

Many of the books that my son was reading on alternative cancer cures seemed to blame the victim and suggest that you, yourself, are solely responsible for your illness or have even 'chosen' it so as to learn something from it.

At first my son was quite euphoric and supremely confident that he would be able to cure himself, that he would be a 'wounded healer' going through a shamanistic death and rebirth and thus help and heal others.

Sean appeared to be getting better during the summer of 1986 and was during this time an inspiration to many as he radiated courage, wisdom and kindness. He took part in gentle forms of therapy, and even psychodrama, recommended by the Cancer Help Centre, and was making plans to enrol with the Open University. At the same time, he became more and more convinced, through his reading and experiences, that it was the unhappiness from his childhood and his own frame of mind (he had actually feared getting cancer ever since adolescence and had had dreams about it early on) that had brought about the illness. Sean had read some books by Janov on the primal scream which had impressed him and he felt that it would take something quite drastic for him to be able to get at the deeply suppressed anger and pain of so many years.

Sean had heard of Rebirthing and thought that he would try it, although neither of us knew what this would entail. He found two Rebirthers, a woman and a man, who practised from a mansion in Portishead near Bristol.

At first he was elated and enthusiastic and felt that it helped him to open up; he felt strange energies rise within his energy/chakra centres and was even able, at times, to cry. He was brimful with uncried tears, as are so many men in this culture.

But, as the weeks went by, I could see him becoming increasingly depressed, despondent, ill and tired; it would take him the whole week to recover before the next session. After six weeks he was in real pain, coughing a lot and sometimes passing out when he did so. He was, by now, feeling weak and very negative. I was getting very worried but in no way would he listen to me as the Rebirthers had told him that he, quite likely and as part of the healing process, would manifest 'pseudo-symptoms' of his illness and that he was to ignore this. Sean was also breathing in a rapid and shallow way. When I asked him about this, he said that he had been taught to do so by the Rebirthers.

He was then offered the chance to take part in a ten-day intensive course ('self-mastery training') at a cost of £400 which he could hardly afford. Being by now so brainwashed by the whole process, he took it into his head that attending this intensive course would finally either make or break him.

The Rebirthers would no doubt claim that they tried to discourage him from taking part, but I clearly remember Sean telling me that he felt pressurised into paying up in advance – as it seems that the Rebirthers wanted to make up the numbers of people who attended the course at any cost. Had they been true healers they would have sent Sean back home and refunded his money when they realised how ill he was. Sean was white as a sheet, in pain, not able to eat or sleep and was often passing out. In spite of this, he took part in this intensive course, which even included periods of being submerged in hot water tubs breathing through a snorkel.

He returned home and took to bed, having still been told to ignore symptoms. He was now told to 'reintegrate' and rest for the next couple of weeks.

I could see him dying in front of my eyes and still he would not listen to me. He had been made to feel that if he was a spiritually advanced person, he should be able to think his way out of his illness, to conquer matter with mind alone.

Fortunately he now had to go for a regular three-monthly check-up at the hospital and somehow he managed to get there, though barely able to stand.

The consultant took one look at him, sent him for an emergency X-ray and it was discovered he had an enormous growth in his lung which was pressing on his heart. If he had not gone to the hospital then, he would have been dead within a week. Added to this, he had caught pneumonia from being in the hot-water tubs.

After a more thorough examination, it was found that he had been wrongly diagnosed and that what he in fact was suffering from was not Hodgkins' disease, which is possible to treat, but the far more lethal and fast-growing non-Hodgkins' lymphoma, that is, cancer of the lymph system, which has a tendency, after relapse, to spread both to the brain and to the bone marrow.

Sean was now in hospital for another couple of months on a far more taxing chemotherapy treatment. He was very close to death several times during the winter months. During this time, none of the Rebirthers bothered to visit him. In contrast, spiritual healers came and gave him healing, refusing to accept any money for so doing.

What was worst was the terrible sense of defeat we both felt, and from then on my son became very dependent on the hospital and no longer had a faith either in his ability to heal himself or in any alternative medicine.

Over yule-tide and the new year he suddenly developed epileptic fits and it was then found that there were a few small cancerous growths on top of his brain.

For a time Sean was having daily radiotherapy on his head as well as chemotherapy, antibiotics and strong anti-epilepsy tablets all at the same time. He also had very uncomfortable lumbar punctures and blood transfusions. It was a miracle that he actually came through all this sane and actually seeming slowly to recover again in the spring.

We hoped that when he finally came off the six-months

long chemotherapy treatment that he would get better. But he relapsed with further growths in the liver and the brain. He was then told by the consultant that he could do nothing further for him and was sent home with painkillers.

Sean arrived home in tears, believing that he had been given a death sentence and that his life-line to the hospital had been cut off. Of course we kept hoping that a mistake had been made in the diagnosis.

My son knew, however, that there had been no mistake because he was having strange dreams and visions. Every time he had been close to dying he had experienced this preparation for entering into the other realms. During a walk with his brother, Toivo (my other son), a week before he finally left us, they had been lying on the grass and looking at the sky when he 'saw' a new-born foetus in the clouds (not a cloud looking like a foetus). He was full of wonderment and awe and it felt to him like a miraculous gift.

During these last weeks and months he had become almost transparent and had a strange beauty, looking like a mixture between a Buddhist monk with his bald head and fine features, and a tall, blond Saxon king, as someone lovingly described him. He shone with an inner light and radiated peace in spite of it all, and never lost his kindness and loving concern and friendliness to other people.

The last two days and nights of his life he was back in hospital because he was delirious and in terrible pain, barely able to recognise anyone or to communicate. My son had had his twenty-eighth birthday on 25 June and two weeks later, on full moon, 10 July 1987, sedated with morphine he stopped breathing.

Sean didn't fear dying; to him it seemed like an adventure into other worlds where he would meet up with his younger brother, Leif. He was well-prepared – by knowing mediums and spiritualists – but he had feared lingering on in unbearable pain like some terminally ill cancer patients. He had his wish and went very fast and was surrounded, as he did so, by loving friends, Toivo and I, who went with him as far as we could, wishing him well on his new journey.

We had a moving non-Christian cremation and wake for him. The wake was in Leigh Woods where we also scattered his ashes, with all our friends in colourful clothes dancing, singing, playing music and celebrating his being – the way he would have wanted it. It felt totally magical and blessed and was a new experience to many people who had not imagined that a wake can be such a dignified, beautiful and joyous occasion. It will long be remembered in Bristol.

Both my sons went to the spiritworld on a full moon.

Rebirthers: Male Mothers and False Rebirth

After my son died I read *Rebirthing in the New Age*,[3] written by Sondra Ray with the help of Leonard Orr, in a tone of breathless California hype. Sondra seems to me to be yet another father-fixated daughter. She herself admits that her father wanted a son and that she spent a life-time trying to prove herself to him. Her book is very patriarchal and Christian in tone and concentrates on divine fathers and sons.

Leonard Orr was the unwanted fifth child of a mother who profoundly resented having children. Until 1968 he worked as a salesman, but being emotionally disturbed, he decided to try to unravel his 'birth-trauma'. He was convinced that his mother had unconsciously wanted to abort him and therefore he suffered from an unconscious 'death-wish'. Orr spent a large part of five years lying around in hot baths, practising connected breathing. In 1974, he worked a short time for the millionaire Werner Ehrhard in EST but soon left to set up the first rebirthing centre in San Francisco. Of the first nine certified Rebirthers, seven were men. They developed a technique of regulated breathing, of hyperventilation and of submersion in hot-water tubs to simulate the womb environment.

Orr had been influenced by the ancient Indian Kriya yoga, the yoga of breath or prana, that had been introduced to the USA and the west by Paramhansa Yogananda who wrote *Autobiography of a Yogi*[4] in the 1920s.

The Rebirthers' 'Five Biggies', as they call them, are: the birth trauma, the parental disapproval syndrome, specific negatives, poverty consciousness and the unconscious death-wish.

They see breath or prana (life force) as the physical connection to life energy that can be used to free all sorts of 'imagined limitations such as poverty, sickness and even death' and as the key to the mystery of life, body and spirit. They believe that 'negative thinking' can be uprooted with breathing and affirmations and, according to them, our birth right is material prosperity and physical immortality.

Their guru whom they worship as a god or avatar, their yogi Christ of India, is, or rather was, Babaji, a Hindu Yogi whom Leonard Orr had encountered in India in 1978. 'Babaji is the Angel of the Lord in the Old Testament, He is the Eternal Father in human form . . . Babaji is the Infinite, Eternal Spirit . . . Fire is the power principle of the universe . . .' Babaji even 'created this planet', according to Orr.[5] Babaji (Baba means 'father') taught the Rebirthers spiritual purifications to clear the energy body and fire rituals even as protection against nuclear war. The biblical symbol for breath is fire, and Jesus talked of the baptism of fire. Babaji claimed that fire, which we have in every cell, burns away death-urge material and anger and demands more consciousness from us than do water purifications because fire flows up while water flows down! Babaji should have lived 9,000 years according to Orr, as an eternal one dwelling in the Himalayas since the world began and could materialise and dematerialise at will. He was claimed to be the same Babaji as Yogananda's guru. Imagine the horror amongst the Rebirthing community when their guru suddenly died in 1984 from a heart attack.

The not-so-immortal Babaji expressed some rather reactionary views to the Rebirthers such as advising them to be 'brave like Mussolini' and as attentive as Scotland Yard or the CIA, according to Nicholas Albery,[6] in his book *How to be Reborn*.[7] He was also, apparently, full of forebodings of coming disasters which didn't comply with the 'positive thinking' favoured by rebirthers.

One might well wonder what Orr would have done if he had grown up in a Third World country with such 'imagined limitations' as no water, much less any running hot water for his bath, and no rich white 'clients' to pay for his very expensive seminars.

Nicholas Albery voices doubts and criticisms about the Rebirthing movement. He says that Leonard Orr's book, *Physical Immortality: The Science of Everlasting Life*, degenerates into something like a fascist discourse. 'Death' is presented as sinful and self-willed, an affront to God whose son, Jesus, said, 'Believe in me and have everlasting life.' Orr believes that all death is suicide since the physical body, the highest expression of universal intelligence, should last as long as the physical universe. 'God has no desire to kill people' (p. 20), 'Nobody can kill you but you' (p. 7), 'all weak-minded people in the past have died' (p. 6), and he actually states that death is the way whereby Earth rids itself of bad or evil people.

In Orr's philosophy you yourself create socially acceptable symptoms such as cancer, so that you'll have an excuse to leave your body. Fear of death is fear of letting go. Cancer is a conflict between your life and your death urge which manifests in your body-cells. We create worry, tension, fear to explain ageing and we sacrifice our natural divinity voluntarily. If you believe that cancer can be cured, you'll live. All you need to do is to change your mind. There are no victims, only people with 'victim consciousness' and, if you die, it is because you have a 'deathist mentality'. Death is only an illusion and by dying you try to kill God since life is the result of thought called 'God'. Original sin is thinking that you are not God.

Some affirmations are: 'I do not give my body a chance

to self-destruct' and 'I no longer need pains and illness to get attention'. (This last is an affirmation which I saw my Sean writing again and again in an exercise book.)

Rebirthing aims at body mastery and the elimination of all sickness and death. Rebirthers see all symptoms as healing in progress, and it was this way of thinking that became so lethal for Sean when he relapsed but was told to ignore the symptoms. Current ideas of death and time are rejected. The Rebirthers think that it is the negative thought that death is inevitable that interferes with the ability of the life-force to build healthy body cells. The ultimate accomplishment would be to be able to materialise and dematerialise the body at will. To them the body is but a loving servant of our minds. Rebirthers seem to retreat back into childhood self-centredness and sense of utter omnipotence. They flatly deny that there exist forces outside of themselves in Earth or nature which cannot be controlled or manipulated by the human mind.

Life is cyclical, however, and death as well as birth are natural. Ancient natural religions celebrate cycles of birth, death and rebirth through the eternal cosmic Mother while Christianity insists that, in one unique historical moment, the cycle reversed and a dead man came back to life in his physical body (the gnostics believed that it was in his 'spirit body' and for this they were burned at the stake).

The concept of immortality in the physical body, as opposed to in the spirit body, is a typically white puritan Christian one with its denial of death and the magical other-world of the Goddess realms.

Under Christianity, anything associated with birth, menstruation and reproduction was unclean and the sacrificial blood of Christ was to take precedence over mother's milk and her sacred blood. The blood of the martyrs was known as the 'seed of the Church'. For Christian theology, it was not birth but rebirth that mattered; the rebirth of the soul in the likeness of the father and the son.[8]

Women's bodies became obstacles to transcendence within the male order. Christian redemption was not the rebirth of the natural cycle – such as spring following the death of winter and Kore returning to her Mother, Demeter, from her stay in the underworld – but a rebirth from the condition of sinfulness and it was accomplished by the 'Son of Man'. The 'new life' entered into by each Christian at baptism is a 'spiritual' life and not a mere physical one. Men's spiritual rebirth was made possible by the sacrifice of the son to the father and this brought grace, to be given out by the Christian priesthood, enabling 'men to become brothers'.

Genuine mystical experience as opposed to the Rebirthing variety, wakes in us true feelings, knowledge and love for creation.

Nicholas Albery writes that the Rebirthers are *not* careful enough in their initial screening of clients and in their assessment of their physical health, and that there is a lack of professional ethics. They do not receive enough training; too much superstition is involved; they are far too expensive; and they keep no records of their clients' progress in mental and physical health. They are ignorant of medical findings but will, in spite of this, take on people who suffer from dangerous diseases such as cancer, epilepsy and heart trouble, and offer Rebirthing as a healing process for all. In fact, the intense breathing can trigger asthmatic attacks, epileptic fits and chest pains.

In rebirthing, everything relates to individual responsibility of the 'you create your own reality' variety, which makes no allowance for oppression by others or by the external world. Furthermore, the breathing process puts people into a suggestible state in which they are particularly open, receptive and vulnerable to being imprinted with new ideas, however crazy, and there is an air of total unreality. An affirmation such as, 'It is totally safe for me to let go' is a bad joke if you are a woman/gay/black, while 'I am an externally radiant being' might be true on other planes of existence, but certainly isn't here. When talking of 'prosperity consciousness', rebirthers teach that the poor are poor simply because they are not capable of receiving. Why is it that the poor are mostly in the Third World amongst non-white peoples? Answer: 'They have lessons to learn in this life-time' and they have brought this upon themselves. Such thinking sits well with the right-wing philosophy of Major, Thatcher, Bush and the white South African rulers, to mention but a few. Inequality, wrong doing, hurt and pain are denied by the Rebirthers. This is a recipe for selfishness and lack of common compassion.

We supposedly choose our parents and future life in a hypothetical, fully conscious existence before birth. This implies that one chooses to be born crippled and deformed or with AIDS or so undernourished, because of one's mother's hunger and starvation, that one dies soon after birth. We are simply working out our karma from former lives and no one must interfere with that. This is the concept of dharma: a reactionary dogma, lifted from Hinduism and Buddhism in India where it served caste society and was an innovation by the privileged Brahmin priestly caste to justify oppression and inequality. There is an unreal and over-optimistic denial of suffering and evil in the world amongst Rebirthers. They invest the specifically human mind with truly incredible and godlike powers. Nothing is mentioned of what happens when you are surrounded by everyone else's mind-created reality. If you question this, however, you are told you are negative and 'to take responsibility for yourself' is always applied to others. If someone feels hurt at being treated without care or consideration s/he is told that s/he is adopting a 'victim stance' or that s/he is 'having expectations' or is 'choosing to be hurt'. Very convenient and very dishonest!

Sean's Rebirthers had the nerve to suggest through intermediaries that I should work on my 'anger' with them – I had a problem (anger at what they had done to my son) but they did not! One is never ever supposed to 'blame' anyone, least of all the oppressors, it seems.

According to Rebirthers, the only thing that exists is pleasure – if you have an experience you find unpleasant, you are living a lie since the present moment is all you have got and you should be grateful for every detail of it, however maiming, horrific and unjust.

By concentrating solely on the individual mind-body-spirit, blame and guilt is thrown straight back on the individual who is made to think that s/he should be able to heal her/himself by mind alone. This takes responsibility away, very conveniently for the rulers, from the obscene and death-dealing structures of imperialism, multinationals, nuclear war industries, coercion of, and violence towards, human beings and the feminisation of poverty. That the universal spirit might be affronted by this worldwide misery, and by those in the USA and the west who perpetuate it, does not seem to occur to Rebirthers and other New Agers. Nor that the western world is building for itself a truly terrible and collective karma by these actions.

Nicholas Albery came across the Rebirthing movement in 1983 and became involved, in spite of feeling that it was sickly; love was treated like treacle and an endless outflow of love, gratitude and forgiveness was professed by people who have no real notion of what these concepts mean or entail. He seemed to develop the usual megalomaniac frame of mind, believing he was moving out on to astral planes, even that he was god and all-powerful. He took part in a one-year seminar and listened to lectures given on New Age spirituality and politics by Americans whose ideas of politics were naive and reactionary in the extreme. He writes that they were exposed to some of the stars of the international Rebirthing movement and found them sadly lacking. They were taken through rushed breathing sessions, submitted to half-baked philosophy, silly games and a class-room atmosphere of conformity. Rebelliousness was not encouraged, it was seen as being caught up in the parental disapproval syndrome – the only reason one rebels against bosses, governments, dictators is because of this – and Albery felt that the Rebirthers were more interested in breaking his spirit than in releasing it.

People experiencing Rebirthing are encouraged to pretend they are not hurt – that life is a miracle where nothing outside oneself can be lethal, where one is safe and immortal and the physical universe exists for the purpose of supporting one's spirit, mind and body in pleasure and comfort forever (what utter arrogance of the privileged), and to say affirmations that do not feel true. There is no true working-out of conflicts and pains. Albery felt that he was colluding in a group fraud.

When Albery started practising, he found that the majority of clients were male, white, middle-class and in their thirties, and that sometimes these men's reports of psychic and spiritual phenomena were unconvincing. He found the shallow breathing was defensive and a way of avoiding the more troublesome underlying painful material in the quest of a weak and premature spiritual orgasm. The theory is that rapid, shallow, unbroken, circular breathing causes complete circuits of energy in the body, bringing all parts of the body into the person's awareness and activating suppressed material. Breath-prana is the link between the spirit body and the physical body, the god within and the god without united through breath.

Albery feels that Phil Laut – whose income is reputed to be in the region of $100,000 a year – is partly to blame for the way Rebirthing philosophy so inadequately comes to terms with pain and suffering.

Laut is the author of *Money is My Friend*[9] and a graduate of Harvard Business School. He served in the Vietnam war as a commanding officer of a coast-guard patrol boat. Albery describes him as a man whose mouth hardly moves and whose eyes do not light up, a man who believes that money simply flows around all the time and all you need to do is to direct its flow towards you. Like Orr he thinks that the more millionaires there are around, the easier it is to become one yourself; that if you spend time with them, their karma will rub off on to you and that the abundance of the universe can make you as rich as you are willing to be. According to Laut, poor people are embarrassed about money and do not, as a rule, negotiate because they do not have enough self-esteem – no questioning of the realities of poverty amongst women and the non-white population in the USA. In New York alone many of the homeless are families headed by black women driven out of their homes through poverty and high rents to live in the streets. Laut seems to be of the opinion that comfort, pleasure, education, affluence and technology have expanded our minds and that spiritual purification is the secret to getting rich fast. A memorable quote from Laut is, 'God might be riding around with you in your Mercedes enjoying it too.'

There are very similar messages about wealth and godliness coming from fundamentalist Christians and Rebirthers alike. Many of the affirmations used by Rebirthers are about making money, such as, 'My personal connection with infinite being and infinite intelligence is adequate enough to yield a huge personal fortune'. Also, 'My job is the pipeline by which I lay the infinite wealth of my US economy for my personal use.'[10]

The Rebirthers seem to think that prosperity and abundance and good health are the birth rights of the west, earned because of good karma and spiritual advancement. All human misery, sickness and death are, according to Rebirthers, caused by ignorance of the law of mind.

There do not seem to be many questions asked about *why* so many people grow up unwanted and unloved, in poverty and real deprivation – in terms of class, sex and race. Neither are questions asked about how we can possibly stay healthy and happy while the Earth is raped and polluted.

It seems to me that Rebirthers envy women's creative powers. Nicholas Albery warns that for some men Rebirthing is a way of competing for attention with pregnant women, that they are trying to give birth to themselves and are jealous of women's ability to give birth and have children. Rebirthing reconstructs birth fantasies, often an imposed and unreal birth experience in which the therapist, if male, takes over the maternal function and acts as the client's 'womb'. Death is the last 'enemy' to conquer and birth is the first.

In the face of all the evidence to the contrary, they insist that life is male-created with its ultimate origin in a divine father god. Since they deny the Mother, they cannot conceive that death is a return to Her from whom we are reborn. It is a mistake, as is birth and all Mother-created life. Men in patriarchal societies often have fantasies of being father-born.

Jim Leonard and Phil Laut spell out clearly their denial of the Mother in *Rebirthing – the Science of Enjoying All of your Life*.[11] They say that essentially the foetus grows itself. According to them, the embryo was formed before the umbilical cord. We form our bodies ourselves out of infinite (male) intelligence and divine (male) energy, with the mother acting as the original 'landlady' (!) who keeps the temperature right, supplies air and takes out waste products. The connection between mother and child is only psychic and no more so than between all of us they say, and claim that no blood or other material flows between mother and placenta. 'God has leased us a body and the Earth' they say.

The reason why Rebirthers like Laut and Leonard deny the importance of the mother is because if they clearly perceived the connection between the oppression of women as mothers, and the profoundly destructive effect this has on the children we bear and on birth itself, they would have to take a firm stand for women's liberation and against patriarchal society.

Hospital births, so often under the supervision of male obstetricians today, symbolise the subversion of female power and are an attempt to destroy women's mysteries. Female reproduction is, today, mostly controlled by men, from the males who make the birth control devices, to the men who do or do not allow us abortions, to the men who deliver our babies. Reproductive engineering is also almost entirely in men's hands, as are governmental and voluntary agencies that fund this research.

Nicholas Albery thinks there is nothing original in Rebirthing; that it is a hotch-potch of theories and techniques borrowed from transpersonal psychology, Kriya yoga, Leboyer's natural birth and Hopi prophecies. It would not be so bad if Rebirthing was simply unoriginal but it is also reactionary and can be downright deadly, as it was for my son, Sean.

The ancient Goddess was the birth and death Goddess and fertility wisdom and shamanism are about crossing between the worlds. The birthing woman is the archetypal shaman as she brings the soul from the other realms into this world, forming and incarnating it within her body. She is mediator between the worlds and magically converts bread and wine into flesh and blood in mysteries of transformation.

Birth without Violence . . . and Birth without Violence

The rebirthing movement has been very influenced by Frédéric Leboyer who asserts that the emotional environment at birth has a profound impact and life-long effect on us.

Frédéric Leboyer is a French obstetrician who wrote *Birth without Violence*[12] in 1974 which advocates natural and gentle birth in dim light and with loving hands. He was rebirthed by Orr in 1974. Leboyer seems to talk of the child born isolated from the needs of the mother and what is happening to her. If women had had any say in the matter, this is the way we would always have given birth. Alienating hospital wards with harsh lights, unloving hands, machinery, loud noises and constantly changing faces are designed to scare the mother as much as the child being born. Because the mother is fearful birth becomes an experience, not of the sacred, but of humiliation, pain and shame.

I had the opportunity to study Leboyer's *Birth without Violence* in great detail during April and May 1989 whilst waiting for my grandson to be born. I had travelled to the Algarve in Southern Portugal to be with my son, his lover and her children who were then living in a small cottage, with no electricity, running water or outside toilet, high up in the breathtakingly beautiful mountains above Monchique. This was glorious springtime and everything was green and lush and vibrant.

I had feared going to the south of Europe ever since Leif's death. Yet I could not stay away from the birth of this child, so precious after the loss of Leif. My son and his lover were 'travellers', living in a big truck, but had decided to live in a cottage for the birth. In no way did they want to have anything to do with hospitals and male medicine, assuming a midwife would be on hand. But in Portugal there are no midwives to attend to women in their homes.

So the child was to be born in a cottage in the mountains, miles from the nearest hospital, which could only be reached by going down winding and bumpy mountain paths. My son, myself and a German woman friend were 'midwives'. No wonder we were anxiously reading up on everything we could find on natural childbirth; if the mother started bleeding too much, or the cord was around the child's neck as it was being born we wanted to know what to do. I do not know who was the most surprised and appalled, I or Annie the expectant mother, when we read Leboyer's description of birth as a battle to the death between mother and child: '. . . the child is thrust into this hell . . . its fear changes to anger . . . it hurls itself against the barrier [the mouth of the womb] . . . this blind, blank wall which is holding it back, confining it is the mother . . . it is she who is the enemy who stands between the child and life . . . only one of them will live . . . it is a fight to death . . . the monster drives the baby lower still. Not satisfied with crushing it, she twists it in a refinement of cruelty . . .'[13]

Leboyer seemed to express his fears and envy of women's sexuality. Neither I nor Annie responded well to Leboyer's description, so negative and aggressive and so contrary to our own experience of the mystery of birth and creation over which women shamans and wise women in all ages presided in the sacred precincts of the Goddess.

The child was born in the dark night on 5 May. It was a three-hour labour. Annie was squatting as he slithered out, and he breathed immediately without difficulty. I had never witnessed someone else's birth before and I had a great sense of wonder and awe and a great respect for this dignified woman and for our great woman powers. It was a moment of true magic and great bliss.

I have, in this life, witnessed the deaths of two sons, children that I bore from my own body, and I have felt the umbilical cord reaching out into the spiritworld where a part of me now dwells forever.[14] We go from the womb of this world into the womb of the otherworld as we return to the light, into Her arms and presence as we die.

I have myself experienced the enormous difference between hospital birth and natural home birth. Sean had been born in a hospital in 1959 in Stockholm and I had – against my will and for no apparent reason as the birth was perfecly straightforward – been made unconscious with ether before he was born. I felt, as a result, totally unconnected to him as a baby. It was as if he was a stranger that I knew not whence he came and I had no loving responses, even though I had wanted him and had felt good being pregnant. As a result, Sean never felt at home in his body that had not been loved and I am sure this greatly contributed to his physical unease and subsequent illness and death.

I had read Dick Read's book *Childbirth without Fear*[15] while pregnant but, living in Sweden during the months before my son was born, there was no way of demanding natural childbirth at home, especially as we had no home of our own and were staying in my mother's tiny flat. I felt worn out from being estranged from my husband at this vulnerable period of my life, poor and having to fight for somewhere to live for us all.

My second son, Toivo, was born two years later, this time at home and naturally, in Britain. This was the experience that put me in touch with the great powers of my woman's body and was my first initiation to the great Mother as I felt connected to both spirit and Earth in visions of great light and darkness as well as body-tearing, pain and joy. Without this, I would never have painted *God Giving Birth* and this time love came naturally to me.

I would defy any Rebirthers to tell me that I or Sean 'created' or 'chose' the reality of alienated hospital birth, homelessness and poverty.

Leboyer and the Rebirthers talk, quite rightly I think, of the first breath of a new-born child being a gasp of fear and panic with the abrupt cutting of the umbilical cord at the hands of an unloving doctor. Breathing becomes ever after associated with closeness to death and pain, and too often in most people remains shallow throughout life. As Sondra Ray writes, if the umbilical cord is cut before you learn to breathe and you were about to strangle to death in your own amniotic fluid, your birth trauma may be the closest to physical death that you ever experience. The baby then suffers from isolation and separation from the mother whose womb had been dark, gentle and blissful. Rebirthers are trying to release and free that first breath and fear. This is all well and good in itself.

But there is no recognition that giving birth in an alienating hospital environment, designed to put fear into the intimidated mother, who is made to feel helpless and out of control, leads to difficulties and traumas as fear and tension create pain and make birth traumatic for both mother and child. Such a situation can in no way be compared to the natural process of giving birth when it takes place in our own chosen space surrounded by the people we love and trust, happening at our own speed, taking the time we need.

Far from Rebirthers clamouring for women's rights to control our 'birthings' and our fertility on our own terms, instead they claim that there is an unavoidable birth trauma that occurs irrespective of the conditions under which a birth takes place.

Otto Rank, in the 1920s, thought that birth itself is necessarily traumatic and that our birth always causes us anxiety in later life. He, like many other psychotherapists, thought that the reason women are feared and hated by men is because in the womb we have all 'suffered the threatening power of the mother'. This is a convenient biological explanation for patriarchy.

This is in the tradition of much psychotherapy. Mothers are always blamed for all the ills in society. We are made the scapegoats, thus diverting attention away from the real causes of illness and oppression. In therapy groups women are reassured and rewarded when they are 'nice', helpless, desperate and suffering, but they are punished or ignored when strong or outspoken. Hatred towards the mother is legitimised. Solidarity between women is destroyed – Demeter and Persephone are forever separated – and women are made 'safe' and not dangerous to the powers that be.

Otto Rank even thought that birth is the first of all dangers to 'Life' – which makes me wonder what he actually means by life, since no life exists without birth – and the prototype of all others to follow.

Janov, whose book *The Primal Scream*[16] had inspired Sean to undertake Rebirthing, doesn't believe that anything that is natural, like birth, can of itself be traumatic. When interviewed by Nicholas Albery, he was very critical of the Rebirthing movement. He feels that it leaves many people with unintegrated experiences, avoiding overwhelmingly strong repressed negative feelings; that it opens up people prematurely and can lead to breakdown and even suicide – in my son's case a relapse of his illness. Janov says that opening up people to their early imprints is a process that requires great skill and is not for a weekend seminar. He also questioned why all other childhood traumas such as incest, abuse, abandonment, etc. are not mentioned and says that rebirthed people have a fixed smile, glazed look and deliriously happy front that one associates with bornagain Christians who live in self-deceptively joyous states.

Orr's answer was that until Janov unravels his own death urge, he will think that everything is dangerous and that what he needs is a good dose of physical immortality. Janov thinks that Rebirthing affirmations are delusory. Here are some typical affirmations, especially useless for women: I forgive my obstetrician for hurting me at birth . . . I forgive all men who hurt me and myself for drawing them to me . . . From now on I am safe in the presence of men because I always attract men who are safe and who pleasure me.[17] The message is that we are to forgive not only individual men but oppressive male power structures that maim us.

Sheila Kitzinger, a feminist and campaigner for natural birth and writer of books such as *The Experience of Childbirth* and the editor of *The Midwife Challenge*,[18] notes that women are not simply containers for babies and asks where the charter is for a woman's right to be only a voluntary mother and for our rights to truly fulfil our true capacities in all fields. Sheila Kitzinger is on the executive committee of the Midwives' Information and Resource Service. She writes that there is much preoccupation with the rights of unborn foetuses, without mention of mothers, reminiscent of arguments put forth by born-again Christian anti-abortionists. Even Nicholas Albery makes this mistake. The focus is entirely on the unborn child without reference to the emotional and social stresses the expectant mother may go through, except in so far as they might affect the child. But what happens to women/mothers happens to our children, whether in or out of the womb, and as long as women are poverty-stricken, violated and suppressed, our children will grow up emotionally and psychically stunted, unloved and often unwanted.

Kitzinger says that because babies' brains are supposed to be too immature to remember anything, all kinds of painful and distressing things are done to them by male obstetricians and unsympathetic doctors. Cords are cut too soon; babies are held upside down and slapped; tubes are forced down their throats; baby boys are circumcised without anaesthetic. There is a veritable torture of the baby at birth which as adults we still 'remember' in our bodies and psyches.

Women in labour in our natural state rely on secretions of natural hormones called endorphines that reduce pain and give a sense of well-being and heightened awareness. The child receives intense rhythmic stimulation as it passes down the birth canal, so essential for good health and development.

It is very likely that post-natal depression is so common because we have been disempowered when giving birth and in our lives.

Matriarchal and Patriarchal Medicine

Medicinal knowledge gives power over life and death, fertility and the right to define what is sanity or madness.

Medicine amongst natural shamanistic peoples is based on an understanding of our relationship with nature, cosmos and our inner selves. Goddesses all over the world were seen as healers – giving knowledge of curative roots, herbs and plants – while priestesses were physicians to those who came to worship at the Goddess's wells and shrines, or to dream-incubate[19] in Her temples as on Malta. They were wise counsellors and oracles.

The Sumerian Goddess Nibada was honoured as the original inventor of clay tablets and writing and Mesopotamian Ninlil taught Her people harvesting and planting.

Ancient women balanced births according to food supplies and so their relationship to nature was ecologically sound. Their concept of healing was based on an understanding of the electromagnetic field's influence on us; they stressed the knowledge of the heart, as opposed to cerebral abstractions, a knowledge that has to be experienced by careful observation. Early peoples had an understanding of the intricate relationship of cellular balances, organ functions, emotional factors, magnetic fields, climatic alterations and radiations that affect the human body and psyche, and used natural remedies that did not suppress but rather healed symptoms gently in the way nature intended.

Women were always the unlicensed doctors, anatomists, herbalists, pharmacists and midwives of the western world. They were the scientists who, using trial and error and actively enquiring, had a far more empirical and humane approach than later male medicine. Herbal medicines developed by the wise women/witches are still in use such as pain-killers, digestive aids, inflammatory agents, ergot for pain in labour, belladonna to stop miscarriage and digitalis for heart disease.[20]

Witch-burnings were part of a calculated ruling-class campaign of terror against women healers who were charged with sexual crimes against men, for being organised or having magical powers to heal and to harm and for possessing medical and obstetrical skills. The burning times coincided with the introduction of a new social order in Europe, one based on a transformation of science and technology, and were a major physical attack on women as reproducers and sexual beings. The wise women gave contraceptive aid, they performed abortions and they attended births. They were the healers of poor women burdened with constant childbirths and brutal husbands and this was interpreted as obstructing the generative force given by god the father.

Mediaeval religious thinkers thought that the homunculus (a miniature human being complete with soul) was to be found in the male semen. It was only incubated in the woman who was not the parent of the child she bore.

The wise women were accused of healing and helping and the blessing witch was seen as the most harmful because she was well loved by the people and had to die. 'No one does more harm to the Catholic Church than the midwives'[21] said the Church fathers who had only prayers to offer to the ill and suffering and whose dogma was that this life is fleeting and unimportant. According to them, magical cures interfere with god's will. The Lord would only work through priests and physicians, who cured the nobility and kings, but he certainly would not work through peasant women healing and assisting the poor and the oppressed. The men of the Church were anti-empirical, they distrusted the senses and hated the material world. They thought that no natural laws govern physical phenomena. Our senses are subject to the power of the devil and carnality. Smells, flavours, sounds and colour are his playground. From early on, but especially from the fourteenth century, there was a campaign against urban, educated women healers. Medicine was to be a male monopoly and women were excluded from universities and medical schools that had their roots and inspiration in Arabic learning.[22]

Midwifery remained, however, a women's domain for another three hundred years. Church, state and male physicians worked together during the witch trials. The physican was the medical 'expert' who would pronounce on whether an illness had been caused by 'bewitchment'. The physician was set up as the moral and intellectual judge who had God and law on his side, while the non-professional woman healer belonged to darkness, practising evil and magic and was branded as a heretic. The physicians proclaimed that any woman who dared cure, but hadn't studied, was a witch and must die. They themselves could then very conveniently say that any illness they were unable to cure was caused by sorcery. The great Paracelsus said, however, in 1527 that he had learned from wise women and sorcerers all that he knew. He was hated by the ruling classes of Europe.

In the seventeenth and eighteenth centuries, barber-surgeons entered into midwifery and with them they brought obstetric forceps. Women midwives protested, but too late, about the dangerous use of these instruments.

Since then, birth has become increasingly treated as an illness. Puerperal (childbirth) fever killed innumerable women as male surgeons went straight from dissecting dead bodies to delivering women without as much as washing their hands in between. The Hungarian obstetrician, Ignaz Semmelweiss, warned in 1847 that such fevers were caused by putrid organisms and he introduced antiseptics. He tried to make surgeons sterilise their hands by washing them in antiseptics. For this he was derided and ridiculed. When anaesthetics came into use at the end of the last century, male obstetricians refused to use them to help women in labour since pain was woman's rightful punishment for Eve's sin. The wise women had also been accused of easing woman's pain in labour, using herbs and hypnotism, thereby interfering with God's will. In Victorian times, it was thought that the reason women found childbirth so unbearable was because humanity had outgrown such 'primitive' animal functions, while the real reason was that Victorian women lived stunted lives. Without physical exercise, and wearing corsets that maimed their bodies and hampered breathing, denied outlets for their sexual or creative energies, giving birth became a terrible ordeal. Never had women been so ignorant of the lunar menstrual rhythm, our fertility and sexuality, as during the last few hundred years after the end of the witch-hunts and the defeat of women healers.

Now, with the advent of male obstetrics and hospital births, we have high-tech births and a production-line. We have foetal-heart monitoring, women wired up and kept on their backs, unable to move even though this reduces the blood-flow to the placenta and oxygen to the child. Women have, in all ages, given birth while squatting which makes birth easier. It suits doctors in the hospitals, however, to have us lying passively on our backs. We have induced births, forceps, Caesarean sections; so common now in the USA; epidurals and episiotomies – most of them unnecessary, harmful, painful and dangerous to mothers and children but convenient for the doctors.

In the USA, midwifery has been virtually outlawed since the early twentieth century, and the popular health movement that flourished in the 1930s and 1940s was destroyed, thus leaving the powers in the hands of white, male, privileged physicans.

Herbal medicines that take into account the whole human being, body, soul and spirit, are under attack from the British Medical Association, and the powers that be will not recognise medicines that have not been 'scientifically' tested on animals.

In the twelfth century, women had known of 200 herbal contraceptive remedies,[23] and we have always known how to space pregnancies.

Because alternative medicine and healing is not covered by the NHS, and receives no economic funding from the state, it is, unfortunately, too expensive for most people's pockets.

From my experience of spending many months visiting my son in hospitals, I would call allopathic doctors and consultants 'body technicians', tinkering as they do with parts of the human body while totally ignoring the whole person. They do not seek to understand why the person becomes ill. And it is a sad fact that almost as many sick people die in hospitals from illnesses caused by the side-effects of toxic synthetic drugs as from the diseases that the drug therapies were supposed to cure.

Some of the holistic therapies and treatments such as acupuncture originated in places like ancient China. Acupuncture treats the body and its energy stream. The accompanying philosophy of life is Confucian which is extremely patriarchal as well as conformist. It is concerned with maintaining the social order, (an order within which women are supposed to stay all through life under the authority of fathers, husbands and sons) and such society is very hierarchical and rigid. According to a Confucian view, illness might be the result of being inadequately adjusted to the rules of society. Since rules had to be obeyed and not questioned, the only way for a person to recover good health was to change and to fit in with the given social order.

The doctors concentrated on the diet of the patient, on herbal medicine and on acupuncture, but did not take into account the outside forces in society that may have made the person ill. It seems to me that there is a similar focus in modern therapies, including the holistic health movement, on the individual to the exclusion of forces in society that drive people crazy or induce illnesses such as cancer.[24] Certainly the constant emphasis in the New Age health movement on yin and yang, without questioning the ways in which this ancient and originally genderless thinking on the interplay of subtle energy systems was used and manipulated by the Confucian Chinese to justify the oppression of women in the father-dominated family, has done nothing for women's sense of self and dignity. There is a constant preoccupation with yang (male, powerful, active, thrusting, solar, positive and light-energy) as opposed to yin (female, dark, negative, passive, receptive and watery non-energy); and it is a way of defining energies devised by men who fear women and is designed to keep women conforming to male projections and misconceptions.

This philosophy is meant to keep us from rebelling, from owning our anger, from breaking out of sado-masochistic heterosexual relationships, from questioning the authority of assorted male gurus.

Today some of the women's spirituality movement is being co-opted and taken over by apolitical Jungians who forever speak with great enthusiasm about the 'feminine in the man' (his 'anima'), and with not quite the same enthusiasm about the 'masculine in women' (her 'animus'), while taking precious little notice of the actual lives of women. Playing at 'being a Goddess', sometimes in expensive therapy courses, becomes a cynical and/or naive sham of the white and rich in the USA when the majority of women in the non-white world, in New York City and other cities up and down the United States of America, are impoverished, disempowered or homeless.

Medicine as a profession has played a central role in defining women as intellectually incapable, lacking in physical stamina, as periodically polluting (when we menstruate and give birth), sexually dangerous and emotionally weak and unfit.

The Twice-Born

In psychiatric and psychology textbooks, the ideas of the afterlife and of the spiritual journey after death have usually, until now, been treated as manifestations of 'primitive magical thinking' or as an inability to accept human impermanence and death. In western patriarchal Christian culture, there is a massive denial and neglect of issues relating to death and ageing, fatal disease and dying; they are not seen as a natural aspect of the life process but as the ultimate defeat and a painful reminder of 'men's inability to master nature'. The dying person is perceived as a loser. I have found that many New Age people are very arrogant and are unable to empathise with grief and illness, old age or dying.

Western mechanistic and materialist science has regarded consciousness as a product solely of the biological brain. Tribal consciousness, with its concept of an afterlife, and ritual to facilitate the transition into another realm, is labelled psychologically immature and a product of wishful and unscientific thinking. But a deep belief in the spiritual existence of the ancestors, the powerful dead, is an important factor in easing the transition to death in most non-western cultures and is far more realistic than the psychotic denials of cultures that have abandoned the

Goddess who is our ultimate ancestor and Mother of the spirits.

Nihilistic and pessimistic western thinking derives from a religion that has lost its function as a vital force in life and claims that only the man called Jesus has this status of immortal ancestor. We are thereby left with no meaningful participation in the process of dying. This leaves survivors in much despair with feelings of bitterness and guilt as they are not able truly to say farewell to their loved ones.

I have known the truth of this in my own life. After the death of my young son in August 1985, I lived very near to the otherworld realms. They appeared so real to me then and I was constantly speaking and thinking of the afterlife. Other people met this with total disbelief and often embarrassment, and they implied that madness had overtaken me, that, as a bereft parent, I had become deranged. It was mostly spiritualists and other bereaved parents who appeared to understand me and to share my views.

Psychotherapists and doctors suffer from unconscious fears and metaphysical anxiety when confronted with physical suffering, biological mortality and death. The transcendental experience of paradise was seen by Freud as a regression into the oceanic bliss of the pre-natal experience in the womb. No recognition that it might actually be the same experience, a return to the cosmic womb of the Great Mother – as above, so below. According to Freud this was not facing up to the 'reality principle' – as defined by himself.

With the modern medical technology of today, such as resuscitation following heart attacks, many people are brought back from states of apparent death and bear witness to near-death and out-of-the-body experiences. Much work was pioneered in this area by the Swiss doctor Elisabeth Kübler-Ross and Dr R Moody, collecting and publishing near-death accounts in *Life after Life* in the USA, as well as Margot Grey in *Return from Death* and David Lorimer in *Survival?* in the UK.[25]

Tibetan Lamas such as Sogyal Rinpoche are now teaching us in the west their ancient traditions of dying based on the *Tibetan Book of the Dead*.

The last rites should make one more conscious instead of less so when we more often than not die in hospitals in a drugged and unconscious state. Dying people have visions and strange dreams – a sense of coming 'home' and being part of an infinite whole, losing sense of time and space, feeling a unity with all beings – and feel elated and joyous when 'seeing' already departed relatives and loved ones coming to greet them.

The *Egyptian Book of the Dead*, (originally *Pert Emhu* or *Manifestation of the Light/Coming Forth*[26] identifies the dead one with the Moon God, Osiris, his journey to the underworld and resurrection through his sister/lover, the universal Goddess, Isis.

The Tibetan Book of the Dead or *Bardo Thödol*, which means liberation by hearing on the after-death plane,[27] based on much older teachings, was written down by Padma Sambhava who introduced tantric Buddhism to Tibet in the eighth century AD. Not being able to defeat bon shamanism, some of its ancient techniques and teachings, such as the Dakinis, are retained in Tibetan Buddhism.

The Tibetans distinguish a total of six intermediary states or bardos. The first is the natural state of bardo whilst in the womb; the second is the bardo dream state, the third is the ecstatic equilibrium attained in deep meditation. The three remaining bardos are associated with death and rebirth and describe the psychic happenings at the moment of death; when the elements of earth, air, fire and water fall away, one reviews one's entire life and finally receives the vision of the primary light of pure reality. If the dying person is, at that moment, prepared and not fearful of the intensity of the great light s/he can then attain instant liberation from the wheel of lifes and deaths. The final bardo is about rebirth which is not seen as desirable, to choose to re-enter the womb is not good to this way of thinking. The experiences in this bardic realm are simply products of one's own hallucinations and of the mind. This seems to be the spiritualists' 'astral realm' which is a thought world, where one has unimpeded movement and can materialise things by thought alone. The Tibetans warn of getting attached to the miraculous powers or sidhis available on this vibratory plane.

It was read aloud to the dying in Tibet, helping and guiding them to make the right decisions on the afterlife planes. It is of paramount importance that the dying person follows the true light emanations and that s/he realises that the wrathful and blissful deities encountered there are only the creations of our own minds, however realistic they may appear.

Stanislaf Grof and LSD Research

Stanislaf Grof is a founder of the transpersonal psychology movement and is on the board of the Trustees at the Esalen Institute of California. His theories have influenced the New Age movement. He has spent thirty years researching into extraordinary states of consciousness induced by LSD, as well as non-drug techniques.

I have studied his books, *Realms of the Human Consciousness – Observations from LSD Research* and *The Human Encounter with Death*[28] which has a foreword by the wonderful Dr Elisabeth Kübler-Ross[29] who has done such pioneering work with the dying. (Both books were co-written with Grof's then wife, Joan Halifax) Together with Christina Grof he also wrote *Beyond Death – the Gates of Consciousness*.[30]

Stanislaf Grof and his co-workers have found that giving LSD to terminally ill cancer patients has helped them immeasurably in achieving inner peace and an understanding of the death process. They have found that deepening experiences in the different stages of the LSD journey help the patient to relieve birth traumas, the oldest and core experiences, before going on to 'transpersonal' and mystical states. They point out the similarities between the birth and death experiences: hearing noises of roaring, buzzing, ringing and/or beautiful music and soothing sounds, passing through a dark enclosed space referred to as a tunnel or cave before emerging out into a great light. (As I see it, death and rebirth through the dark womb of the Mother who is both dark and light.)

LSD research was initiated by the military and Grof has received requests for papers from hundreds of military centres from all over the world. Psychic research has also long been on their agenda.

When LSD was made illegal, even when used for serious research, Grof and Halifax started using hyperventilation-breathing, shamanistic music and sounds and meditation to achieve altered states in their patients.

Grof and Halifax believe that the matrices for religious LSD (*peyote*, mescaline, mushrooms) experiences of death and rebirth are an intrinsic part of our perception and must be recognised and explored.

When interviewed by Nicholas Albery in *How to Feel Reborn*, Stanislaf Grof said that breathing is a powerful tool for changing consciousness and has been used in this way for millennia. That hyperventilation, as used by the Rebirthers, can bring about states of serenity with visions of light, feelings of love and even, if persisted with, a reliving of past events and mystical states.

Grof also said, however, that as long as Leonard Orr talks of the 'Five Biggies' or physical immortality – of death as the ultimate hypocrisy, and uses simple-minded affirmations combined with an emphasis on financial success – Rebirthers will not be taken seriously.

But Grof does not seem to question the patriarchal basis for what passes as religious thinking and spiritual concepts in his otherwise very interesting work. He appears to share with the Rebirthers and many other therapies a contempt for women as mothers.

In Grof's philosophy, the pre-natal experience in the womb is the gateway into transpersonal experience. He talks of four pre-natal matrices:

1 Within the womb – cosmic unity.
2 Beginning of labour – 'no exit' or hell.
3 Passage down the birth canal – death and rebirth struggle.
4 Exit from the womb – experience of ego death and rebirth reflecting the child's reunion with its mother as it lets go and surrenders.

In all cultures there have been rites of passage involving separation, transition and incorporation, but in present-day western society the major transitions of life are viewed negatively and no support is given. Feminists have recognised that the onset of menstruation in a young girl, and that of menopause in an older woman, become traumatic because there is no support or celebration at these important transitions in every woman's life. Suicidal tendencies as well as drugs, sex and alcohol are often unrecognised manifestations of spiritual longing.

Referring to the four pre-natal matrices Grof says that the womb is paradise, with primordial bliss and primal union with the mother, oceanic and total oneness, feelings of sacredness and transcendence of time and space. At the onset of biological delivery, however, the world becomes hostile and there is an experience of cosmic engulfment. Travelling down the birth canal, there is paranoia, crushing movements, suffocation and a sense of being trapped, of 'no exit', and an experience of hell and purgatory, of torture and darkness, before emerging into the light.

Grof claims that scenes of unbridled aggression and of mass destruction, as well as sado-masochistic orgies, are standard components of pre-natal development and he talks of the baby's desire to fight back and to kick its way out of the birth canal. Sometimes the baby feels hatred for the mother and/or a fear of killing her while being born. Grof uses words like 'brutal', 'obscene', 'monstrous' and 'disgusting' when describing birth and talks of men's desire or need to revenge themselves on the 'female element' that had caused them such agony. Grof even suggests that similar psychodynamic mechanisms might be at work in cases of sadistic murders of women.

It is, however, not nature's intention for women to give the gift of life to our sons, only for those sons to turn around and commit matricide which was considered to be the most heinous crime in ancient communities.

Grof, like so many other male therapists, is clearly speaking from his own sexual fears of women as he dwells on the blood, faeces and urine that accompany birth, as if those perfectly natural bodily products are somehow intrinsically revolting.

To me it is amazing that women, in spite of all this abuse heaped upon our heads, have gone on giving birth to, and loving, our boy children.

Yet boy children are not born patriarchs, nor is it through a natural process that men become such. The reason women have carried on is because deep in our beings the Goddess dwells, and we know, on some level, just what a lie patriarchal society is – a true obscenity and abomination and so contrary to nature's ways and intentions. And our boy children are alienated from us by patriarchy; or they are taken from us and turned against us.

During LSD trips people have relived traumatic ancestral memories, past incarnations, cellular memories of ovum and sperm, of tissue and cells, the operation of karmic laws, identification with insects, plants and animals, precognition, clairvoyance, time travel, visits from UFOs and beings and gods from outer space, multiple universes, and consciousness as a basic cosmic phenomenon at one with the organisation of energy that exists throughout the universe. Women on LSD are often not able to tell whether they are being born or giving birth.

Grof says that there is a karmic hurricane blowing through the centuries and the universal emotional pattern of greed, jealousy, hatred and aggression all resemble each other and that the hurricane is the force that perpetuates the cycles of death and rebirth and is responsible for all suffering. There appears to be no difference between whether the person is the oppressor or the oppressed because it is the traumatic pattern that is imprinted, the inability to forgive and transcend one's suffering appears to be conducive to karmic imprinting as effectively as is actively performed injustice and violence. The resolution of a single karmic pattern can result in feelings of indescribable bliss.

Grof does not recognise that fear and confusion in an inexperienced mother, and alienating hospital surroundings, make delivery difficult and, he claims, creates in the child a combination of libidinal feelings, painful physical sensations and aggression. With a typical Christian puritan sentiment he says that confusion in the adult heterosexual male arises from the fact that the genitals and thighs of the woman are both the place of love and sex as well as 'where this nightmare of birth and filth had happened', the place of 'dangerous evil filled with the power of the witch'. He could not be more unequivocal than this. He writes that hospital birth is remembered vividly in LSD sessions down to the odours of anaesthetics, sounds of surgical instruments, use of forceps, bright lights and uncaring hands.

The misogyny of therapists like Grof and of the Rebirthers makes it impossible for them to join hands with women demanding willing motherhood, an end to the oppression of women and the cruelty to women and our new-born babies involved in male-controlled hospital births. Not willing to question their own privileged positions as white males in oppressive societies, they end up blaming the mothers.

Man-made Life and Biological Engineering

Male scientists are now working on making life 'father-born', the age-old dream of patriarchal men. These scientific 'fathers' today speak of mothers in terms of 'foetal environments', as egg farms and foetal supermarkets.

They see women as raw materials for experiments in tes-tube babies and cloning. Geneticists, embryologists, cell biologists and biochemists are working on altering the genetic material so as to be able to manufacture human beings to desired specifications.

The new reproductive techniques are presented as benevolent, such as in vitro fertilisation given to infertile women. But the future that is actually being planned for women by geneticists is truly sinister and is an attempt to gain total control over women's fertility and over life itself.

New reproductive techniques are heralded as providing choice, but what is actually planned for women is the loss of autonomous reproduction leading to an even further loss of self and of motherhood dismembered into its components. Doctors routinely remove healthy ovaries, our eggs being their raw material as well as the genetic material for future populations, in women undergoing increasingly common hysterectomy operations.

Feminist women scientists warn that artificial insemination and embryo transfers will change human reproduction and the scenario could be that in the future, planned for by genetic scientists, there would be three types of mothers: genetic mothers who provide eggs, surrogate mothers who provide the uterus and are the human incubators for the babies that men make, and social mothers to look after children.

In 1984 there were more than seventy in vitro fertilisation clinics established around the world, within only seven years of the first 'test-tube baby' being born in Britain in 1978. There is a race to produce artificial placentas. To be the 'father' of the first test-tube baby would bring fame and fortune to the scientists involved, while women who have always given birth are simply regarded as 'battery hens'.

Because women have so little control over our lives in patriarchal societies, such reproductive techniques threaten our survival. There are indeed already male scientists who see women as obsolete and are looking forward to a world populated by mostly men and of women's lives being utterly curtailed, living impoverished as the abased servants of males. Hitler's dream of genetically engineered populations could now become a reality.

This is the manifestation of the Christian notion of 'son of man' born into a brave new world. Men are to be the parents of cloned offspring simply by donating a set of chromosomes, whilst a class of under-privileged women are to donate their nourishing wombs – this time as 'hostesses' – for implantations of man-made life.

In India and China and elsewhere throughout the world women are already offered abortions if the foetus is established to be female, using the latest techniques of amniocentesis and sonography.

Women scientists are fighting back, and the first international conference of FINRRAGE (The Feminist International Network of Resistance to Reproductive and Genetic Engineering) was held in 1985 in Sweden, followed by conferences in Spain in 1986 and in Eire in 1987.

Feminist scientists feel that decisions about women's future lives are taken behind locked doors and that we are utterly unaware of what is being planned for us by science. They are repeatedly warning us that we must take action and know what is being planned for us before it is too late, and have written about the issues involved.[31] My horror is that eastern male gurus, Christians and New Agers alike – as well as assorted therapists – seem to look forward to a male-engineered future – which is one very good reason why we should resist them.

West German feminists have attempted to sabotage genetic and reproductive engineering. The German state, however, obviously sees this research as supremely important, and two women were persecuted and imprisoned as 'terrorists', while the women's 'Gene-Archive' in Essen was raided, and much material invaluable to women was confiscated in December 1987.

Truly when Jehovah took the credit for creation he cursed the Earth; when a creator-god lays claim to our lifegiving powers, women's experience of the sacred – as in childbirth and menstruation – is declared profane and obscene and has no place in the scheme of things as planned by the priesthoods of the godfather.

In the name of all our foremothers who were burnt as 'witches' while resisting the oppressive Church and its male priesthoods we must now resist the mysogynist scientific brotherhoods of our day.

8
Traditional Shamanism and its New Age Manifestations

Shamanism as Women's Experience

Shaman is a Tungus word meaning 'specialist in the sacred' among Siberian reindeer herders and hunter-gatherers. The shaman is a healer, transformer, artist, soul guide and mediator between the seen and unseen worlds, the living and the ancestors/the dead.

The shaman is a 'wounded healer', who usually has gone through a terrible illness or psychic breakdown similar to mental illness, and who has gone to the 'lower and upper worlds' emerging from this initiatory experience healed. The shaman will have been helped along the way by others who have travelled the same path. The shaman's personal experience of suffering and near death makes for compassion and understanding. The shaman's world is a nature infused with 'beingness' and inhabited by spirits and ancestors.

Shamanism was originally women's ecstatic experience. One of the earliest researchers into Aboriginal shamanism was Mary Antoinette Crispine Czaplicka who wrote about shamanism in *Aboriginal Siberia*[1] in 1914. Her work was used by Mircea Eliade in *Shamanism: Archaic Techniques of Ecstasy*.[2] But Eliade is now considered the expert on Aboriginal shamanism, while Czaplicka's pathmaking and important work is all but forgotten.

Geoffrey Ashe has pointed out to me that it is common, unfortunately, that when men make use of women's work and research, hers is not acknowledged while his becomes

217

famous. And Mircea Eliade barely mentions the women shamans.

It seems that nearly all early writers on Siberian shamanism agreed that the position of the female shaman in the early twentieth century was often more important than that of the male shaman.

Among the Kamchada the shamanistic gift was almost exclusively women's; amongst the Tungus an eighteen-year-old woman was held superior to any man shaman.

There were traditions existing amongst tribes that the shaman's gift was first bestowed on women, and in Mongolian myths goddesses – daughters of the moon – were shamans themselves as well as givers of the 'technique of ecstasy' to humankind.

Nearly all neo-Siberian peoples have a common name for the woman shaman, indicating how ancient it is, while each of the tribes has a special name for the male shaman. The word for woman shaman relates to the Mongol word for Earth Goddess, and in different Altaic and Finno-Ugric tribes it relates to the names for the Two Bear star constellations.

Among tribes such as the Siberian Chukchee, which practised family shamanism, the mother was in charge of the magic drum and the amulets. It is/was very common for the male shaman to wear female dress – two iron circles represent breasts on his coat and his hair is braided as a woman's – and even to marry another man. He changes his sex 'in obedience to the command of the spirits'. It is less common for a woman shaman to adopt male attire and role, but this also happens.

Lynn Andrews writes in *Teachings around the Wheel* that she has been taught in the ancient and sacred women's way and that her teachers are the sisterhood of the shields. According to them, the 'star nations' came down to Mother Earth from the Pleiades 300,000 years ago and they invested great knowledge in this planet. This knowledge was planted like seeds in the mountains, trees and oceans and sometimes during our her/history this wisdom has been uncoverd when societies have been ready to hear it. Much of this knowledge was memorised by certain women representing the indigenous cultures on Earth and they, in their turn, transmitted this wisdom, via the oral tradition, to daughters and apprentices all through time until now.

Barbara Walker writes in *The Woman's Dictionary of Symbols and Sacred Objects* that seven legendary priestesses were said to have founded major oracle shrines throughout the ancient world. They were the seven sisters who were the guardians of the sacred Earth. They were the seven stars of Ursa Major/the Great Bear – sacred to Siberian shamans – or the Pleiades which in Greek means 'a flock of doves'. They were the Seven Pillars of Wisdom in the Middle East and in south-east Asia they were the Krittikas or Seven Mothers of the World. To the Egyptians they were the Seven Hathors, the 'seven beings who make decrees' whom the dead meet in their journeying through the seven spheres of the afterlife. To the Arabians they were the elder Seven Sages who were originally female – 'imam' meaning 'sage' which comes from 'ima' meaning 'mother' – but now masculinised.

Michelle Jamal explores in her *Shape Shifters – Shaman Women in Contemporary Society*[3] the lives, practices and beliefs of contemporary women shamans amongst whom are Joan Halifax, Lynn Andrews, Luisah Teish (the Afro-American Woudon priestess), Tsultrim Allione, Starhawk, Brooke Medicine Eagle and Vicki Noble.

Vicki Noble, a healer and teacher of 'lunar yoga', also teaches classes and courses. She is the author of *Motherpeace – a Way to the Goddess through Myth, Art and Tarot* and *Shakti Woman*.[4] Vicki Noble feels that the glossy west-coast journal *Shaman's Drum* is male-biassed; she herself publishes a journal of women and shamanism called *Snake Power*. She speaks movingly in *Shape Shifters* of women's sexuality as sacred, how out of women's sexual experience comes creativity and a sacred understanding of the cosmos. She speaks of the birthing woman as being the original shaman as she mediates between the worlds: 'We go from the womb of this world into the womb of the other world.'

As she says 'Feminism as a spiritual path is awakening to what is real and what is authentic and what is truly spiritual.'

Brooke Medicine Eagle, speaking of herself in *Shape Shifters*, says that she was never taught her native tongue as a child, growing up as she did on an isolated ranch on the Crow Reservation in Montana. She draws from a 'rainbow blend of Native American teachings', as well as New Age therapies and the 'Masters of light'. This mixture of white New Age therapies with ancient native teachings seems to be common practice amongst many Metis or mixed-heritage shamans. Brooke Medicine Eagle sees modern shamans as 'bridge persons', combining therapy, counselling and healing. She says she has often wished that things had been made easy for her, that she has wished for an elder to teach her and tell her that 'this is how things are'. She thinks that hers is a new way . . . that she is one who will help bring us gracefully over the rainbow bridge into a new age . . . to step into a pattern we have never had before. Brooke Medicine Eagle says that she has been called and guided and confirmed by light, illumination, radiance. That much of shamanic experience describes going into the darkness and coming out again. She says we are all of us living in a time of darkness, compared to 'the radiant world that is coming to us'.

Joan Halifax has written two books on shamanism, *Shamanic Voices* and *Shaman – the Wounded Healer*[5] and has worked with shamans and healers from Greenland to South America. She gives workshops, one of which I attended with Sean in London in 1986. She is a medical anthropologist, specialising in psychiatry and religion and has worked closely with Joseph Campbell. She is the director of the Ojai Foundation which is based on the original land, named 'Happy Valley', that Annie Besant had bought for her prodigy Krishnamurti.

In an interesting article called 'Shamanism, Mind and No-Self' from 1986, Joan Halifax compares Buddhist and shamanic religious concepts. She says that it is not surprising that 'the most archaic of mystical practices' are of such interest to many today, at the very time when shamanistic cultures are being overtaken by western technology. The attraction of shamanism – as well as eastern spiritual paths like Buddhism, yoga and Taoism – is because both we and our society need healing. We in the west need psychophysical integration and we need to rebalance our relationship with nature and to reverse the threat that our culture poses to all sentient beings on this earth.

Halifax writes that there is an astonishing similarity between the narratives by shamans about their initiatory ordeals and their inner experiences the world over, and that they can give us a greater understanding of psychology, parapsychology as well as near-death and mystical states. She writes that we in the western world have lost our traditions but that we now have available to us nearly all of the spiritual and esoteric traditions of the world. Traditions that formerly were kept secret from those outside the particular society in which they originated. Western New Agers are involved in creating a kind of 'Buddhishamanism', although there are difficulties in reconciling the Buddhist doctrine of non-self with the animistic worldview of shamanism which posits many souls in, for example, rocks, trees, rivers. Shamanism also deals much more with mind-display or phenomena, while Buddhism emphasises 'suchness' or emptiness. But in some shamanistic cultures the primordial ground of being is perceived as Great Grandmother Space, regarded as the feminine emptiness, in which the creative matrix of all phenomenal manifestation is embedded. In the new shamanism there is more of an emphasis on the 'unreality' (created by your own mind), of the terrifying phenomena encountered during initiatory crisis in the lower world (or 'hells' of Tibetan Buddhism).

It is not usual for shamans to conceive of the mind

as emptiness or suchness, however. In the Shambhala teachings ('the sacred path of the warrior') of Chögyam Trungpa there is a great emphasis on working with fear – especially the fear of death, by transforming it into an 'ally' – derived from the Tibetan pre-Buddhist tradition of bon shamanism warriorship. The task is to face the fear and not invent endless strategies to avoid it or to deny its presence. In shamanism there are the ideas of the kinship and relatedness of all life and there is a respect and reverence for every form of life, including trees and rocks. There is also great importance attached to the cultivation of 'life energy force'. In Tibetan Buddhism, this is seen as the 'instinctual side' or 'lower chakras' and the emphasis is on the 'higher chakras' for the development of compassion and wisdom. The shamans have to be psychophysically powerful to be able to heal skilfully and there are many practices for developing life energy force. The 'energy garden' below the navel has to be a 'strong focus in the initiatory crisis, without which there might be a total shattering of the psyche or even death . . .'. However, as Halifax points out, energy in itself can be used for beneficial or harmful purposes and she feels that our western non-tribal cultures do not have the guidelines for using these 'instinctual energies'. This is why she thinks that 'Earth philosophies' like shamanism and 'sky philosophies' like Buddhism which emphasise the mind should be woven together. She writes that the shaman who is a technician of the sacred can communicate with the world of the spirits while s/he is also a mystical and priestly/political figure. S/he has 'mastered death' and is the carrier of her/his culture's traditions and history.

'Seeing in the sacred manner', as Halifax says, goes beyond materialistic science and reaches towards a new science that embraces the greater mind.

Walter L Williams, an ethno-historian living in California, has written *The Spirit and the Flesh – Sexual Diversity in American Indian Culture*[6] in which he explores the public rituals and private lives of various 'Berdaches'. These men are holy people and shaman/healers of their tribes; they are cross-gender and live their lives as respected outsiders. They are a sort of third sex. It would appear that the Berdache is inspired by a female spirit, or that he has a 'supernatural husband' who speaks through him.

When I heard my friend Bel Bucca – a Celtic shaman and artist/craftsman – speak truly inspired about the Nordic runes during a pagan gathering in the mid 1980s in Sherwood Forest, the runes seemed to talk to me; reminding me of the north of Sweden, where I come from, with its vast open spaces, wild and dramatic mountains, of the winters of snow and ice that are so breathtakingly beautiful.

I have celebrated full moon and quarterday festivals, on occasion, with a coven close to where I lived in Wales, and also with women's groups. However, I have had to walk my own long, sometimes joyful and ecstatic but often very painful, path of initiation and have never been initiated into the Craft officially. So I can see I might be disapproved of by traditional Celtic elders who think I am an upstart – not even from this land and and not grounded in time-worn tradition; therefore that I am not entitled to speak for the old religion. My reply is that my 'tradition' is of the ancient women cultures and spirituality and the great cosmic Mother of time immemorial – of past, present and future.

In my own life I have never set out to have 'shamanic experiences' but there seems to be a pattern to my life wherein I have been led to, or been made to, go through many transformative experiences and have had strange insights because of often very painful, as well as joyous, events. I have also learned when journeying to sacred sites that the way and how of travelling is as important as the arrival; that they way one travels influences the experiences one has upon arrival.

My Pilgrimage to the Bleeding Yew at Nevern in March 1983

I set off with my friend Val on a mild spring day. We hitched on the beautiful coastal road towards Cardigan, and ancient Bay of Rhiannon, to where a smaller road branches off on one side up to Pentre Ifan cromlech and on the other side down to Nevern, which lies in a valley by a river. It turned into a day when nothing could go wrong and we felt as if we were guided all the way. We walked the three-mile-long lane and paths leading to the cromlech and found ourselves by 'mistake' taking the 'wrong' path, one leading to the farm of Pentre Ifan. We both became convinced this was a fairy path snaking its way through the very ancient forest and here and there crossing a winding serpentine stream. The atmosphere was such that we both felt as if we were stoned and our hands tingled as if from hidden energies. The mood became meditative and trance-like. We had, however, to return down the path to find the road to the cromlech which is placed on high with a view of the Preselau mountains beyond and the sea below. I later learned that 'Pentre' means village and that there was formerly an ancient settlement where the farm now stands.

This cromlech is different from any other I have seen: it is not at all an enclosed shape but, on the contrary, gives the distinct impression of being a 'gateway' to the earthmound that no longer exists. One can see the traces of a large oblong mound – the 'Womb of Cerridwen' – and it must have been truly impressive when it stood there in all its glory. Through the high 'gateway' one can see a holy mountain beyond. The capstone of the cromlech gives the impression of floating in space, so finely balanced on the tips of the supporting stones. A few stones still remain of the original enclosing lunar/horned entrance to the mound.[7]

From Pentre Ifan we made our way down the hill, across the road and into the valley where the village of Nevern nestles by the river of the same name. It was getting towards dusk by the time we finally entered the graveyard which, within the embrace of the yew trees, is always dark, even on a sunny day. This is truly the abode of the death Goddess. The place felt even more eerie and weird than I had remembered it.

I again felt the wonder of seeing the amberglowing Celtic cross of St Brynach by the church wall. It is extraordinarily powerful and barbarically beautiful. We went searching for the bleeding yew among the dark, gnarled, gigantic tree trunks. I had not seen it when I had previously visited the graveyard. But now, as I turned around one of the trunks, I found it!

I was not prepared for its impact; my reaction was one of amazement and wonder: my hair stood on end. I felt a chill up and down my spine, a split-second feeling of unreality as I saw the dark red, tacky, blood-like substance seeping out as from a cunt or a wound in the trunk of the tree. It was truly astonishing. A moment of time out of time.

It was indeed an otherworld realm that we stumbled upon that day, that magical spring day in 1983.

On a later visit that summer there were four of us women who went with candles at midnight on the full moon (which was also the summer solstice) to communicate with the menstruating yew Mother. We felt a wonderful maternal presence, of peace and of healing, as we sat meditating around Her trunk, our little candles burning in the darkness. We felt absolutely no fear at being there in the graveyard at the 'witching hour'.

Spider Woman and Corn Mother

Spider Woman is the spiritual Mother of all beings.[8]

The matrilinear Pueblo peoples (the Hopis and Zunis) called Her Thought or Thinking Woman. She creates life, sound and joy as She sings the creation song and Her white substance cape is creative wisdom. She created the two twins who live at the Earth's poles and keep the balance of all the vibratory centres along the Earth's axis. She created all plants, birds, sea creatures and animals as well as humans in Her dark purple light. She gave birth to two daughters (Her other selves) who became Ut Set, the Corn Mother of the Pueblo people – corn was the milk from Her breasts – and Nau Ut Set who became the Mother of all others. Earth was our Mother, we are made of Her flesh and we suckle at Her breasts. The Aztecs called Her Tonantzin, Our (Pachamama) Mother and later still she became the dark Virgin of Guadelupe, worshipped by all Indian America.

The corn that feeds the people is utterly sacred and is worshipped as a sacred being. Ut Set and Nau Ut Set formed the sun, moon and the star people who have clear crystals for eyes, while human beings were made from different coloured clays. Upon them Spider Woman put the covering of creative wisdom, Her white substance cape is spun from Her spider-being and to each human being She attaches a thread that leads from the top of the head to Her own shimmering web. The Hopis refer to the chakras – of our spiritual bodies as well as that of the Earth and its and our vibrational centres – and emphasise greatly the need to keep the 'hole on top of the head' open as this is the way we are connected to the inner vision and the web.

Earth is destroyed in catastrophes of fire and floods but always the Hopis, who are the chosen people, migrate and re-emerge to keep the spiritual quest alive.

We can keep the door to the spirit realms on the top of our heads open by chanting through it. But many forget about the door and allow it to close, and because they then forget the ancient creative wisdom Spider Woman brought the flood. After a very long time people emerged through the Sipapuni or womb hole into the fourth world which we now inhabit. The Hopi place of worship is the kiva which is an underground cave-like shrine and the central opening in the ground of the kiva is the symbolic place of emergence, the vagina and womb of the Earth Mother, from which we emerged. The whole myth and meaning of the emergence is expressed in the Labyrinth/Mother Earth symbol that has been found carved in the rock at the ancient sacred Oraibi and Shipaulovi. It is known as Tápu'at (mother and child) and represents spiritual rebirth and the spirit of the placenta. The kiva itself is the Earth Mother within whose womb all the important rituals take place. The thread binding us to Spider Woman is the web of destiny that we travel as long as She weaves it.

The Hopi Prophecies

There is a tradition that there is in existence one half of an ancient stone tablet inscribed with pictures and symbols. The legend has it that one day the true white brother – a race of light-skinned people from the east – will arrive with the matching piece of the tablet and that 'he will remember who "he" is'. The Hopi of light skin, called the White Brother, had travelled in the beginning of time when the different peoples went separate ways in the direction of the rising sun, and it was foreseen that 'he' might have forgotten their original purpose and thus become dangerous. The coming of the Hopis' White Brother Pahana is like the return of the Maya's bearded white god Kukulcan (Quetzalcoatl), a myth common throughout the pre-Columbian American world. The year that the Aztecs in Mexico had foretold that the White Brother, or Quetzalcoatl, would return, was 1519 when Cortés and his conquistadors arrived. Alas, the White Brother had forgotten the pact and Cortés betrayed Moctezuma's hospitality at the court in Tenochtitlan (now Mexico City) and laid seige to the Aztec capital. The same happened to the Hopis. One can imagine just how many stoned male hippies have arrived over the years in Hopi lands claiming to be the true white brother! (Perhaps the white sister will remember more and fare better?)

Besieged by white missionaries and by the powerful Navajo people who, with the encouragement of the US government, have been encroaching on Hopi lands, the Hopis have still retained their ancient religious teachings and practice. The US government has set Navajos and Hopis against each other in the past with a policy of divide and rule.

Hopi means 'one who follows the peaceful path' and the Hopis believe that they play a key role in our survival because of their vital communication with the unseen forces that hold nature in balance. They still hold the key to the supernatural and to the survival of all beings. They have remained the guardians of life and live in accordance with the infinite plan implied in the name Hopi. They believe we became stuck in our present physical form. Before we had been able to materialise and dematerialise at will, then we became arrogant and neglected the creator's plan. There is, within us, a continual struggle between our left- and right-side brains – to our detriment. This suicidal split has carried on throughout world after world until we are now opposing the very order of the universe. Even the Hopis are now beset by signs of disintegration from within, as well as bribery and threats from without, aimed at forcing them to join the rest of the materialistic world.

The Hopis consider themselves to be the caretakers of a fine balance between life and death. Throughout countless centuries, they have recalled in their ceremonies the previous world, our emergence into this present world and our purpose in coming here. Every so often they renew their vow with Masaw, the guardian, to live the simple life and to preserve the sacred balance with nature. They believe that we will only survive the coming purification if we change our ways to go with the energy of truth itself. We have tampered with the sun, moon, stars, Earth and the ozone layer, and great catastrophes and pestilence will come about as a result.

The Hopis believe they have been entrusted to guard

the land (the Black Mesa in North Arizona and the dreaded power of natural resources like uranium beneath the land) for future generations; that they must live simple lives and maintain a loving sense of relatedness to the Earth, the living Mother-organism and its life forms, so maintaining harmony and balance in an attempt to counteract the prevailing patriarchal destructive behaviour and thought-forms that have such a powerfully negative influence on the Earth's energy processes.

The Black Mesa symbolises to them the spiritual centre of the American continent. It is the vibratory centre on top of the head, the soft place that is the doorway between body and spirit, and it has belonged to the Hopis now for perhaps ten thousand years. The Hopis' dwellings, the pueblos, were constructed by and inspired by people known as the Anasazi, the ancient ones, and the Sinagua people in Arizona who flourished from about 300 AD to about 1300 AD.[9] The Hopi and the Zuni still retain customs from that period.[10]

The US government is now attempting to regain this holy land on which they have found uranium, and rumours of land disputes are being spread to unsettle relationships between the Hopi and the Navajo peoples.

Knowledge of world events has been handed down in secret religious societies amongst the Hopis who keep watch as each stage unfolds. On their ceremonial gourd-rattle, which moves the force of life when used in ritual, are drawn the ancient symbol of the swastika – showing the spirals of force sprouting from a seed in all directions – surrounded by a ring of red fire which symbolises the encircling penetration of the sun's warmth which causes the seed to sprout and grow. The symbols of the swastika, the sun and the colour red are mystical signs that bring about either/or total annihilation or great purification, either of which would be violent. When the Hopis saw the German swastika – which is an ancient symbol of transformation and immortality found throughout the world – together with the Japanese sun – they began to communicate their prophecies and warnings. In 1976 the Hopis spoke to the UN-sponsored habitat conference in Vancouver. There is a rumour that the prophecies mention a gourd full of ashes that would eventually be invented and if dropped from the sky would boil the oceans and burn the land. This is taken to mean the atomic bomb and the great horned water serpent will churn the oceans until the lands are swallowed up and drowned. Hopi prophecies warn of the dangers of extracting the multicoloured uranium (the rainbow serpent of the Australian Aborigines) from under their sacred sites. They seem to have always known, as have the Aboriginal people of Australia, that this metal has a sacred function embedded within the Earth Mother, but if taken out of Her it would cause nothing but utter destruction and disease.[11]

New Age Shamanism

New Age shamanism claims to be dedicated to putting the power of ancient shamanic knowledge and healing techniques into the context of our times and culture without losing shamanism's transformative alchemy and magic.

But this is being done without relating to those indigenous cultures that shamanism actually comes from. Nor is its use in the context of the dominant society that is exploiting those cultures, and is attempting to destroy them, ever considered. The majority of New Age 'shamans' are the product of the white, western, exploitative world. This is sinister.

The New Age shamanism movement, now relatively widespread in Britain, originated in the USA which has long been a cauldron or melting pot for peoples of different races, cultures and religious beliefs. Such a fusion is potentially very vital and can give birth to great creativity and energy. One vision it has given birth to is the concept of the rainbow warriors of the New Age who are people of many colours, multicoloured, and another is the new shamans, both women and men.

The problem is that in the USA, the wealthiest and most politically oppressive imperialist power on earth today, spiritual experiences easily become corrupted. Prosperous white people tend to believe that instant vision quests and other shamanic experiences can be bought. The American New Age scene lacks awareness of where shamanic traditions come from and how they were ripped off from the Native Americans in a form of spiritual imperialism. What is more, the money paid out to expensive workshops on shamanism does not go back to support the Hopis and other indigenous peoples in their struggles to keep their ancestral lands from US military and economic domination. However much we who live in industrial capitalist societies try to suppress our own western cultural background, we are deeply affected by the consumer-orientated, instant gratification ideology of our culture. People who rip off eastern and Native American traditions are usually not willing to change their own social environment and work for their ideals; instead they isolate themselves and pay money for the offering of supposed wisdom. You can now become a 'shaman' without going through years of seaching, pain, and true vision quests – as long as you can pay for expensive weekend courses.

Alawn Tickhill, who publishes *Medicine Ways*, a British shamanism journal, sees the danger in taking too much from other traditions because what is taken often becomes superficial and simplistic. He writes in 'Shamanism in Britain – Being our Grandfathers'[12] (what became of our grandmothers?) that it is very easy to adopt the customs and ways of other peoples and 'not to face the guardians of the underworld naked and earning the power'. He speaks of the increasing glossiness and 'supermarket style' of the more public manifestations of shamanism, both in the USA and in the UK, and the 'occult grasshoppers' whose 'thing' shamanism has become, and he has noticed the anger of Native Americans whose indigenous traditions are being stolen by whites who 'huddle like tourists around someone else's fire'.

Tickhill writes: 'gifts of the spirit cannot be bought, not now or ever', and he points out that there has been systematic destruction, ever since the Druids resisted the Roman invasions, of our own European indigenous shamanic tradition of the Craft. We have, as a result, no elders to turn to for guidance and inspiration, though we still have the sacred calendar of seasonal festivals that give us a holistic and living continuity from the past.

Having been in the USA, I understand the complexities and difficulties experienced by white young Americans who are on a spiritual quest. They feel that they are aliens and without real roots in the land where they grew up, a land in which all the places of power and sacredness belong not to them but to the indigenous peoples.[13] The whites have inherited the uncomfortable knowledge that their ancestors carried out genocide against the Native Americans and attempted to wipe out their shamanic traditions.

The practice of traditional Native American spirituality-shamanism was illegal until 1978 when Congress passed the Freedom of Religion Act. The Native American Church, a legally protected church since 1910, uses *peyote* ritually. Since the end of the last century the *peyote* ritual has been adopted widely by Native American peoples all over the States and is seen as most healing and sacred.

In his books, published from 1968 onwards, Carlos Castaneda writes of his apprenticeship to the wonderful, witty and wise Yaqui shaman, Don Juan. His books have influenced a whole generation, including my sons and myself.[14] We found *Don Juan* delightful with his wisdom and great sense of humour.

Matthias Neitsch wrote a paper for the 'Third conference of European Indian supporters', held in Vienna in Austria in 1987.[15] He says that the shamanism described in Castaneda's books (the experiences of other worlds of consciousness induced by sacred roots and mushrooms and the techniques of individual self-realisation and healing) unleashed a tremendous run on the last centres of Native American traditions. Many 'Indians' experienced this as hurtful and disgraceful. But apparently this had been prophesied in the Native people's own traditions. People from the alternative, ecology and peace movements, who wanted to abandon ways which they saw were corrupt and had led to the destruction of the Earth, integrated more and more Native American ways of thinking into their vision.

We yearn for spiritual/esoteric secrets and to live in harmony with Mother Earth. But, as Neitsch writes, we have failed to develop a spirituality based in our own European pagan traditions, although this is now beginning to happen in the contemporary Goddess, Green and Pagan movements. The alternative movements have found it easier and more comfortable to adopt eastern and Native-American traditions.

A few Native-American men were willing to give a little spiritual help to the young white seekers. To start with this went only so far, but the whites insisted on being taught every secret and in the end a very few 'Indians' were willing to offer this also. None of these individuals was really initiated into the secrets and ceremonies of the tribe however, writes Neitsch, and what they knew they mixed with their own visions and interpretations. These men passed on ceremonies such as the sweat lodge, the sacred pipe, the vision quest – all of which were given by White Buffalo Cow Woman to the Lakota people – and they did this for money in gatherings organised by white people for whites.

These non-traditional shamans often claim to be authorised by the great spirit in a vision as medicine people, and thus try to justify their unauthorised passing on of ceremonies for payment. What Neitsch calls 'instant medicine people' are sponsored, with only a few exceptions, by persons and organisations involved in the New Age.

Neitsch says that one of the most important principles

of the New Age movement is never ever to resist anything, but always to be for something. This means that you should not protest against uranium mining, genocide, forced relocation of indigenous peoples, environmental pollution, etc. Instead you should work for alternative energy projects such as solar power, ecological forms of economy and a more humane society.

The theory is that by talking about, or thinking of, negative things that are happening in the world you set free negative energies which only intensify these situations.

An *Open Letter to the Pagan Community* from Bob Gustafson, who calls himself an elder and warrior of the Mohawk nation which fought the historic battle of Wounded Knee and is a leader of the United American Indians of New England, was published some years ago in the Welsh-based *PAN* (Pagans Against Nukes) journal. Gustafson is also a founder member of the Thomas Morton Alliance, which is a radical and politically minded group of revolutionary pagan activists. He says that the Alliance condemns the practice of selling shamanships, vision quests and sweat lodges, a practice that is becoming more and more common, both in the USA and in Europe. This is a theft of Native American spiritual traditions and is an attempt to accomplish in a short period of time that which it takes the authentic shaman a lifetime to learn. It is an affront to Native tradition.

There is a common agreement amongst both Native American and European pagans that one does not sell medicine or magical services as spiritual teachings are a gift from the spirit. To make quick money in this way is an unforgivable insult to the memory of native warriors who have been killed whilst defending their people and traditions. Gustafson says in the *Open Letter*:

> Before delving into native traditions, be they the way of the longhouse, the sun dance, or the kiva, non-Indian pagans should keep in mind the following points. First and foremost is the fact that our warriors

have fought and died as recently as the last decade to defend and preserve our old ways. This struggle continues. Second is the fact that all our medicine ways are tribal and intended to serve the people. Ours is not a tradition where 'you do your own thing'. Third, true sharing comes only between equals – not between oppressors and oppressed. Let there be no mistake; we are still an oppressed people in our own homeland. Fourth, our traditional elders do not advertise in the pages of New Age or pagan publications. Indeed, our traditional elders are among our most militant political leaders. Many of them urge total separation from the dominant society. Fifth, Europe was once as tribal as we continue to be. *Non-Indian pagans have their own roots to draw upon.* (My emphases.)[16]

Amongst the ancient Celts, their shamans, the druids, led their people in resistance against the Romans; the Wicce in Europe fought the imperialising Church and coordinated and led the peasant rebellions. Amongst many indigenous peoples, the shamans are seen as the greatest threat against global imperialism by the west and the USA.

Marilyn Ferguson wrote in *The Aquarian Conspiracy*[17] with enthusiasm of how top US officials were discussing shamanic healing, but she does not mention that the US government is intent on dumping nuclear waste on, and to mine for uranium in, Native American ancestral and sacred homelands, both in the Black Hills as well as in Hopi lands.

Frank Waters published his *The Book of Hopis* in 1963.[18] It was billed as the first revelation of the Hopis' historical and religious worldview of life. Unfortunately Frank Waters' book sparked off the trend for whites to journey to Hopi-land looking for new-found gurus. It soon became part of the counter-culture. This new kind of spiritual imperialism had the effect of causing divisions among the Hopis themselves – between so-called Traditionalists and

Progressives – and some Hopis even took on some of the occult and mystical beliefs of their followers.

Whereas in the first world of Hopi religious belief, Grandmother Space, or Tokpela/Endless Space, was the creatrix, some Hopis now elevated Masaw, who had been the caretaker god and guardian of the Third and Fourth Worlds, and called him the Great Spirit. Frank Waters speaks of a male creator, Taiowa, within whose mind everything exists and of Thought/Spider Woman, the original Mother Goddess of the Hopis, as his 'helper'. In his version She is blamed for leading the clans in disobedience against the male 'creator'.

The Open Gate Trust, which is connected with the Bristol Cancer Help Centre, organises expensive seminars and retreats which they call 'education for new times'. In September/October 1987, Don Eduardo Calderon, a shaman from Peru, was to give a five-day residential training costing £210, together with his apprentice, Dr Alberto Villaldo, a professor at San Francisco University. In the Open Gate catalogue it says that Calderon, who owns a small restaurant in Northern Peru, is also a shaman and practitioner of ancient Native American arts of healing. In a vision, he saw that the sacred knowledge of the American Indian peoples must be revealed and shared, and that the new shamans and caretakers of the world 'are to come from the west'.

Dr Alberto Villaldo was also to lead a 'journey of initiation' to visit the sacred sites of Peru and to study the ritual healing methods of Don Eduardo and other shamans. Sites to be visited included the Nazca plains where ancient giant etchings are carved into the desert floor, the dramatic ridgetop ruin of Machu Picchu, the 'lost city of the Incas', and the ruins of the Temple of the Sun in the mountain city of Cuzco. To the shaman, these sites are ancient power centres and Don Eduardo was to introduce participants into the manner in which such places are used in healing ceremonies. Group participants became honorary apprentices to Don Eduardo and were to take part in various spiritual and healing rituals.

If Don Eduardo Calderon is honest, and I do not doubt this, in saying he had a 'vision', why is he passing on his knowledge to privileged whites who can pay high prices for his teachings and go on 'metaphysical' jet-set tours? Why does he think that these kind of people can be trusted with ancient Native American wisdom?

In 1988 the Open Gate Trust ran a course in 'shamanistic studies' at a cost of £940, which included three weekends, three five-days and a concluding three-days over a period of several months.

Shamanism seems to be lifted out of its context of tribal life and native people's struggle for survival and sacral communication with the Earth, Her plants and animals and cosmos, and used by wealthy and privileged white people as another form of 'healing' and therapy. It is seen 'as a spiritual practice of unique value for our time and culture'.

I was very disappointed when I read Lynn Andrews' books *Medicine Woman* and *Flight of the Seventh Moon*.[19] These had been enthusiastically recommended to me by feminists excited about a woman writing of shamanism from a woman's perspective and perceptions. So I did not approach her in a negative frame of mind. But I was appalled by what seemed to me the superficial, sensational and breathless California-speak that pervades these books. They did not ring true though I would have loved to have been able to think otherwise. To be fair, Andrews can conjure up wonderful imagery in her books and shows knowledge of shamanism and reverence for the Earth and for darkness. Some women I spoke to in the USA felt that Lynn Andrews' writings have given a certain protection to Native Americans. I do not doubt that the Native women's secret societies that she speaks of exist, but I do doubt how far such women would entrust a rich, white, glamorous woman from exclusive Beverly Hills in Los Angeles with their knowledge. I might, of course, be wrong.

Anne Cameron, the Canadian author of the wonderful *Daughters of Copperwoman*[20] in which she communicated some of the Native Canadian women's legends and teachings, has sent out a 'message for those who would steal Native traditions' in an Open Letter to the alternative movement.[21] She says that the journal *Moccasin Line* published an article called 'Indians Protest Andrews' Books' and the letter 'Indian Women Confront Lynn Andrews'. They express anger at the 'theft' and 'appropriation' of Native spirituality, at the way non-Native people seem to feel that they have a right to share in the culture and religion of Native peoples, at the lack of spirituality in non-Native society. Cameron says that 'many of those who want to "share" think they are well-meaning and liberal', that they are worthy to be taught by Native teachers just because their need is so great. When told that they cannot have what they want, they become angry and defensive. When told they have to learn the basics before they can learn the secrets, they always say, 'Yes, *but* . . .' When told they should go to their own pre-Christian religion (the Craft), they say it is lost. In a previous life they were Indian, 'usually an Indian princess, Indian chief or Indian shaman, never an ordinary person, never a victim of smallpox or rape'.[22] She goes on to say that the Celts had a culture very similar to that of the Native American, with a medicine wheel, sacred-bundle guardians, shield carriers, and used colour and crystals, drums and sweats, protective familiars, dream search, etc.

White people wanting Native shamanic wisdom were never taught any personal responsibility and never had to wait for things. They expect to get things handed to them and do not know how to 'seek'. But, for a price, there are people, and not all white either, who are willing to hand it to them.

> Most of these 'native teachers' are men who claim tribal and lodge affiliation, who charge high prices for workshops and seminars, and who are

accompanied by throngs of starry-eyed young women. Very starry-eyed, very young. Perhaps these men should be confronted too. Their opinion of women is made very obvious by the way they treat the youngsters who follow them; and the many children they leave behind but never help support or educate.

The many Native Canadian women who told Cameron their stories were

'. . . taught by example and lived lives of spiritual focus; none of them set up workshops or seminars in exotic places and charged small and large fortunes to introduce the leisured middle-class to the truth. Those women worked in fish canneries for disgustingly low wages, they cooked in camps, they picked berries, they were politically involved for land claims, fishing rights and child protection. What they had, they shared; they did not get rich and travel around in rarified circles being worshipped by a clique of devotees. They didn't have nice long lacquered nails or have their hair styled, and for the most part they were not verbally clever.

When asking these women what they would do about the current abuse of Native teachings they told Cameron that everything gets settled in the end . . . but also not to condone the abuse; that we must protect and preserve the dream. As a feminist Anne Cameron says that she finds the New Age movement to be merely a collection and mish-mash of all the worst of the lies inflicted on women such as passivity, gentleness, patience and, above all, 'romantic love'. She comments on how popular the movement is in a society 'which prefers to have its citizens sitting around not making any kind of protest'. The money from sales of *Daughters of Copperwoman* goes, apparently, to Native women's organisations, to land claims defence funds and a fund to make it possible for Native Canadian women to write and publish.[23]

The traditional elders' circle has sent out a number of warnings about such false medicine people. For this, they are accused by the New Agers of being a reactionary minority among Native Americans, and the native resistance movement against white US imperialism is described as 'racist'.

Contemporary Shamans

Shamans of mixed heritage and/or cultures, with often divided loyalties and living in the belly of the beast itself, more easily throw in their lot with US politics, unfortunately.

There are 'myths of spiritual wisdom' bandied about, according to Matthias Neitsch, one being that many pupils of 'false medicine men' believe that they are, in fact, 'reincarnated Indians'. Also very commonly known is the 'Indian prophecy' that obliges Indians since 1981 to share their esoteric wisdom with white people. Therefore in the consciousness of these people 'plastic medicine men' are 'good' while traditional Indians are 'bad' or have 'racial hatred' because they do not 'share' with the white New Age shamans. New Age shamans 'do not teach traditional Indian spirituality and ceremonies' which are closely connected to the land and the community. In most cases they teach a mixture of a New Age Mother Earth philosophy and elements of European occult traditions.

Sun Bear is a Chippewa medicine man who grew up on the White Earth reservation in Minnesota. At an early age he had a vision of the medicine wheel and was instructed to spread its teachings to the world outside the reservation. I heard Sun Bear speak in Bristol on 23 May 1988, who said that the elders of his tribe had told him to go out and teach, that he had to try to communicate with the white people who were polluting their land and fishing grounds.

Sun Bear spoke with a great deal of feeling and warmth, and what came across was that he did have a genuine vision and has got something to teach us.

Since the end of his youth, Sun Bear has not lived amongst his people.

In 1970 Sun Bear and Wabun, his white American wife and comrade, founded the Intertribal Bear Tribe Medicine Society near Spokane, Washington, an alternative land-commune of mainly whites. The 'Bear Tribe' has developed itself into a profitable mail-order business for sacred objects and ceremonies. Sun Bear has, together with Wabun, written a number of books such as the influential *The Medicine Wheel-Earth Astrology* (1980), as well as books covering the path of power, the vision quest[24] etc.

Sun Bear is probably one of the most famous Native American gurus and is therefore much exposed to criticism from the Traditional Elders' circle. In 1983 he had a meeting with the elders that ended in impasse.

In quick courses he teaches whites whom he then authorises to conduct ceremonies. His daughter, Winona Laduke, is very active working for the economic and political rights of her people. She was a member of the founding group of 'Women of All Red Nations' and is the director of the Ashinabe Oral history project in the Chippewa White Earth reservation where she lives and works. She is also a co-director of the Institute for Natural Progress. Her mother, Sun Bear's first wife, is the wonderful artist, Betty Laduke, whose work I very much admire.

Hyemeyohsts (Chuck) Storm is, according to Neitsch, a Southern Cheyenne, author of *Seven Arrows* and *Song of Heyoehkah*.[25]

He does not claim to be a medicine man, but rather a 'warrior' or 'sundancer', and is also a guru to white people.

Harley Swiftdeer Reagan is one of the Native Americans who are not aligned with their own traditions and who therefore have most influenced the New Age movement. Instead of defending the integrity of the traditional ways and teachings, according to Neitsch they have been co-opted into the New Age to work with white folk. It is probably true that some genuine Native American shamans have chosen to do this because they have found many of their people divorced from their own traditions and because of visions or dreams that have pointed them in this direction.

Matthias Neitsch writes that Harley Swiftdeer is probably the most dangerous of the so-called 'false shamans' and that his preferred audiences are amongst the 'alternative aristocracy' of the upper-class New Agers. He says that Swiftdeer admits to practising 'black magic' and is the only one who claims he allows women during our moontime/menstruation to take part in his shamanic ceremonies.

In this I disagree with Neitsch's unquestioning acceptance of all that the Elders teach, since what is often called 'black magic' is sometimes the left-hand path of ancient women's sexual/menstrual magic. We women are, in my own experience as an artist, most deeply feeling and thinking, as well as most psychically, sexually, magically creative during, or close to (before and after) the menstrual period. To exclude women at this very time, of heightened energies and magical insights, from ritual activity seems to me to be a sign of wanting to disempower women and of male fears of women's great powers. Therefore I would, in this case, go along with Swiftdeer rather than the Traditional Elders.

Swiftdeer's teachers are Hyemeyohsts Storm and Don Genaro whom he calls 'grandfather'. Neitsch writes that Swiftdeer mentions some 'dubious', and 'maybe not really existing persons', such as 'The Sundance Council', 'The Black Widow Society' and its members or leaders called Grace Walkingstick and Ruby Morningstar, whom he claims have authorised him. Swiftdeer calls these women 'grandmothers'. However, I see nothing dubious about the existence of indigenous women's secret societies.

Together with his wife Mary Shy Deer and some followers, Swiftdeer operates the Deer Tribe Metis Medicine Society in Los Angeles. He travels worldwide and has 'unleashed his first rank of unauthorised followers upon the Europeans' who spread his teachings, including ceremonies, for a high price. Some call him 'Swiftbuck'!

It says in a leaflet advertising one of Harley Swiftdeer's workshops in Britain that he had a traditional medicine upbringing. His background includes being a martial arts champion, Shinto warrior and shaman. It says that his vision is of the coming together of the wisdom-traditions of the eight rainbow powers of the planet and of the sundance beauty-way of walking the Earth Mother in harmony and balance with Her.

Together with Hyemeyohsts Storm, Swiftdeer is the founder of the National American Metis Association (NAMA) of which Sun Bear is also a member and which, according to Neitsch, advocates a pro-US ideology and can be seen as an umbrella organisation for the 'instant medicine people and their followers'. Followers of Swiftdeer in Germany, Austria and in Switzerland founded the 'Nameless Network' in 1985 that is based on Swiftdeer's teachings. This Network is based in the privileged New Age scene and Neitsch guesses that some of its members are bound to have key positions in politics, economics and science in their various countries.

Other shamans who remain living with their tribes quarrel with their elders' circle but do not invent any 'Native philosophy' of their own and do not refuse to work politically as they do take part in political actions and work for Native prisoners. (These are Native people imprisoned for resisting the racist US laws and for defending their land against its exploitation by, for example, multinational companies mining uranium.) Their audience is more with the freak and alternative scene, and not so much in the bourgeois New Age movement.

Heather Campbell (or 'Moon Owl') is, in her own words, the co-chief of the British Lodge of Swiftdeer's Deer Tribe Metis Medicine Society and is an 'authorised fourth-fifth gateway and road and sacred pipe carrier'. She is founder of both the British and Australian lodges of the Deer Tribe. She says she is interested in passing on these teachings which she claims are based in alchemy and are therefore transferable. She was appointed West Rainbow Bridger whose task it is to carry the shields, wheels and keys of sweet medicine sundance to different places on the planet.[26] She is offering these teachings to those involved in the Celtic and Wiccan paths who have lost many of their own Native ancient shamanic traditions owing to persecutions.

The 'Dream Weavers' – Arwyn Larkin (Dream Walker) and Bridget Clansing (Fire Wolf) – are two North American New Age shamans who have quite a following in Britain. They no longer work together but Arwyn Dream Walker, who studied with Swiftdeer and Lynn Andrews amongst others, is still teaching courses in the UK. She has been a practising therapist for eighteen years and aims to bring together shamanic teachings and the Celtic traditions of both the wheel and the web, thereby awakening the sacred symbols of the Rainbow dance within us. She works within the Dream Weavers Star lodge and teaches the Rainbow sundance medicine in which there are three laws, one of which states that 'all things are born of woman', and claims to want to help women to rediscover our conceptive/creative power in a world that no longer even recognises its existence. 'Crystal knowledge' is part of the teaching and the crystal is seen as the matrix and doorway into other dimensions of time and space.

It was the Dream Weavers who, some years back, travelled around the sacred places in Britain planting crystals by the standing stones. I share the unease felt by pagans and people involved in Earth mysteries at this.[27] (Crystals are universally used and exploited by New Agers, are invested with extraordinary powers, and are sold at high prices in fashionable New Age shops.)

I attended a workshop evening led by Arwyn, held during the Merlin conference in Bath in September 1990 and it became clear that she, like Swiftdeer, also thinks we came from other planets from out of space, and that in the future we are to return there. At one point she even called Earth 'the hostess' and presumably therefore considers Her expendable. I find this kind of teaching dangerous and reactionary.[28] I also had a disturbing account from a woman friend of mine who, having taken part in one of Arwyn's weekend worshops, had felt totally demolished and utterly disempowered as a woman. On that occasion, cruel therapy games mixed up with demanding shamanic training proved to be a dangerous mixture for her. (Though it has to be admitted that other women who have attended her workshops have found them empowering.)

Fighting for Survival

Because of China's invasion of Tibet, many of its learned lamas and teachers have come to the west and are teaching their ancient occult/magical knowledge, while shamans of many cultures feel that the time has come to reveal some of the, until now, hidden teachings before it is too late. We live in dangerous times and Earth is fighting for Her survival; indigenous peoples and women everywhere are her guardians.

Christian fundamentalists such as the New Tribes Mission, are sending out their missionaries to remote places like Papua New Guinea, looking for the last remaining natural living shamanic peoples to teach them that their nature spirits are evil. The shamanic tribal peoples of the Brazilian Amazon forests, who are the guardians and caretakers of those wonderful and complex ecosystems, are threatened by extinction, along with the forests which are now fast diminishing.

Large areas of the Earth are being turned into deserts because of the 'green revolution' and 'development'. Vandana Shiva, a feminist and radical scientist from India, writes movingly in *Women, Ecology and Development*[29] of the ancient Indian concept of nature as *prakriti*, a living, active and creative process, the feminine principle that creates all life. She writes of maldevelopment as the death of the feminine principle and that the green revolution is a western paradigm imposed on Third World peoples. She also writes that women's age-old knowledge of agriculture is being eroded and erased as the green revolution, designed by multinational corporations and western male experts, attempts to streamline nature's diversity into producing crops that are dependent on seeds and chemicals coming from the west. This is a biotechnological revolution that ties Third World peoples to multinational chemical companies and spells disaster for women, their children and the Earth itself. Vandana Shiva speaks of the violence inherent in the green revolution and how modernisation and development are associated with new forms of patriarchal dominance of nature, *prakriti*, and of women whose traditional land-use rights and ability to sustain their families are eroded.

In the Third World women's access to economic resources has worsened and their burden of work has increased. Ecological destruction and the marginalisation of women go hand in hand as the western misogynist scientific worldview is introduced to other cultures. Commodities grow and nature shrinks and dies as the 'virtues' of capitalism and the free market are preached and practised, to the detriment of women and all indigenous peoples. Vandana Shiva writes that, after suppressing and destroying women's skills and knowledge during the witch-hunts in Europe, this process is carried on as even more violent ways of excluding women's knowledge, and of the knowledge and expertise of tribal and peasant cultures, is happening worldwide.

She speaks of the vanishing waters, soil, plants and trees. Forests were worshipped as Aranyani, Goddess of the forest, who is the primal source of life and of fertility.

Women and indigenous peoples are organising themselves and in many places are fighting back. Vandana

Shiva[30] is active in the Indian women's Chipko (women hugging the trees) movement, a movement to save the trees and forests from further destruction.

There is a group called *DAWNE* (Development Alternatives with Women for a New Era), based in Rio de Janeiro which consists of a network of activists and researchers from Third World countries.[31] They and others are speaking out about the relationship between women and economic 'development' internationally, facts which are entirely ignored in official statistics and planning generally.

It is possibly significant that new shamans, even the New Agers, are emerging from the USA with a non-Christian message which reveres nature and her spirits. If New Age shamans could disentangle themselves from US politics, commercialism and patriarchal occult thinking, they would have a positive message for the world today.

9
The Harmonic Convergence

A Background History of the Harmonic Convergence

Dr José Argüelles of Boulder, Colorado in the USA is credited with having originated the idea for the Harmonic Convergence, although it seems that many other New Age groups had been promoting this August date in 1987.

José Argüelles has a PhD in the history of art which he teaches. He is forty-seven years old, a practising artist and the author of several books, including *The Mayan Factor: Path Beyond Technology*.[1] In it he describes how he spent his childhood in Mexico and writes that he had been on a thirty-three-year search for the Maya people of ancient Mexico.

Argüelles first came across the Maya in 1953 when he was taken to Teotihuacan, the 'place where the gods touch the Earth', the great pyramid city. He later suffered an alcoholic breakdown in the late 1970s. On his emergence from that he saw clearly that there was an endemic crisis and that the Earth as an organism was threatened, that either the 'divine intervenes or extinction becomes our legacy'.[2] In 1972 he met the traditional Hopi spokesman, Thomas Bayaca, who is involved in formulating Hopi prophecies. Bayaca told him that only those who are spiritually strong will survive the passing of the Fourth World and the coming of the Fifth.[3]

In 1968 he met the 'renegade' Native American Tony Shearer who was involved with the prophecies of Quetzalcoatl and the sacred calendar, which he wrote about in his book *Lord of the Dawn*. He taught Argüelles the significance of the 1987 date in relation to the prophecies concerning the return of Quetzalcoatl, the white-feathered serpent god, who was called Kukulkan ('place where the serpent dwells') by the Maya. Kukulkan, the white god who was the same being as Quetzalcoatl, appears to have been an historical figure, a great teacher (born c. 947 AD) who founded Tula and revitalised Chichen Itza in Yucatan. He is known to have prophesied the coming of Cortés in 1519 AD. On another level, Kukulkan/Quetzalcoatl is, like the Christ spirit or entity, perceived of as an invisible and immanent force that has always been with us and transcends myth. His is a religion of mystical unification based in the sacred mushroom cult. Quetzalcoatl is also associated with the morning/evening star that was always the home of Venus/Ishtar or the star Goddess.

Argüelles visited Palenque in 1976 and had experiences of entering into past lives and of communing with the ancient Maya. He had intimations of presences, of star beings or guardians, when visiting the Mayan monuments and felt that his writing was being 'channelled' through him.

A neo-shamanic think-tank in April 1985 at the Ojai Foundation called 'Council of Quetzalcoatl' made it clear that the Mayan factor lets us know that we are now twenty-six years short of a major 'galactic synchronisation', and that either we face up to this or we have lost the opportunity.

The Mayans had an obsession with time. Their civilisation lies scattered across the jungles of the Yucatan and the highlands of present-day Guatemala in great numbers of ancient cities and temple-sites. They suddenly abandoned their centres by c. 830 AD after 500–600 years of intense activity – we do not know why. They left behind their calendrical, mathematical and astronomical data encoded in hieroglyphic inscriptions that have defeated every would-be interpreter until now. José Argüelles thinks, however, that he is the medium through whom the Maya have revealed the meaning of their knowledge, and he comments on how similar the Mayan Calendar is to the 'I Ching' which he thinks is the code form of a science based in 'holomonic resonance rather than atom physics', and the DNA. He thinks that the Maya have the capacity to identify consciousness with resonance and ride the frequencies of different levels of reality – transmitting themselves as DNA-code information from one star system to another. Transcending bodily form, their return can occur within and through us now. According to Argüelles, the Maya were/are planetary navigators and mappers of the larger psychic field of the Earth, the solar system and the galaxy beyond. The 'solar cult' of the Maya (also of the Incas and Egyptians) is not only about the sun as source and sustainer of life but also about the sun as the mediator of information beamed to us from other star systems. Primarily he thinks it is from the Pleiades (the seven daughters of Pleione, the brightest of its stars called Maia) and from Arcturus. Higher knowledge and wisdom is transmitted through the sun and primarily through its sun spot cycles. The Tzolkin or Mayan solar calendar is a means of tracking the information through the knowledge of these cycles. The Maya kept calendars of the lunations and eclipse cycles and computed the length of the Earth's revolution around the sun to within a thousandth of a decimal point of the calculations of modern science. Argüelles thinks that the calendar might have been a numbers system, a means of recording harmonic calibrations that relate not only to space-time positionings but also to resonant qualities of being – an experience that our materialistic pre-disposition blinds us to.

The Maya were the first people known to have used the concept of zero and their mathematical and astronomical achievements were unparalleled until the eighteenth century.

The central thesis of Argüelles book is that the Mayan 5125 year 'great cycle' represents the time it takes for the

Earth to pass through a 'synchronisation beam' emanating from the galactic core. Further, he argues that we are now entering the last phase of one of these cycles to be called the 'solar age' when technology will harmonise with the galactic community. If we manage to do this right (if 'we' don't destroy ourselves and the planet) our collective organism will come into resonant attunement with the sun and through the sun with the galactic core, called Hunub Ku – 'one giver of movement and measure' – the principle of life beyond the sun.

According to Argüelles, human history is shaped in a large part by a galactic beam through which the Earth and sun have been passing for the last 5000 years and a great moment of transformation possibly awaits us at the beam's end in 2012 AD.

In modern physics, the universe is a single multiform energy event, an organism involved in its own development, one numinous cosmic process. Argüelles writes that hydrogen atoms and stars and ourselves and our psychic lives are not disconnected as we have believed.

I disagree with Argüelles, and would say that it is not 'we' who have believed this but patriarchal thinkers, Christian and otherwise, who have forced us (women and all oppressed and disinherited of the Earth) to accept this disconnectedness from nature and cosmos, and our very selves, through witch-hunts and persecutions. That all events are at the same time physical and psychical was, I believe, always known to ancient women and men.

The galaxy has intelligence and purpose and Argüelles says the Maya were engaged with the mind of the sun. Only when we re-awaken to our psychic sensitivities will we stop our assault on life and live ecstatically. He asks, 'Why do we not hear as the living world howls in anguish?' I would answer because men simply do not seem to hear the anguish of women who are the mothers and who sustain life and nurture nature on this planet – and they have, as yet, no solidarity with us.

José Argüelles has recently sent out an 'Open Letter to

the World Community regarding UFOs'[4] in which he says he thinks that 'the most significant event of the twentieth century is the advent (since the end of the last war) of unprecedented and massive UFO phenomena' with the 'widest possible implications for our evolutionary future now facing us'. He is convinced that the UFOs are benevolent and are here to benefit us and he thinks that we could have learned immeasurably from 'the interdimensional nature of reality by which UFOs possess their tremendous capabilities' instead of 'us' continuing to spew out ever-more toxic and lethal technologies which is happening now to the detriment of the Earth, our biosphere. No official communication of welcome has been extended to the UFOs who are still 'waiting for an intelligent signal from us in the form of a public welcome' and assurance of mutually benevolent intentions.

Argüelles suggested that people should come together – on 144 key sites, seventy-two each in the northern and southern hemispheres – on 31 December 1989 to meditate, consciously linking those sites which will then 'create the harmonic grip in resonance with the Earth's geomagnetic field', in the same way as at the Harmonic Convergence. 'The creation of this harmonic grid will precipitate the mind-shift necessary to radically alter the public attitude towards the UFOs' and 'the materialistic one-dimensional attitude that has created the grim psychic and environmental condition of this planet will dissolve' and give way to a more 'spiritual, interdimensional life-style . . .'

Robert Coon, an American 'physical immortalist', writing in the *Glastonbury Communicator* before the Convergence, claimed that in 1967 he was involved with this same prophecy concerning the return of Quetzalcoatl in 1987. In that summer, like Argüelles, he met Tony Shearer, a Lakota 'Indian', with whom Coon experienced (*peyote* or mushroom-induced?) prophetic visions in the Denver/Boulder, Colorado area. They felt inspired to share their visions, of the transformation of this Earth in the 1980s by two great 'fire serpents', with the public. Coon's vision focussed on the activation of the first great fire serpent at Glastonbury Tor at Easter sunrise of 1984 (Glastonbury being the Earth body's 'heart chakra' and the 'new Jerusalem' according to him) and Tony's vision was of the second great fire serpent being activated at dawn on 17 August 1987 at Palenque and El Thule in southern Mexico. According to Coon, the two great serpents are the primary circles of vital energy prana or chi that embrace the Earth. Famous spiritual centres or Earth chakras, such as Glastonbury Tor, Mount Kailash in Tibet and Lake Titicaca in the Andes, are located on these cosmic dragon-sites. The St Michael ley line in England – on which Glastonbury Tor and Avebury are situated – is a segment of the fire serpent. The second fire serpent is assumed to be that of Quetzalcoatl and its ley energy nourishes El Thule, the mythical tree of life, that grows in Mexico.

Robert Coon wrote of 144,000 priests and priestesses of Melchizedek (an Atlantean priest?) that were to gather and that the key theme of the Mayan millennium was the abolition of death and for us to 'rise above mortality'. He believes that we will, in the Aquarian age, be able to express ourselves in a spiritualised or light body at will, and that this will establish peace on Earth.

I have heard all this before. The language and male megalomania is similar to that of the days of the 'acid revolution' in the 1960s; once again men play the role of interpreting the sacred. I am not denying experiences I myself have had in the past and have benefited from in terms of altered states and mind-expanding substances such as LSD, magic mushrooms, etc. that can vastly enhance one's understanding. But with unbalanced patriarchal men, such experiences seem to blow their egos out of all proportion; indeed, just living in Glastonbury itself seems to have the same effect.

To these patriarchal men, the Earth Mother is a pathetic and helplessly grieving mother who willingly dies to fulfil the plan of her creator, the lord of life – Mother Earth labouring to bring forth Christ-consciousness. According to some New Age thinking, the planet is to die and rise again a reborn 'radiant new Earth', and we will become divinely improved mutants or high-frequency beings – a product of revelation and transformation. This transmutation or genetic mutation will be brought about through the increased radiation reaching Earth via the weakening ozone layer, thus creating the 'sixth root race' of New Age beings. 'Physical immortality' will be bestowed on a 'light-transformed humanity', and the message to us is 'purify thy heart before the fire of heaven'. It has even been said that 'the bomb is the Second Coming in wrath'. The Earth will be a planet of light like the sun's nuclear furnace, it will be brilliant and fiery and under the 'direct rulership of God'. The 'end of the world', is but a healing crisis within the natural order of cosmic progression for the advancement of us as spiritual beings.

I gather that the old and secret Hopi prophecies are warning of disasters to come.[5] They warn especially about uranium, the multicoloured rainbow serpent of the Australian Aborigines, being disturbed. The elders see themselves as the guardians of Mother Earth and Her magical dragon serpent powers, as were the shaman priestesses of the Mother Goddess in the ancient cultures.

It is clear that the aims and aspirations and hopes for the future, the Aquarian age, of New Age white lighters are hardly compatible to those of pagans who revere the Earth as a powerful and self-creating Mother. Nor to women rediscovering our spirituality who desire to return as the lost daughters to Mother Demeter so that the Earth will green again after the thousands of years we have suffered of a parched and patriarchal wasteland.

Surely the 'Harmonic Convergence' of 16 and 17 August 1987 should have been about the fiery energies of the subterranean Mother in conjunction with the major lunar standstill that happened that summer, and in interaction with other planetary beings?

Instead of this, New Age male gurus advocated the return of assorted transcendant male sun/son entities and refused to recognise them as divine messengers of the divine Mother transforming Herself.

Who Was Quetzalcoatl?

The religious structure which the Aztecs called the Pyramid of the Sun at Teotihuacan, the ancient pyramid city in Mexico, may have originally been dedicated to the symbolic entrance to the underworld and the fundamental Mother Goddess,[6] and could equally well be called pyramid of the moon. An underground cave with four chambers has apparently been discovered in recent times. This is the navel of the Earth, centre of supernatural power of the divine death and Earth, toothless giant toad Goddess, the great nocturnal hunter, who with spiralling tongue devours the dead and gives birth to the sun. This is the place where the great Goddess resides and where, as at Her womb/tomb/temple Newgrange in Ireland/Eire, she gives birth to the sun.

The Incas' Sun temple was called Amaruncancha, which means 'the place of the serpents' and was another name for the Goddess/god Meru, the owner of the original sun disc or 'winged serpent wheel'. Meru was both female and male.

The cave represents the four quarters of the many tiered universe; the surface of the Earth supported by an upper and an under world. This is the sacred navel centre with its world tree or cosmic axis, with four trees holding up the sky at the cardinal points. There is no primordial 'void' in Indian myth as phenomena pre-exist in some other form. In south America the Goddess or Pachamama, is corn and Earth, shining like the moon yet found in sacred caves. Her essence is known as both eagle and serpent as in old neolithic Europe where she was both water-bird and serpent.[7]

The Earth Goddess, Mother of the sun, is at the centre of the calendar stones.

The Aztec Goddess Coatlicue, lady of the serpent skirt

('coatl' means serpent) is of earth, rain and the underworld. She wears a snake belt and has a flayed face. She wears a necklace of skulls around Her neck like Kali of India or the Tibetan Dakini.

Maize sacrifices were given to Her and there are life size ceramic sculptures of Her at El Zapotal in Vera Cruz. As serpent Goddess Her nature is that of fire and clouds and She lives on a high mountain where She is revered at altars made of volcanic lava that comes up from the underworld created by the internal fires of the Earth.

The serpents live with Her in the caves whence She brings forth the sun, the moon and the stars. She is Pachamama of the Ayamara people of Bolivia and Peru.

In Christian times She becomes Our Lady of Guadelupe Hidalgo. She is the native and dark-skinned Madonna or Virgin Morena. She is the great divine grandmother and the male gods are Her sons and lovers. She is the receiver of their sacrifice. Originally She was the pre-Aztec snake-mantled Mother-daughter Goddess, source of serpents, wind and sun. The serpent is a symbol of universal and life-creating electromagnetic cosmic energies.

In patriarchal times, however, the original and indivisible Goddess is given many forms and many of them are cruel and grim. To give the Goddess many forms, often contradictory, was a way in which the emerging patriarchs attempted to divest Her of Her powers, playing a game of divide and rule with the shaman priestesses.

It is interesting to see what qualities and powers have been assigned to supposedly different Goddesses, and to speculate how much these are the products of male fears and projections in cultures which were abandoning the Goddess and therefore feared Her revenge.

Chantico was Goddess of fire, both domestic and volcanic, as was Pélé in Hawaii, Mahuea of Aotearoa or New Zealand and Fuji of the Ainu people of aboriginal Japan. Chantico was also Goddess of maize, of rain and moon.

The Moon Goddess is weaver of destiny and of our

lives, as were the Norns of the Nordic lands and Spider Woman of the Hopis.

The Goddess Tlazolteotl, who dies in childbirth, was the Aztec Mother of the male maize deity and of the young Mother Goddess in the fifteenth and sixteenth centuries AD.

Chicomecoatl (which means seven serpents) was a corn Mother also associated with childbirth and the sun. There was Teten Innan, Goddess of childbirth, healing and prophecy, as well as Chalchihuhtlicue who was Goddess of rain and waters.

Quetzalcoatl was the feathered Aztec serpent-saviour god. José Argüelles writes in *The Mayan Factor* that he was born of a Virgin, or three mystical sisters, who represented the corn. Like Christ, he is a spirit entity that stands for death, resurrection and the Second Coming. He is one of the 'castrated fathers' and the blood from his penis supposedly recreated the human race after the flood. He is an Osiris figure, it seems. With his brother 'death' he is a two-faced deity, a dual god, of creation and destruction, as is the white and dark Manitu of North America.

As time went on, the male god Quetzalcoatl took on an increasingly generative luminous aspect or character and he became the culture-bringer and hero king, a prince of light and humanity. As Morning Star, Quetzalcoatl is the positive symbol of the ascending power belonging to the male-spiritual aspect of heaven and the sun.[8]

Quetzalcoatl is a symbol of the east and is the eagle of the luminous sky which devours the serpent of darkness. He is the god of knowledge and the plumed serpent.

Quetzalcoatl is also the fertility king of the old ritual who must die to fertilise the world with his sacrifice, the penitent who transforms himself. Her sacrificed himself to the fire and prophesied his return in the east. Quetzali means 'tail feather' and he is son of both heaven and Earth (bird and serpent), a dual god, typical of the ancient gods of the moon, vegetation and transformation. He is also Xolotl Nanuatzin who burns himself up by way of atonement and whose heart is turned into the rising Morning Star. But there is a loss of paradise, the Toltec 'Golden Age', and he is defeated by the demonic primary powers of an anti-god. In the patriarchal interpretation of the myth, his 'sin' was that of intoxication and sexual pleasure in immoderation. He commits incest and suffers death and 'succumbs to the terrible demonic powers of the Great Mother'.[9] The more luminous and 'light' he becomes the more terrible, 'dark' and demonic is the Goddess.

Thus we have the split in the psyche of all patriarchal societies who cannot then handle the dualistic systems they have themselves created. They proceed to try to slay the mothers to 'free' themselves of their own-created monstrous dreams. The 'demons' bring Quetzalcoatl the 'harlot' Xochiquetzal, who is called 'Precious Flower' and is the great Goddess of love. She 'seduces' him and he then becomes Xochipilli, Prince of Flowers, and he 'regresses' to becoming Her son/lover, which to the patriarchs is the ultimate 'sin'. She is the 'intoxicating sister – beloved' who becomes his 'doom'. 'The Goddess, with Her mantle of snakes, is taking me with Her as Her child. I weep,'[10] he cried and was not able to defeat Her power, although he almost became supreme god of the Aztecs.

Thus, once again: 'man' is not to become as one with the woman/Goddess in sexual embrace, neither must he use mind-expanding drugs that might cause him to remember the blissful and undivided state of the Mother's womb. He must at all times be in control.

'Man loses his power of rational thought in orgasm', said St Augustine.

According to Mayan prophecy, Quetzalcoatl/Kukulkan, the lord of dawn, is due to return and he represents a force of cosmic intelligence.

On 17 August 1987, the Earth spirit of Quetzalcoatl would ascend from the roots of El Thule, the tree of life, at Palenque and transform itself into the thunderbird or eagle and start to fly around the world. 144,000 'sun dancers' or rainbow warriors had then to unite their minds in harmony to begin an energy shift, to avert cataclysms at this time when Earth would enter a new alignment. They had to create an energy field promoting world peace and make contact with beings from other planets in the future. Celebrations occurred in places as distant as South Africa, Australia, the USA and Britain.

No mention anywhere of the Goddess or of the fact that the summer of 1987 was also the time of the major lunar standstill that happens once every eighteen to nineteen years. The ancients experienced this time of exceptionally powerful lunar energies as a most important magical event of great spiritual/psychic significance. The 'Convergence' was one of a line-up of planets in the fire sign.

A Hopi Prophecy

A Hopi Prophecy: A Rainbow Prophecy which seems to have originated with Harley Swiftdeer's tribe, was widely read and circulated in the summer of 1987 before the Harmonic Convergence took place. The 'Prophecy' is set out below:

1980: the year of the creation of the teachings of the eight great powers, (the new circle of law which will include the UN). The star-maiden circle and the flowering tree teachings began the evolution of the distribution of the wheels and keys (the esoteric teachings of the North American Indians) of Turtle Island.

1981: the teachings begin to open to the rainbow people known as the Meti (mixed blood – the rainbow people).

1982: the year of planting the seeds of light of the higher self.

1983: mythologies of the world and all the eight great powers are finally revealing secrets and are brought out in the open.

1984: the year of the dark force, of the animal. Rainbow people now exist everywhere, and the dark forces are threatened and will use their power and their power exists in technology. The technology can be both a threat and a blessing. The dark forces are trying to create an artificial sun – nuclear war. We – the rainbow people – must not give our energy in protesting and being against something. Instead of protesting uranium, promote solar. By using our energy positively we can change things for the better.

1985: we will re-establish contact with our ancestors from the stars. The first wave will come from the Pleiades and will be known to all the world powers. The second wave will come from Sirius.

1986: is when the enlightened teachers begin to open the veil of the cracks between the worlds. All Kivas and sacred power spots will come alive. The order of the golden dawn will have ceremonies in the inner room of the great pyramid – now opened – for the first time in 20,000 years. Old traditional ceremonies that are still applicable today will be renewed. Many of the ceremonies that are so-called traditionalist, but are trying to keep us locked in the past, will fail. The traditionalists of the medicine societies, who are not willing to change their ways will either have to change or die. 'Many teachers who have been seen as great teachers who have literally kept us in the dark as worshippers of the sacrament orders will physically die and go over because it's the only way they can find light.'[11]

1987: 144,000 sun-dance enlightened teachers will totally awaken in their dream mind bodies. They will begin to meet in their feathered serpent or winged serpent wheels and become a major force of the light to help the rest of humanity to dance their dream awake. On 17 August the various winged serpent wheels will begin to turn, to dance once again; the rainbow lights will be seen in dreams all over the world.

1988: science will once again become metaphysics, become again magic. Social and civil laws will tumble and will have to be in conformity with natural laws or the people will not accept them.

1989: we will see the star people come out of the

illusion of their two-legged form and into their actual great sleeper-dreamer form. This is the year of very powerful masters and the second coming of Christ spoken of in the Book of Revelations. Christ means circle – sacred circle.

1990: a shift in planetary consciousness. The first migration to the next world will begin by the pathfinders willing to step out into the totally unknown from grandmother Earth.

1991: those who stay will totally gain the light of the great light wheel.[12]

1992: Earth will join the sisterhood of planets, the daughters of Copperwoman and will be in total harmony.

1993: a whole new way of perfection. No more starvation etc.

1994: total balance and peace. Humans still in their physical bodies.

1995: 'The new race of humans will begin to design their new reality of life on this planet as they intended it to be when they came from the stars.'

1996: second migration to the new world.

1997: Earth is part of the great council of planets, part of the intergalactic international brotherhood and sisterhood of humanity and keepers of the light circles.

1998: the Earth becomes a star ship.

1999: third migration leaves this planet for the other new worlds and this world is now a star/spaceship harmonised with its sister planets.

2000: 'the great spirit will have left its seed and the egg of everything here on this planet and it will create itself twenty times over at the speed of light and thus the prophecy ends as I have been given it by the grandmothers that I share with you now.'[13]

It should be noted that, as I understand it, Hopis themselves would have nothing to do with the above 'prophecies', and refused to take part in the Harmonic Convergence celebrations.

Metaphysical Jetsetters

A list of sacred sites had been sent out, having been compiled by Jim Berenholtz from New Mexico in the USA, to prepare the way for the Harmonic Convergence. Below are some of Jim's words:

> Sacred peaks of Mount Shasta, the Grand Teton, and Taos Mountain, its centre on the island of the buffalo in the Great Salt Lake. A ceremony at Pyramid Lake grounds the historical roots of the vision, and a linking from Mount Tamalpais, San Francisco Bay, to Hatney Peak, the Black Hills, allowing the new energy to stream in as the Buffalo come out of the west. An old order is dying, and our ceremonies at ancient sites are partly a cleansing – a healing of thought forms that allow such sites to be destroyed, to prepare the fields for an entirely new cycle. New sacred sites shall emerge and new ley lines shall be forged. We are learning to work in harmony with the planetary being to co-create our shared reality. Like our ancestors were, we are again technicians of the sacred . . . Perhaps most crucial in the year ahead is our ability to embrace the unknown. Political and natural upheavals may test our abilities to adapt and release. We may be guided to go to certain sites or do certain things without knowing precisely why. But revelations will come with each step along the way.

I read in Jim Berenholtz's *Commemorative Book of the harmonic convergence and International Sacred Sites Festival of 1987*[14] that he had most certainly been metaphysically jetsetting to sacred sites from Kilimanjaro and the temples and pyramids of Egypt to the Pacific islands and MesoAmerica.

Jim, who lived in New Mexico, had travelled and formed a musical duo in 1984 with an Aztec friend and they were inspired by visits to the many sacred sites of Mexico where they, in Jim Berenholtz words, 'remembered' the music still embedded in the stones and temples. They developed a performance ritual that 'wove pre-Columbian instruments together with native chanting, Aztec dance, ancient poetry, animal ally masks and burning incense like copal'. Jim clearly sees himself as a latterday white shaman priest of Quetzalcoatl and his mission to bring this spirit-force energy back into this Earth realm. He believes that his ceremonies 'activate' and link sacred sites and even influence volcanoes and the weather. He writes that the ancient Aztec/Toltec calendar prophesied that the end of the fifth planetary age which we are now in is associated with earthquakes, shifts in the Earth's axis, volcanic eruptions – Pélé the volcanic Goddess of Hawaii destroying to recreate and give new birth – and Earth changes that involve the element fire.

I wonder, though, if increasing earthquakes are not brought about by underground nuclear testing upsetting Earth's balance? Jim acknowledges the negative forces that have been at work around the time of the Harmonic Convergence (violence, accidents, plane crashes, economic collapse of Wall Street, etc.) but says they are toxins coming to the surface when the body is beginning to heal itself. Berenholtz is aware that many received the impression that the convergence involved mainly white, middle-class New Agers, but writes that there was in fact a widespread participation on the part of Native Americans, Latin Americans, Polynesians, Aboriginal Australians, Asians and Africans. This, however, went mainly unreported. I do not know how true this is. He also claims there were many sightings of spaceships, many visions and miraculous signs from nature and deep spiritual awakenings.[15]

It is true that, as we are now approaching the millennium, great numbers of people are having visions and strange dreams. Many are becoming aware of latent psychic powers, capacities and talents, and there is an expectation in the air. But there is also mounting violence, both verbal and physical, towards women and our children, aggression and warfare in all corners of the Earth and an increasing feminisation of poverty worldwide.

Why is it that New Agers are so obsessed with Second Comings of assorted male spirit beings – of Quetzalcoatl, Horus, Christ, Mithras, Osiris? Why are they not speaking of the emerging Goddess consciousness within us all if they really want a different and blessed world? (To be fair, Jim Berenholtz writes of the Native American prophecy concerning the return of White Buffalo Cow Woman at this time.)

Contrary to what New Agers think, the re-emergence of the Goddess in women's and men's consciousness and dreams *is* the symbol for the transformation of our culture, and of the Earth. And if we welcome Her, within and without us, She will guide us through great and positive changes. If we refuse Her, however, we will all die in unimaginable destruction and catastrophes which we ourselves have helped to unleash.

The Harmonic Convergence at Glastonbury

The 'Harmonic Convergence' on 16 and 17 August 1987 was the largest participatory New Age worldwide event so far. Large gatherings of people congregated on innumerable 'sacred sites' in many parts of the world, officially with the intention of 'healing the Earth' and preparing themselves and the Earth for coming cosmic events.

Another aim seems to have been to welcome in beings or entities – intergalactic travellers – from outer space.

I and other women had an uncomfortable feeling that behind the official benevolent front of Earth-healing, there might be yet another sinister and imperialistic intention, this time to co-opt sacred sites for the purpose of directing their magical energies towards the specific aim of promoting US-led world domination by the white west.[16]

The various serpent wheels were to start turning and dance again, and when they did so the rainbow lights would be seen by dreamers all over the world and would help to awaken the rest of humanity.

One of the largest convergences was held in Glastonbury and one of its main organisers was Robert Coon. In the months leading up to the Harmonic Convergence in Glastonbury, the local journal *Glastonbury Communicator* was full of his writings of a most messianic kind, proclaiming the return of the 'Lord of Dawn', Quetzalcoatl, on 16 and 17 of August and the birth of the new millennium.

Robert Coon says of himself that he has been working and teaching as an 'immortalist' for more than nineteen years. He taught the physical immortality portion of the 1985 'god training' (at around £450) in Glastonbury.

During the Harmonic Convergence, a feminist friend went up to Robert Coon while celebrations were happening on the Tor, and said that she would like the Goddess to be sometimes mentioned (in amongst all the glorification of assumed maleness of spirits and light), only to be told by him that she should concentrate on 'gratitude'.

Robert Coon was a friend of Anthony Roberts[17] who distinguished himself by publishing anti-feminist and anti-Goddess pamphlets as well as writing letters of the most abusive and threatening kind to women whom he singled out (I am included) as 'mad matriarchs'. Roberts was a writer and geomancer and saw himself as a guardian of the Tor which, to him, was the abode of the Archangel Michael. To Roberts, Glastonbury was the New Jerusualem.

Robert Coon, presuming to speak for Quetzalcoatl himself, wrote at the time of the convergence in *Glastonbury Communicator* that Quetzalcoatl, the lord of dawn, would once again shine as the 'rising sun of life triumphant and immortal'. That Mother Earth is now labouring to bring forth Christ consciousness, a divine son yet again, thereby opening the 'flood waters of creation'.

The main speaker at Glastonbury was Sir George Trevelyan who wanted the Harmonic Convergence to activate the network of so-called light centres such as Findhorn and Glastonbury. To my mind this is not the same as wanting to heal the Earth – which was the official reason for the convergence and the worldwide web of invocations. To Trevelyan, the object of the exercise was to attune ourselves and to raise our consciousness so that the spiritual light could flood into the darkened Earth and drive away the 'beings of darkness'.

Eternal light and no darkness would, however, drive us all mad as we would not be able to sleep and dream. Life is created and grows within the dark womb of cosmos, of Earth and of mothers. The seed germinates in the dark soil and human life and mind developed in the alternating light and darkness of day and night.

According to George Trevelyan, new light is now coming flooding into the planet and will sweep away much that is dark and wicked, 'those elements which of their free will have preferred egoism, violence and separation'. It would be wonderful, but unlikely, if he meant by this that at last we will now see the end of patriarchal greed and exploitation of the Earth and Her plants, animals and peoples, the end of male religions and the return of the Goddess.

However, Trevelyan claims that our higher self is in touch with the Christ-power, which is the 'power of universal life and love'. The new humanity will enter into the vibration of the fourth dimension and will 'see' Christ through our spiritual or third eye. Before this happens there will be a purge but those who are really attuned and think positive thoughts will not be affected by the disasters to come while the planet is being cleansed. But it is the Mother Goddess who is the universal life and love and Christ partakes in this Her essence only so far as He is and remains the son of the divine Mother.

The New Age is to be cosmic summertime, a higher vibrational rate and light from the sun's aura beyond the ultraviolet . . . whatever that is supposed to mean. It sounds ominous to me in this time of increasing greenhouse effects and unnatural heating up of the climate. To me, a northerner and born in the darkest winter in the north of Sweden, eternal summer, cosmic or otherwise, would be utterly intolerable.

Trevelyan thinks that Sai Baba, the holy man and healer in Southern India, is the nearest thing to being a god incarnate and that he is an avatar come to redeem our planet Earth. He also thinks that his own most recent book *New Teachings for an Awakened Humanity* has been channelled to him from the 'living Christ'!

Treading the Maze – Labyrinth and Spiral of Glastonbury Tor

Let me now say something about Glastonbury Tor as I have experienced it and of what I know of its true purpose and the legends that surround it.

In September 1989, women held an exhibition called 'The Goddess Re-emerging' in Glastonbury Assembly Rooms. I, together with Philippa Bowers, Jill Smith and Joanna Gorner, exhibited sculptures, images in different graphics and other media and paintings. We also had a programme of performances and rituals by Jill Smith as well as slideshows and talks. During this time the Assembly Rooms became a magical and beautiful Goddess temple. Glastonbury is again and again reclaimed by those who love Her ancient Mother spirit.

The Tor was in ancient times a powerful and primordial place of Earth-dragon, Goddess, serpent-power energies. It was a heaven mountain, out of time and place, where separate realities meet and shamanic journeys were undertaken. It is a three-dimensional labyrinth of vast proportions, as pointed out by Geoffrey Ashe in his book *Avalonian Quest*[18] he says labyrinths universally belong to the Goddess. They represent Her heart and womb into which one dances symbolically to die within Her still centre, to re-emerge new born as one winds one's way – dancing sometimes to the left and sometimes to the right, thereby connecting the energies of our own minds with those of the Earth – back out of Her womb.

The Tor labyrinth terraces are neolithic and were built by women-led farming communities in the mists of time before the emergence of warlike partriarchal tribes in the Bronze Age.

To the Hopis the labyrinth represents 'Mother Earth', the divine giver of life. To them it is the place of emergence and of death and to tread its pathways leads to rebirth, an enactment by the individual of the emergence. The spiralling hole – the foetal membrane and umbilical cord of the Earth Mother giving birth to Her children – is the birth canal through which the ancestors emerged into this fourth world. The Hopis believe that earlier worlds have been destroyed because humans have lost touch with the creator/creatrix and strayed from their spiritual path. Glastonbury Tor was to the ancients such a place of death and rebirth and represents the spiral/serpent force that gives birth to the universe.

The DNA molecule is a twin spiral; the Milky Way gives birth to new stars from its spiralling and rotating wave pattern. The spiral and the circle and the labyrinth – primaeval symbols in all ages for the great cosmic Mother – are life energy itself. She is Chi or Prana, she is the subtle energy force of cosmos and of life itself and our bodies, water, air, wood and minerals dance in spiral formation. Ancient snake dances are still performed by the Hopis and in Africa, and the Egyptian hieroglyph for 'Goddess' is an upraised cobra.

The most universal legend is that of the power of the serpent/dragon, the magic powers of water. She dwells in rivers and seas, in pools and wells, in the clouds above the mountain peaks, in caves and underground caverns. She regulates the tides, the menstrual flow, the rainfall and the thunder and lightning. Her energies are mostly beneficial, but they embody powers for both 'good' or 'ill'. To the Christians, however, she came to represent Satan, and women and men who still communicated with and were consciously in tune with her energies were vilified as 'witches', said to be in league with evil powers. Her barrows, stone circles and mounds have been found as far apart as Arabia, Africa, Tibet, China, India and also North America, where the famous great-serpent mound at Ohio is thought to date from the first century BC.

From St Michael's Mount at Penzance in Cornwall/ Kernow there runs a 200-mile 'dragon path' through Glastonbury and Avebury. It goes through clusters of stone circles on the heights of Dartmoor and Bodmin Moor and there are powerful collections of dragon images in local churches dedicated to St Michael and also appearing in folklore along this path. In Avebury church there is a famous carving on the font of a bishop killing a dragon. The early Christians took over the pagan places of worship, healing and ritual. On many high places there are churches dedicated to Michael, like the one at Glastonbury Tor, and dolmens and standing stones are included in many of these well-nigh inaccessible churches perched as they are on high hilltops. St Michael's Mount, supposedly linked with the stone row alignments at Carnac in Brittany/Bretagne, is a large human-made mound.

One of my many journeys of pilgrimage over the years was to Carnac where many stone rows cross the land for miles. While Ireland/Eire was the land of the fairies, the Shining Ones, Brittany was the land of the blessed dead . . . and they are one and the same. There is Mont St Michel off the coast of Normandy. On many of these flat-topped mounds there originally stood stone circles. These hills with artificially flattened tops, and with coils of serpent-like earth works encircling them and leading to the summits, were known as Dragon Hills. It appears that the ancients danced the serpentine stone avenues that led into the stone circles.

Did the Mount contain a hidden treasure/power which could bring riches to the surrounding countryside?

On the Dragon hills the Beltane fires were lit on the night before 1 May. The ancients used to roll fiery discs of straw down the hills, and torchlight processions descended from them to cleanse and fertilise the cattle and crops with her magic and life-giving energies on the night to the midsummer solstice.

On May Eve/Beltane, the sun rises at Glastonbury Tor exactly in line with Avebury forty miles away. The Tor was surrounded by marshes and isolated lake villages as late as 1000 BC. It was worshipped by the Celts as the entrance to the otherworld (Annwn) and was the sacred Isle of Avalon, the Isle of the Dead and of the fairies. It is the only known three-dimensional labyrinth, with its serpentine path winding to the summit in seven full circuits. There are rumours of there being a labyrinth also within the Tor and it is the legendary resting place of King Arthur. If so, he rests within the womb of the Great Mother, awaiting rebirth from Her.

The Tor was also called 'the Island of Glass' (Ynys-Witrin) or Caer Sidi, the spiral castle where the magical wonder-working Cauldron of Cerridwen was housed. The Cauldron of inspiration, and of the menstrual blood or waters of life, later became the mythical Holy Grail of Arthurian legend and finally the chalice of the Christian church. The original Cauldron of Cerridwen contains her magical and transformative blood of life, while the Christian chalice contains the blood of the dying and wounded Jesus figure. Geoffrey Ashe writes that Madron or Matrona was the name or expression for the indwelling Goddess of the Tor. She later became transformed into Morgen of the Celts and She dwelt here in Her island community of nine shaman women who were healers and shapeshifters.

Glastonbury Tor is a natural hill that was formed and pushed 500 feet high by geological forces in ancient times. It has been shaped into terraces by human hands. Its original shape has been altered to create mind-bending perspectives and visual experiences of being out of space and time. This is in common with other sacred places of the Goddess that were moulded and altered by the neolithic peoples. The seven labyrinthine paths on both sides of the Tor were once walked for ritual and magical purposes by the entire farming community.

It is likely that the ancient peoples buried their dead on the Tor, it being a dry area in an otherwise marshy land. In Celtic lore, Avalon was the meeting place of the dead, where people passed over into another existence. It is also thought to be surrounded by a vast zodiac engraved within the landscape and is called by some 'The Temple of the Stars'. By its foot lies a sacred well, Chalice Well, and nearby is the ancient city of Glastonbury.

The journey through the maze or labyrinth was everywhere central to the Goddess religion and to the regeneration of the soul and of nature.

On May Day Eve – Taurus full moon – 1980, a group of us set out to walk the maze of the Tor. It was led by Geoffrey Ashe, Kathy Jones (a creator of theatre and a healer) and members of the local Glastonbury Matriarchy Study Group who had taken the initiative and organised the walk. Geoffrey Ashe had after many years of living at Chalice Orchard, in the shadow of the Tor, finally walked the labyrinth in its entirety and managed to make a coherent plan of its winding paths.[19] He had a vision of groups of like-minded people re-treading the maze and thereby recreating the ritual of the neolithic peoples.

May Day is one of the ancient festivals of the Goddess, and in Sweden bonfires are lit everywhere on this night. This was my experience of that night.

> Walking in torchlight procession – or at least attempting to do so – we could not at first find the others. We started walking in what seemed to us the direction that felt good, seeing the moon, darkness, damp grass, slippery slopes, having difficulty walking with our feet all the time at an odd angle. The paths not very clear after thousands of years of neglect, cows and sheep being the only creatures to wander and stumble to the summit. Time and again in the past I have found cows congregating on top of the Tor,

their calm heads and horns outlined against the sky. Cow shit everywhere.

Although the Tor is always represented as a cone surmounted by the phallic tower, the only part left of an old church of St Michael, the dragon-slayer, it is in fact shaped as a vast elongated humped dragon which increasingly rises from hump to hump. Or as a recumbent female figure with the Tor forming its breast. From a distance the church tower looks like a nipple on this breast. Each terraced spiral is vast in its length . . . it takes some time to find the others and the torches, although we see the dark figures scrambling up and down the slopes in various places. One of my friends is menstruating, feels tired, has backache. We have to rest with her from time to time. We join the procession only to find it walking back the way we originally came from, slowly winding our way up and up. I feel: Who are most of these strangers, women and men, walking here with me? What have we in common? As most of us have never met before, do not know each other's intentions, how can we possibly experience and enact an ancient mystery? We cannot possibly act collectively as one body, one mind, which is necessary if we are to re-awaken the ancient power.

The labyrinth is not fully walked by most of us, and when everyone finally gathers on the summit there is only an aimless wandering about, exhaustion, trying to shelter from the increasingly furious wind. Feeble attempt at making a bonfire . . . We had not been given permission to do so by the National Trust who 'own' the land. On the tower, however, there is carved an image of Brigid milking a cow.

The original plan had been for all of us to spend the night on the Tor by a bonfire, and then walk down the maze again at dawn. As it worked out, most people went off after a while, feeling cold and vaguely frustrated, feeling the lack of some form of celebration or ritual that the long walk seemed to have been leading up to. Someone even suggested that what followed was, in fact, some form of punishment for unleashing powers that we are not able to channel or give form to.

Only a few of us remained on the Tor: four women and two men. We huddled closely together in our sleeping bags, and got some shelter from the wind at the foot of the tower. Everything was now in total darkness. I could, after a while, hear snores around me, but I was unable to get to sleep myself. I found myself trying to hang on to our covers with fists and teeth . . . heard strange sounds like rumblings and bells in the distance. This is a place of high magic, and this was a powerful night of the year. I seemed to be waiting for something: weird fantasies of UFOs arriving (and yet I am not in any way prone to this particular fantasy), and enormous giants climbing across the Tor. All sounds are magnified up here, and so is climatic change; the Tor is utterly exposed, unprotected and naked. Through my closed eyes I seemed to see strange lights, and when I looked up I discovered the most wild and amazing lightning constantly criss-crossing the sky. All the years I have been in Britain I have never seen anything like this!

Some of the others also woke up, and someone said she had heard stories of the lightning having been seen to strike the tower and spiral its way down to its base. We thought we might get fried alive if we remained where we were, so we scrambled out of our sleeping bags, stumbling half-awake away from the tower. Slithered, ran and fell the very long bumpy road down the dragon's backside, while all the while, every few seconds, we were as if in broad daylight while the next moment in total darkness: on – off, on – off . . . Figures illuminated against the sky . . . weird visual experiences. Total light but absolutely no sense of colour, like a photographic negative/positive. This added to our sense of fantastic unreality . . . Was this the Kundalini energy of the Tor awakened by our unfinished spiral walk? We felt as if we were being actively driven off the Tor. It was about three o'clock in the morning, now. When we arrived at her base, torrential rain fell.

(It is strange that I was writing this account late one night and the very next morning a letter arrived from Geoffrey Ashe in which he said, 'Yes, I heard of the storm on the Tor after the maze-treading. A demonstration by the thunder god who is said to be the Goddess's arch enemy?' Was this a coincidence?)

We drove away, all of us wet and cold, cramped into the one available car. We arrived back to a warm flat, with a fire and hot tea and food. Somehow we felt an amazing energy in spite of everything, as if we had been storing the discharged energy or electricity of the storm within our bodies and psyches. At dawn a few of us drove back again to the Tor. We climbed up yet again, but this time took the shortest path. The sun was not visible, and this time we found ourselves pelted by a hailstorm! Yet again we fled down the slopes and arrived back at the flat absolutely soaked to the skin.

What was amazing about that night was not only the wild storm but also what happened to some of us in the weeks following; the profound effects it seemed to have on us.

I kept seeing images of the out-of-time-and-space distortions of the Tor that can clearly be seen and felt up there.

St Michael, the Archangel of the Christians, so highly thought of at Findhorn and to whom so many churches were dedicated – especially the ones built on ancient sacred Goddess sites – was described in the *Book of Revelation* as the leader of the band of angels who went to war against the dragon ('Satan') and her/his demon cohorts. Like St George, he was the successor of the god Wotan, the pagan Germanic killer of dragons. He was a sun god or solar spirit, an 'heroic' slayer of the ancient Mother Goddess who was the mistress of the labyrinth of the Tor. Pre-Christian Glastonbury was a very important goddess and other/underworld sanctuary that had to be conquered, taken over and suppressed. But even with the coming of

Christianity, Glastonbury remained a Goddess place as the first wattle-built little church there was dedicated to Maria, the queen of heaven. It has always been a pilgrimage place for those who worship the blessed Virgin.

Almost everywhere in the early churches one finds the images of St Michael or St George slaying the dragon, and the Madonna is shown crushing the serpent under her feet. The serpent tempting Eve in paradise has a woman's torso and head.

John Michell writes that the Church used this dragon symbolism to represent the ancient power which is contained in the ley lines, wells and megalithic monuments.[20] The monuments – focal centres of local customs and magic – were in this way assimilated and consecrated by the early missionaries.

The Glastonbury Tor labyrinthine terraces would be contempoary with Silbury, with Newgrange and with the Goddess temples on Malta. As Nick Mann points out,[21] it was only during the peaceful neolithic times that great collective ritual centres such as these were being, or could have been, built. The later patriarchal peoples were preoccupied with building embattled hill forts.

Chalice Well or Blood Well as it was called because of the red water stained by a high iron content, at the foot of nearby Chalice Hill, would have been perceived as the menstrual flow emanating from the vaginal-shaped Tor. Seen from an aerial view, this is distinctly what the outline of the Tor looks like. Its sister-well of white waters, which is no longer there, would have symbolised the white, ovulatory flow.

To the Iron Age Celts, the tor was the entrance to the magical otherworld, home of the dead ancestors or the fairy folk, and ruled over by Gwyn Ap Nudd, Lord of Annwn and leader of the wild hunt summoning the souls of the newly dead.

However, it seems to be St Michael the archangel that attracts partriarchal men to Glastonbury. They see the phallic church tower on its summit as a needle to hold the

Dragon Goddess and channelling St Michael's energies into the Earth to subdue Her. Michael, the dragon slayer, is to them a champion for the 'forces of light', fighting the 'forces of darkness'.

I had no intention of going to Glastonbury for the (Disharmonic?) Convergence, since I knew it would be led by patriarchal and reactionary men.

I found myself unexpectedly taking part instead in a two-day sun dance and fast in the tipi village in the Black Mountains near Landeilo in South Wales. We danced to drumming from sunrise to sunset. All of us then slept in the large lodge or tipi, attempting to dream together. I 'happened' to arrive there just in time for this wonderful and magical celebration. There I was amongst people whom I love and trust and who try honestly to live in a sacred relationship with nature learnt from natural peoples – as far as it is possible in the industrial west.

My young son's ashes are buried there in a little African drum within the medicine wheel in a field surrounded by two streams and many beautiful trees. Had my son lived, he would definitely have been one of the Rainbow tribe in its true sense, being as he was of mixed race heritage and having great intelligence and a fast and creative mind.

Full Moon at Callanish

We are not longing for an eternal light world, or an irradiated Earth scorched by a nuclear sun . . . we are lovers of the radiant moon, giver of dreams and visions and mind and psychic powers, in the luminous darkness of the fertile nights.

Summer 1987 was the year of the major lunar standstill and this is the cosmic event that is particularly spectacular and powerful when witnessed from Callanish stone circle on the Isle of Lewis on the outer Hebrides. It occurs every 18.61 years at the extreme of the lunar cycle.

Lewis is an uncanny place of strange powers, of people with 'second sight'.

In the lunar cycle, year by year the moon rises a bit closer to the Earth every summer until the standstill is reached. She then starts to rise higher and higher again.

Twenty miles or so beyond Callanish stones is the sacred mountain called locally 'the Silver Maiden' or 'the Sleeping Beauty' because the body of the mountain resembles the recumbent figure of a gigantic woman. She is the primordial Mother and was venerated long before Callanish and the other nearby stone circles were raised by the neolithic peoples. The stone circles were, in fact, placed in relationship to lunar risings and settings seen over the body of the Silver Maiden. According to Jill Smith, poet and Earth-mysteries artist who lives on Lewis,[22] during the major lunar standstill the moon barely rose above the horizon. She observed from Callanish that it moved slowly and gently along the body of the mountain-woman, causing her to turn silver and then setting on her brow. The mountain is sometimes pregnant and her finely modelled head and profile is very clear to see for miles around the island. I have walked on her breasts and belly far above the world experiencing extraordinary states of being on a summer solstice in 1982. I was there with Jill and her young son watching the moon for many hours amongst the Callanish stones on the full moon in September 1987, the summer of the standstill and of the Harmonic Convergence and felt as if I was given some ancient knowledge. I again remembered something nearly lost during these last years of grieving and sorrow. Thank you Mother.

10
False Transcendence: the Gurus or the Goddess?

New Agers and Transcendence

New Age men grew up in societies with Christian notions of contempt for the body and for nature and its spirits. They consider transcendence to be of a higher order than immanence, and that it is a release from the Earth which is seen as the prison of the soul.

Some of the ideas of the present-day New Age were around in what Dr Christoher Evans calls *Cults of Unreason*[1] in movements such as the Church of Scientology and the UFO cult of the Aetherius Society. There is a preoccupation with gadgetry, such as the E meter of L Ron Hubbard, the prana box of George King, black boxes, antigravity machines, dynamisers, psyonic or radionic instruments, the EEG (electro-encephalograph) of the feedback cult, and so on.

George King, founder of the Aetherius Society, is a medium with a long training in yoga and the occult. King believes himself to be the primary terrestrial channel, the chosen servant of the 'cosmic masters', the voice of the interplanetary parliament. The first message from the masters from out of space reached him in 1954, and from 1955 he produced the journal *Aetherius Speaks to Earth*, later called *Cosmic Voices*. According to George King, Aetherius comes from Venus as does the master Jesus, who is not a son of god but a wise master, and where all the planetary masters are born via parthogenesis or virgin birth. The

'Star of Bethlehem' was a star ship which brought Jesus to Earth.

The cosmic masters are labouring to save Earth (Terra) from damnation and disaster and are urging suspension of nuclear tests and they warn that Earth is rushing headlong into another major war. The universe is a battlefield for forces of good and evil, not on the astral plane but in the actual physical universe, and opposing forces are moving from galaxy to galaxy, planet to planet, on space ships (UFOs), or are even teleported. Members of the Aetherius Society are involved in providing spiritual 'pushes' of vital energies – the beaming of 'magnetic energies' – for the masters to do battle with. According to King it is up to us to recharge Earth's weak spiritual energies, because beings from outer space are attempting to annihilate all humanoid life on Earth by drawing the atmospheric belt away from our planet. We have to relearn the use of prana (wind, breath, spirit, orgone energy, vital force) which we have lost the capacity to use, except in entirely automatic ways.

The Aetherius Society practises personal revelation, prayers, rituals, chants and pilgrimages. Prana, or spiritual energy-radiation, is collected and concentrated in a box/machine. The energy charged within the box can then be emanated when required. From 1959 to 1961 the Society undertook the most spectacular religious ritual ever undertaken, called Operation Starlight, when King and members of the Society personally ascended a number of holy mountains (again worldwide and according to a pre-made list) to 'charge' them with spiritual power. They have also carried out Operation Karmalight, Operation Bluewater, etc.

The teachings of the Aetherius Society claim that Flying Saucers (UFOs) are interplanetary spacecraft from other planets in our system, which are inhabited by cultures far more highly evolved than us and whose 'peoples' are compassionate and peace-loving. King has repeatedly been attacked and criticised in *Psychic News*, the newspaper of the spiritualist movement, because of his claim that the actual location of 'summerland' (or the spirit-world) is not in some non-physical or extra-terrestrial sphere but on a separate planet either in the solar system or other galaxy. Spiritualists claim that their messages are from spirit guides and the 'dead', while George King would say that they are from space beings.

George King prophecies that another 'Master' will come whose magic will be greater than any known upon Earth, and that those who do not listen to his words will be removed from Earth. He will not come 'in mystery', as Jesus did, but openly in a UFO, and everyone will know of his coming. He will guide us into the new millennium or world. King claims that great teachers such as Buddha and Sri Krishna were masters such as this and that the solar system is ruled by a cosmic hierarchy or interplanetary parliament. One day, after many lifetimes, we will all become enlightened masters.

I went to a meeting of the Aetherius Society in Bristol and I found their claims contradictory. I failed to understand how one was to distinguish whether a 'voice' was speaking from other planets or from the spirit realms. When asked this question, some members became quite irate. The Aetherius Society has, however, gathered an impressive amount of information on sightings of so-called UFOs and of communications with beings from outer space, all of which has apprently been kept secret from us for military and political reasons. It is believed that cosmic masters are guiding us from other planetary cultures and that some of them already live here on Earth.

There are other scenarios by the more paranoid, such as Anthony Roberts and Geoff Gilbertson in *The Dark Gods*[2] who take inspiration from the weird *Tales of Horror and Fascination* by H P Lovecraft.[3] They believe that evil entities existing in other dimensions collaborate with evil groups of humans with the eventual aim of forming an unholy alliance to take over Earth.

Carl Jung believed that UFOs are psychic projections of

the human mind, and it is now thought that UFOs materialise near ley lines and sacred places. When people of old thought they saw fairies and dragons, white ladies, ghosts and balls of white light, Earth lights, they now 'see' UFOs. There are strong auric forcefields at such sacred places situated on fault lines in the Earth's crust; these are 'windows' or gateways into other realities and are trance-inducing.[4]

Is the New Age Movement Imperialist?

How much collaboration is there between US military and imperialist establishments and some New Age groups? Are some groups backed by the CIA? I have no definite answers, only suspicions.

These suspicions are, however, shared by others I know, and I quote below from a letter from a feminist friend of mine, an Earth mysteries and Goddess artist who lives in Australia.[5] My friend wrote in connection with the Harmonic Convergence that the New Age has everything to do with American consumerism and that since everything else has been exploited it is now the turn of the sacred sites.

My friend had been present at a meeting in Australia of Fountain International, which was founded in Brighton in 1981 but is now an international movement. I gather that it was named after a famous Brighton fountain of geomantic significance that stands on the Steine, a town square and centre of Brighton. ('Steine' is a Saxon word for stones.) Around the base of the fountain are placed large stones that were dug up here and quite likely belonged to a former stone circle on this once sacred site.[6]

One of the things the Fountain group does on a local level is to try to diffuse the violence and petty crime in the towns and cities where they live through the use of meditation. They broadcast 'thoughts of love' using the ley system of geomagnetic energies that emanate from the fountain on the Steine and that they conceive of as pathways of consciousness that can be influenced and altered.

The members of the group seem to have no conception of the background to this increasing violence, rooted as it is in unemployment, homelessness, poverty and the despair of the young at the smugness and lack of caring in Britain today.

The 'Fountain group' seems to be the 'brainchild' of dowser Colin Bloy who sees 'Fountain' as devoted to liberating people from 'negativity' and as fighting on the side of light with St Michael as their patron. The group claims to be trying to remove previous psychic manipulations of the Earth energies, and Colin Bloy and many Fountain people are involved in attempting to reverse 'the outrageous manipulations which have been carried out by dark forces over centuries'.

It seems that Colin Bloy has been well-known for many years as a dowser and geomancer in the Earth mysteries movement. His fellow Earth mysteries researchers Paul Deveraux and Nigel Pennick feel, however, that he is misusing his powers for reactionary and near-fascist purposes. They accuse him, in a letter to *The Fountain Journal*[7] of anti-democratic right-wing attitudes and of attempting to magically alter the geomancy of political Britain, using geomancy and Earth energies for political control, in favour of the Tory government. As Pennick writes: 'Evil often starts off with the intention of being good and pure, then goes down hill to the holocaust. The Christian witch- and Jew-hunts prove this.' Pennick asks (as I do) how the nuclear and military build-up ties in with 'prayer for peace' and he calls magic done with the intention of controlling others, their thoughts and actions, 'black magic'.

Paul Deveraux writes that true geomantic research is about listening to the land, seeking to learn and understand from ancient sites and landscapes 'rather than choosing to project thought forms all over them'. He also writes that Fountain group members leave 'psychic litter' and 'Coke cans of the mind' at sacred sites, and that they can

FALSE TRANSCENDENCE: THE GURUS OR THE GODDESS?

even be dowsed as thoughts do have reality and Devereaux feels they are inspired by the New Age movement. He calls this 'plastic geomancy', garbled notions of quicky geomancy, and that behind the façade of 'sweetness and light' that Colin Bloy presents there are other motives. Deveraux thinks that many members of the group are unaware of the fact that they are members of a cult (the Alphaega group) with right-wing views and spiritual pretensions.

Colin Bloy writes in his own defence that 'Fountain has no system to offer, other than the applied knowledge of pure love and the discipline that that implies. I have no political claims, other than liberty . . .' He also writes that 'we must create a new ley system in which the collective consciousness is not the victim of archetypes of the past'.

Radio and TV stations are seen as node points that can transmit spiritual energy and the Fountain group planned yet another global event to take place on St Michael's day, 29 September 1990. They hope that Radio and TV stations all around the world will be open for all New Age groups to combine their energies in the healing of the Earth and, in Colin Bloy's words, the complete rebuilding of its etheric body and the subtle spiritual fields that surround it in 'an act of mutual love between the planet and its people'. The language throughout *The Fountain* journal is that of man/he and of 'mankind'. And words such as 'love' and 'good' are used indiscriminately by New Agers without a thought that everything is relative.

My Australian Earth mysteries friend wrote that the Fountain group she attended in 1987 had been run by two very dominant men who kept talking of St Michael and dragon-energies, and of churches of St Michael the dragonslayer situated on ley lines. They did a series of guided meditations of local sacred sites that they had marked out through dowsing and which bore no relationship to the notions of Aboriginal people whose land it is.

The two men talked of places being 'black', i.e. bad and corrupted; meditation was to be used to heal the 'blackness' and to give them 'light'. 'They had identified buildings in Adelaide as energy-sites – all with towers – never mentioning the Earth at all. It was all about focussing new energy into places via phallic towerlike structures.' All dragon–killing stuff, with St. Michael's phallic sword rammed into the Earth, controlling and manipulating Her energies.

My friend bought a publication at the meeting by Vincent Selleck who lives in Queensland. According to her, all his writings are illustrated with the SS insignia used by the Nazis[8] who 'activated' the ancient sacred sites during the Second World War. 'It's all to do with directing a large group of people to focus on special sites already powerful – raising the energy and then directing it for some specific purpose. I believe it is to empower the US military and social takeover of the world.' She also comments on how so many of the supposedly great psychics seem utterly unaware of, or are positively afraid of, lunar powers, and knew nothing of the major lunar standstill in the summer of 1987.

In a further and more recent communication[9] from my Australian friend, she writes that she was horrified by what the Fountain group was trying to do in Australia:

> You may be interested to hear that recently the guy behind the groups here was approached by Aboriginal people in Adelaide and told to stop his lectures and workshops on Earth energy and rainbow-serpent stuff. Aboriginal people are very disturbed by what the group is doing, i.e. re-directing energy for their own ego-centred power trips and taking over Aboriginal symbols without permission.

She writes that the group has been told to stop as they are not aware of what they are doing and that the leader is a German man very much into fascist methods, who completely ignores feminine energy.

This neo-fascist attitude to women was highlighted

recently in a report in the feminist newsletter *Media Watch* in California. Women write that Roy Masters' nationally syndicated New Age radio show 'New Dimensions' in Los Angeles is broadcasting the message that women continually tempt men to evil because of women's satanic past. Furthermore, feminists are wanting to castrate men because they have stepped from their predestined role as men's helpers.

There seem to be any number of New Age groups like Fountain International that claim to be working for Earth healing and peace. Many of them are listed in the *Link Up* journal, such as 'the Earth Stewards Network' and 'the New Group of World Servers', inspired by Alice Bailey and her Lucis Trust which was formed as a registered charity in 1922. World Goodwill which aims to establish 'right human relations' to aid 'spiritual awakening', is part of Lucis Trust which in 1989 was granted consultative status at the Economic and Social Council of the UN. The World Goodwill Foundation has prestigious addresses in London, Geneva and the United Nations Plaza.

I would, among other things, like to know what such groups do with the money they amass and what their political affiliations are.

In a pamphlet called *Resonance Returning*,[10] Selleck writes of José Argüelles' concept of Earth and us passing through the last stage of the galactic synchronisation-beam, thereby becoming radiant beings in alliance with the 'Galactic Federation of the Higher Evolution'. He writes that either we evolve consciously to become radiant with the light of the universal intelligence or we become radiant and radioactive as a result of nuclear war. That in either case matter will be transformed into light and that from the universal perspective it might not make any difference since light would be released in either case!

Vincent Selleck does mention the dangers created by scientists and by the global industrial and military technology. But he also writes of how the incredible tension implied in all of this will ultimately 'shatter the shell of our form-limited concept of being' and, like the splitting of the atom, will release 'potent pure-light energy into our collective unconsciousness'. Selleck is, in his own words, involved in evolving planetary ritual, in attempting to key energy into the Earth through a network of sacred sites (Earth acupuncture) that will create a 'collective resonance' to unite the globe in a pulse of light. Selleck calls this 'Festivals of World Peace' which he claims are apolitical. He believes that once we are aware of our true nature as spirit beings, our fallen terrestrial consciousness will be transformed into the light body, we will be able to heal the world and to restore balance to nature and to ecology.

In phrases such as 'light will impregnate matter' the white light is clearly seen as male by definition and has been called 'the divine radiance of the father of the cosmos'.

Later in his pamphlet Selleck starts tripping out on a light-pyramid starship from Arcturus laser-beaming light at him on the autumn equinox. According to him this was a threshold command vehicle that operates in a similar way to 'the CIA advising a revolutionary army training, providing information and supplying new psychic and spiritual powers (weaponry) without directly or physically becoming involved in conflict.'

I find this a most extraordinary statement. It makes me wonder what some of these New Agers are truly thinking if the CIA can be spoken about in such glowing terms. It bodes ill for the New Age movement. The function of the CIA worldwide is to protect the interests of US multinationals and global domination. Here it is again important to note that both David Spangler and W. I. Thompson suggest that US corporations utilise methods which serve strategies for establishing planetary consciousness, the electronic global brain.

It is true that worldwide there are many people with good intentions involved in meditating, praying for 'peace' and who take part in world healing days. Their intention seems to be for a critical mass to be focussed and achieved

FALSE TRANSCENDENCE: THE GURUS OR THE GODDESS?

to create a field of resonance. Colin Bloy wrote in *The Fountain* that the Cambridge biologist Rupert Sheldrake's concept of the 'morpho-genetic field'[11] has shown that these are subtle energies which unite species and make 'the hundredth monkey syndrome'[12] explicable. This has given us new understanding of the collective consciousness. The idea being that if a certain critical mass is achieved by vast numbers of people around the Earth meditating and concentrating on peace, then real changes will happen. The only problem is that people are then given the distinct impression that this is all that is needed for 'world peace' to be achieved, which is all very convenient for the west.

The question that does not seem to be asked is what sort of 'peace' is being suggested/requested; and on whose terms? After all, millions of women and children are raped, abused and murdered in 'peacetime'. 'Peace', in our unjust world, seems to mean within the status quo of poverty and starvation in large parts of the Third World. When the oppressed rise up and demand food, the return of their land and justice, they are told they have broken the peace; and should they arm themselves, they are called 'terrorists'.

If the New Agers, as well as meditating and praying for peace, would also set about dismantling the multinationals and the arms industries in the United States and other western countries that are causing such havoc to the world, I would then believe that they wanted genuine peace. If they took apart the nuclear power stations and destroyed the missiles as well as demanded an end to the disgraceful debt-repayment that is breaking the backs of Third World countries, it would be even better. And considering the class and family connections that many American New Agers enjoy they could have a very real impact if they all said no to US imperialism. Instead, we have groups such as Americans Working for the Light and New Agers undergoing expensive therapies which reassure them that it is just fine to be wealthy and privileged in a world where the majority are suffering from lack of food and basic necessities.

New Agers adopt religious veiws which teach that whatever happens it is simply a matter of one's personal karma and that each of us creates his or her own realities. The message is that you don't need to feel responsibility for your oppressed sisters and brothers.

There is no recognition in New Age writings that it is not our DNA that is incorrectly coded, neither is it because we are genetically imperfect or because the planets are in this or that position or conjunction that things are wrong.

What is wrong, and has been wrong now for thousands of years, is that deadly patriarchal worldviews and exploitive systems have dried up the sources of life on this Earth and have disconnected us from the radiant web of Spider Woman. We have forgotten to keep the hole on the top of our heads open. We must now go through a change of heart and open our psychic eyes to the greater nature and mind of the Mother.

The Re-Emergence of the Goddess

Olivia Durdin-Robertson of the Fellowship of Isis[13] says, 'The Second coming is the re-emergence of the Goddess.' The Goddess is re-awakening from Her long and cosmic sleep in the underworld and as Kore, the Maiden, She re-emerges to unite again with Her Mother Demeter and women worldwide are rising. A critical mass is indeed being reached in women's consciousness worldwide.

I believe in the power of thought and of thought-forms. I know the importance of meditation and visualisation. I believe in the reality of communication with the spirits, of the spiritworld and of reincarnation. I have experienced many times the oracular power of wells and of the sacred places of the Goddess. I do believe that we are indivisbly and holistically whole. I believe that we must open our second sight and 'see' again. I believe that if we work with Earth's places of power and Her evolutionary lights, we

FALSE TRANSCENDENCE: THE GURUS OR THE GODDESS?

ourselves will be deeply affected and great changes will come about. I believe in synchronicity – as above, so below – and in multiple universes.

Superficially, one might think that I have much in common with New Age thinking. But, as I have tried to show throughout this book, there are great differences indeed between being open to psychic changes on many levels and adopting the fundamentally reactionary, anti-Earth and anti-Goddess, patriarchal religious views of so many New Agers. I do not believe that they truly love Earth, our sorrowing Mother.

I sense that we are having a mass near-death experience at this time.

Ever since I experienced flying with my son Leif into the great light, I have longed to be in the otherworld with him and, now, Sean. Having two sons gone into that world it is as familiar and as much 'home' to me as is this physical Earth. Yet I also love this beautiful Earth, our Mother of the life-giving dark soil, internal fires and sacred waters, and I love the magical and radiant moon in her luminous darkness, Our Lady of light and her horned son. This is one of the contradictions I have to live with now.

I also love intensely the all-embracing and life-giving solar Mother who brings ecstatic new life and new beginnings in the joyous spring after the long winter months.

I do believe that the Goddess is re-emerging, that Persephone is returning to Her mother Demeter/Gaia at last, and that the Earth will rejoice and that She will green again.

The New Age is the Second Coming of the Goddess and only then will there be true peace and another Golden Age as experienced in ancient Atlantis.

Now is the time for all visionaries – women and men – to come to the aid of our ancient Earth Mother. We must struggle to make far-reaching changes politically and economically if we are to survive, and we must indeed also meditate worldwide and dream Her alive.

It is only through Her that we have our being and are

reborn. It is into Her magical otherworld that we enter at death. It is through Her that we become truly immortal spirits.

Blessed Be
Monica Sjöö
Bristol, August, 1991

Notes

Introduction

1 From a statement in *PAN*, the Pagans against Nukes journal, (now called *Pandora's Jar*) founded in 1980.
2 From Ed McGaa/Eagle Man, *Mother Earth Spirituality*, Harper & Row, San Francisco, 1989.
3 Bob Stewart has written several books on Merlin, on the ancient Celtic gods and goddesses as well as *The Underworld Initiation: A Journey Towards Psychic Transformation*, Aquarian Press, Wellingborough, 1985.
4 I do not mean to imply that all New Agers hold the views I explore in this book. There are obviously also areas of New Age thinking that are not well known to me; however, most New Agers hold some of the views expressed here.
5 See Peter Russell's *The Earth Awakening: The Global Brain*, Arkana, Harmondsworth, 1988.
6 Described thus by Michael Green, a fan of Alice Bailey, in his very patriarchal contribution to the anthology *The Crop Circles Enigma*, Gateways Books, Bath, 1990.
7 *A Course in Miracles* (Arkana, Harmondsworth, 1985), has become Holy Writ to many New Agers. This book was published in 1976 and 'channelled' over a period of seven years through Dr Helen Shucman, a professor of medical psychology at Columbia University School of Physicians. 'As patriarchal as the Bible', my sick son Sean said when the Rebirthers required him to read it.
8 David Spangler, *Towards a Planetary Vision*, Findhorn Publications, Findhorn, 1977, p. 22. (See Martin Bernal's *Black Athena: The Afro-Asiatic Roots of Classical Civilization*, Free Association Books, London, 1987 for an exposé of European ethnocentric and racist thought.)
9 The quotes are from pp. 88–104 of David Spangler's *Explorations*.

10 See *The Star People* by Brad and Francie Steiger, Berkley Books, New York, 1981.
11 Paramhansa Yogananda discusses such paranormal abilities in his *Autobiography of a Yogi*, Rider, London, 1977.
12 From *Angels*, by Peter Lamborn Wilson, Pantheon Books, New York, 1980.
13 According to Merlin Stone in *Paradise Papers (When God Was a Woman)*, Virago, London, 1976.
14 For information on these ancient Goddess cultures, see *Goddess – Mother of All Living*, by Adele Getty, Thames & Hudson, London, 1990.
15 Teilhard de Chardin, *The Future of Man*, Harper & Row, New York, 1964.
16 Read *The Great Cosmic Mother: Resdiscovering the Religion of the Earth*, by Monica Sjöö and Barbara Mor, Harper & Row, San Francisco, 1987, for information on the Lunar Mother and women's mysteries.
17 James Lovelock introduced the 'Gaia Hypothesis', the self-creating living Earth, in his book *Gaia: A New Look at Life on Earth*, Oxford University Press, Oxford, 1979. He cannot, however, bring himself to recognise Earth as a spiritual being with consciousness. Other popular New Age theories, such as those of Peter Russell (see note 5), is that the collective human mind and the electronic mass media are now supplying Her with consciousness.
18 Read Janet McCrickard's book *Eclipse of the Sun*, Gothic Image, Glastonbury, 1990, for its wonderful information on the sun Goddess/es, although she does see fit to attack women who write of the Lunar Mother and singles out *The Great Cosmic Mother* book for special and vicious attention.
19 See Leonard Orr, *Physical Immortality: The Science of Everlasting Life*, Inspiration University, Sierraville, CA, 1980, for information on the Yogi Babaji.
20 Brian Easlea discusses this in various books; see the bibliography and chapter 4.
21 Ajit Mookerjee, *Kali: The Feminine Force*, Destiny Books, New York, 1988. He has also written beautiful books on Tantra.
22 Michael Dames wrote *Silbury Treasure – The Great Goddess Rediscovered* and *Avebury Circle*, Thames & Hudson, London, in 1976 and 1977, respectively. These are two books which have greatly inspired me.
23 So called by Alexander Thom in *Megalithic Lunar Observatories*, Oxford University Press, Oxford, 1971.
24 The title of a book by Paul Devereux, *Places of Power: Secret Energies at Ancient Sites*, Blandford Press, Dorset, 1990.

Deveraux is the editor of the *Ley Hunter Journal* and the main force behind the Dragon Project which set out to investigate the energies and emanations at sacred sites, especially the Rollright Stones.

25 Paul Deveraux, *Earth Lights Revelation*, Blandford Press, Dorset, 1989.

26 Paula Gunn Allen, *The Sacred Hoop – Recovering the Feminine in American Indian Tradition*, Beacon Press, Boston, 1986.

27 Shown on British television, Channel 4, 5 December 1990. See also, Alan Ereira, *The Heart of the World*, Jonathan Cape, London, 1990, a book about the Kogi by the television producer, who is also an historian.

28 Suggested by Vicki Noble in her women and Shamanism journal *Snake Power*, published in the USA. Her book *Shakti Woman* was published in 1991 by Harper & Row, San Franciso.

29 Recent good books on ecofeminism are *Healing the Wounds: the Promise of Ecofeminism*, edited by Judith Plant, Greenprint, London, 1989; and *The Recurring Silent Spring*, by Patricia Hynes, Pergamon Press, Oxford, 1989.

1 Questioning the New Age Movement

1 This poem was published in PAN (Pagans Against Nukes) journal in 1985, and also in *Greenline*.

2 I have written in detail and in great pain about these experiences and of Leif's short life and early death in 'Darkness in my Mind/Journeying through the Underworld', first published in *Arachne*, journal of the Matriarchy Research and Resource Network (MRRN), in 1986 and then included (edited) in *Glancing Fires: An Investigation into Women's Creativity*, edited by Lesley Saunders, The Women's Press, 1987.

3 See *Great Moments in Medicine*, by George A Bender, Parke-Davis, Detroit 1961.

4 In 1984 I wrote a long article called 'The Goddess/es of the North', published in *Arachne*.

5 *Peyote* is a psychotropic plant, a sort of cactus, very common in Mexico and used in ritual to experience altered states.

6 R J Stewart explores the fairy/otherworld realm in his many books. His *Robert Kirk: Walker Between the Worlds*, Element Books, Dorset, 1990, is particularly interesting, as is his *Celtic Gods, Celtic Goddesses*, Blandford Press, Dorset, 1990. Caitlin Matthews, *The Celtric Tradition*, Element Books, Dorset, 1989, is also a good source book.

7   Robert Graves, *The White Goddess*, Faber and Faber, London, 1948.
8   Pointed out by Barbara Walker in *Women's Rituals*, Harper & Row, San Franciso, 1990. Until the seventeenth century, public meetings in Corsica took place in cemeteries to ensure the presence of the invisible dead or ancestors in the decision-making.
9   Luisah Teish, *Jambalaya: The Natural Women's Book of Personal Charms and Practical Ritual*, Harper & Row, San Francisco, 1988. Another important book is *The Voodoo Gods/Divine Horsemen*, by American film-maker and dancer Maya Deren, Thames & Hudson, London, 1953.
10 Marija Gimbutas, *Goddesses and Gods of Old Europe: 6500–3500 BC*, Thames & Hudson, London, 1968 (updated in 1982). *Oya: In Praise of the Goddess*, Judith Gleason, Shambhala, Boston, 1987, is also a fine source book. See *The Language of The Goddess*, Harper & Row, San Francisco, 1989, also by Marija Gimbutas. Marija Gimbutas' most recent book is called *The Civilization of the Goddess: The World of Old Europe*, edited with Joan Marler.
11 The Orishas are the consciousness of the forces of nature while the Egun are the spirits of the dead and of the ancestors.
12 One fascinating account is in Matthew Manning's *The Link: The Extraordinary Gifts of a Teenage Psychic*, Colin Smythe, Gerrards Cross, Bucks, 1974; also his *The Strangers: My Conversations with a Ghost*, W H Allen, London, 1974. Both books are autobiographical. He is a natural medium and psychic who now practises as a healer.
13 Virago, London, 1989.
14 'Active' spiritual healing is considered a male occupation, although today there are many great women healers. The most revered healer of modern times was Harry Edwards who was also mediumistic. In ancient times, healing was always a woman's occupation, as the priestesses of the Goddesses were herbalists and psychics.
15 Anthony Borgia, *Life in the World Unseen*, Odhams Press, London, 1954, and *More About the World Unseen*, Psychic Press, London, 1956.
16 Elaine Pagels, *The Gnostic Gospels*, Penguin, Harmondsworth, 1982.
17 *The Case of Helen Duncan*, Maurice Barbanell, Spiritualist Press, London, 1945.
18 I understand that The Witchcraft Act of 1735 was repealed thanks to the efforts of influential and respected spiritualists

such as Lord Dowding and Sir Arthur Conan Doyle (both of whom had lost sons during the First World War). It was replaced in 1951 by the Fraudulent Mediums Act, which is hardly ever used.

19 Wicce applies to women of the Craft and Wicca to the men, which is why I alternate between the two terms.
20 Tony Ortzen, *Psychic News*, the London-based spiritualist journal, July 1987, p. 2.
21 *Psychic News*, 4 July 1987.
22 *Ibid*. Shirley MacLaine has written a number of autobiographical books and conducts spiritual seminars in the USA.
23 Tony Ortzen, *Psychic News*, 2 May 1987, p. 21.
24 I agree with this organisation's perspective on women's unpaid work, but having been a member for two years I left, disillusioned with the top-heavy method of organisation.
25 There are two lengthy interviews with me, the first in *We are Here: Conversations with Lesbian Women* with Angela Stuart-Park and Jules Cassidy, Quartet Books, London, 1977; and then Moira Vincentelli's interview with me in Wales in 1984 in *Visibly Female: Feminism and Art Today*, edited by Hilary Robinson, Camden Press, London, 1987.
26 'Woman as Warrior', in *Women of Power* journal, no. 3, Winter/Spring, Cambridge, MA, 1986, pp. 80–81.
27 Marilyn Ferguson, *Aquarian Conspiracy: Personal and Social Transformation in the 1980s*, Paladin, London, 1982. Another book influential at the time was *The Six O'clock Bus: A Guide to Armageddon and the New Age*, Moira Timms, Turnstone Books, London, 1971.
28 Marshall McLuhan, *Understanding Media: The Extensions of Man*, McGraw Hill, New York, 1965.
29 Pluto Press, London, 1976.
30 Peggy Kornegger, 'The Spirituality Rip-Off', *Second Wave* journal, 1976.
31 Susan George, *How the Other Half Dies: The Real Reasons for World Hunger*, Penguin, Harmondsworth, 1976, and *A Fate Worse Than Debt*, Penguin, Harmondsworth, 1988. As early as 1970 Esther Boserup had written *Women's Role in Economic Development* (Allen & Unwin, London), warning of what was happening to Third World women.
32 *Aquarian Conspiracy*, p. 387.
33 *Ibid.*, p. 389.
34 There are a number of radical books by black and Native American writers. One is *Marxism and Native Americans*, edited by Ward Churchill, South End Press, Boston, MA, 1982.

35 Archbishop Desmond Tutu of South Africa in *The Hunger Machine* by Jon Bennett with Susan George, Polity Press, London, 1987, p. 110.
36 On Alice Walker's recommendation, I read the very interesting *Indian Givers: How the Indians of the Americas Transformed the World*, by Jack Weatherford, Fawcett Columbine, New York, 1988. He shows how silver robbed from the Americas fuelled western capitalism, how Indian agriculture and pharmacology gave the world many food plants and medicines, and how Indian federalist and truly democratic institutions and tribal living influenced Marx and Engels. *Bury my Heart at Wounded Knee* by Dee Brown is a history of pain, humilation and genocide of the Native American tribes (published by Picador, London, 1972).
37 Paula Gunn Allen teaches Native American studies at the University of California, Berkeley. She has also written *The Woman who Owned the Shadows*, Spinsters ink, San Francisco, 1983, and edited the anthology *Spider Woman's Granddaughters*, The Women's Press, London, 1990.
38 The USA wants to set up a geothermal scheme, drilling into the active vulcano Mauna Loa, a manifestation of the goddess Pélé. Native Hawaiians and conservationists are trying to block this. Noxious gases produced would threaten the remaining rain forests. The Nevada desert, where innumerable nuclear bomb tests have been and are still being carried out, belongs to the Sheshone people who have protested again and again against their land being used in this way. Cancers are very common amongst the people living in the area.
39 'Even though . . . the radioactive contamination of Rongelop Island is considered perfectly safe for human habitation, the levels of activity are higher than those found on other inhabited islands in the world. The habitation of these people on the island will afford most valuable ecological radiation data on human beings.' Brookhaven National Laboratory, the US Atomic Energy Commission's three-year report on Rongelop and Utirik, 1957, quoted in 'Women Working for a Nuclear Free and Independent Pacific', *Pacific Paradise, Nuclear Nightmare*, a CND publication, 1987, p. 36. Marshallese children have been born without arms and legs, others are called 'jellyfish babies'. These are beings that breathe but bear no resemblance to human form and die within hours of birth.
40 See Diane Bell's *Daughters of the Dreaming*, Allen & Unwin, Australia, 1983, about aboriginal women's rites and lives.

41　Amongst others, *Pacific Paradise, Nuclear Nightmare*, CND publication, 1987 (see note 38 above) and 'Pacific Women Speak: Why Haven't You Known?', *Greenline*, 1987.

2 Dreaming the Sacred Land

1　See Diane Bell, *Daughters of the Dreaming*.
2　See Michael Dames, *Silbury Treasure – The Great Goddess Rediscovered*.
3　'My Initiation at Silbury/Avebury' prose-poem was published in an early *Arachne* Matriarchy journal in 1978 and is included in the anthology *Voices of the Goddess*, edited by Caitlin Matthews, Aquarian Press, London, 1990, in my 'Tested by the Dark/Light Mother of the Otherworld'.
4　Starhawk is the author of, amongst other books, *The Spiral Dance: A Rebirth of the Ancient Religion of the Great Goddess: Rituals, Invocations, Exercises, Magic*, Harper & Row, San Francisco, 1989, and *Dreaming the Dark: Magic, Sex and Politics*, Beacon Press, Boston, 1982.
5　On 16 August 1989 I watched the full moon lunar eclipse at Silbury all night. I felt as if I had come full circle.
6　The 'Battle of the Beanfield' followed soon after when police wrecked travellers' vehicles and many dreams were smashed.
7　This is an edited and re-written version of an article originally published in 1985 in PAN and in *Greenline*.
8　I got to know those tors when I was one of the teachers of the ancient Albion camp held by the Oak Dragon Camps on Dartmoor in the summer of 1989 and we explored the stone circles, rocks and stone rows on the magical moor.
9　See *The Great Cosmic Mother*, pp. 53–4 and p. 436 end note 5 for a full discussion of this subject.
10　Marija Gimbutas, *Language of the Goddess*, Harper & Row, San Francisco, 1989.
11　Martin Brennan, *The Boyne Valley Vision*, Dolmen Press, London, 1980; *The Stars and the Stones*, Thames & Hudson, London, 1983.
12　Janet McCrickard, *Eclipse of the Sun*.
13　Rider, London, 1988. Ron Williams of Surrey and James Harrod in the MS 'The Acheulian Goddess: Symbol of the Transformation of the Early Paleolithic', suggest that there were flint sculptures of the Goddess as far back as 600,000 BC.
14　British Museum Publications, London, 1989.
15　*Ibid.*, p. 50.

16 Monica Sjöö and Barbara Mor, *The Great Cosmic Mother: Rediscovering the Religion of the Earth*.

3 Explorations of Consciousness

1 Luisah Teish, *Jambalaya: The Natural Woman's Book of Personal Charms and Practical Rituals*.
2 Basil Davidson, *Africa in History*, Paladin Books, London, 1974. Also of interest is *Black Athena: The Afro-Asiatic Roots of Classical Civilization* by Martin Bernal.
3 Routledge & Kegan Paul, London, 1984.
4 According to Janet Gyatso in *Feminine Ground: Essays on Women in Tibet*, published by Snow Lion Publications, New York in 1989, the Bonpo also had suppressed an earlier, female-centred religion. Buddhists saw Tibet as female, demonic and dangerous, like a demoness.
5 I had been put off by misogynist and life-denying Buddhist and Upanishad thinking when I came across it at the age of sixteen in Sweden in the Beat scene of the late 1950s. The existentialists were equally negative, misogynist and life-denying. This left many scars.
6 Harper & Row, San Francisco, 1988.
7 Harper & Row, San Francisco, 1989.
8 According to Mary Condren, the great pagan minds of the time fled to the non-Christian near east from a Europe where women could now be tortured, murdered and raped with impunity. The Church preached that the world is evil and literally the devil's cesspit. Christianity set cultures back thousands of years.
9 Swallow Press, Athens, Ohio, 1984.
10 Raphael Patai, *The Hebrew Goddess*, Avon Books, New York, 1978.
11 Shekinah re-emerges as a powerful Goddess of creative wisdom (the holy spirit) in the Kabbala of Jewish mediaeval European mysticism and inspired European occult and magical thinking.
12 See Elaine Pagels, *The Gnostic Gospels*, for information on the beliefs of the gnostics.
13 Rider, London, 1973.
14 W I Thompson, *The Time Falling Bodies Take to Light: Mythology, Sexuality and the Origins of Culture*, St Martin's Press, New York, 1981.
15 Sri Aurobindo, a devotee of the Mother, believed that humanity would create a new global spiritual culture. The Esalen Institute in the USA was inspired by his example.

4 Banishing Darkness: Findhorn's Plan of Light

1. William Irwin Thompson, *Passages About the Earth: An Exploration of the New Planetary Culture*, Rider, London, 1973, pp. 165–6.
2. Element Books, 1988. Also, *God Spoke to Me*, Findhorn Press, 1971.
3. Originally published both in *Greenline* and in *Spare Rib* in the UK.
4. Turnstone Press, London, 1984.
5. For Theosophist writings by A P Sinnett, see the bibliography.
6. W I Thompson, *Passages About the Earth*.
7. Helena Blavatsky, *The Secret Doctrine: The Synthesis of Science, Religion and Philosophy – Key to the Mysteries of the Ancient and Modern Science of Theology*, original version in six volumes, 1888. Abridged version by Elisabeth Preston and Christmas Humphreys, 1964.
8. From the abridged version of *The Secret Doctrine*, p. 159.
9. *Ibid.*, p. 172.
10. *Ibid.*, p. 163.
11. From Blavatsky's discussion on 'The Civilization and Destruction of the Third and Fourth Race', in *The Secret Doctrine* (abridged version), pp. 224–34.
12. *Ibid.*, p. 28.
13. Nigel Pennick, *Hitler's Secret Sciences – His Quest for the Hidden Knowledge of the Ancients*, Neville Spearman, Saffron Walden, 1981, pp. 132–3.
14. Annie Besant, *An Autobiography*, Nasanta Press, Adyar, Madras, 1893.
15. Merlin Stone has much information about this in her *Paradise Papers (When God Was a Woman)*; see also, Monica Sjöö and Barbara Mor, *The Great Cosmic Mother: Rediscovering the Religion of the Earth*.
16. Avon Books, New York, 1961.
17. See Val Remy, 'The Legal Right to Steal, Burn and Kill: the Criminal Fraternity and its Men's Huts States', PAN, 1986.
18. Sir John R Sinclair, *The Alice Bailey Inheritance*, Turnstone Press, London, 1984.
19. Lucis Press, London, 1925.
20. It is suggested that these Secret Masters direct world events and human evolution by influencing the minds of key people through visions and dreams and sudden flashes of insight

and inspiration. For instance, Niels Bohr, the Danish physicist, 'saw' the structure of the atom in a dream.

21 Alice Bailey, *The Externalisation of the Hierarchy*, Lucis Press, London, 1957, p. 497. In the same book, DK says in connection with the release of atomic energy: 'I would like at this time to touch upon the greatest spiritual event which has taken place since the fourth kingdom of nature, the human kingdom, appeared. I refer to the release of atomic energy as related in the newspapers this week, August 6, 1945, in connection with the bombing of Japan.' DK says that scientists are impressed by and motivated from Shambhala 'and scientific work is then started and carried through into the stages of experimentation and final success', pp. 492–3.

22 See the bibliography for a list of Brian Easlea's books. Easlea has taught on science and gender studies at the Department of History and Social Science at the University of Sussex. This department was closed in 1987 and Easlea was forced to take 'early retirement'.

23 An important book by Carolyn Merchant, *The Death of Nature: Women, Ecology and the Scientific Revolution*, Harper & Row, San Francisco, 1980.

24 Brian Easlea, *Science and Sexual Oppression – Patriarchy's Confrontation with Women and Nature*, Weidenfeld & Nicholson, London 1981, pp. 120–1. Bacon (1561–1626) was the 'Father of Modern Science' and was the inspiration behind the Royal Society founded in 1660.

25 See Lindsay River and Sally Gillespie, *The Knot of Time – Astrology and Female Experience*, The Women's Press, London, 1987.

26 Souvenir Press, London, 1988.

27 Taken from the title of the book by Dr Thelma Moss, *The Body Electric: A Personal Journey into the Mysteries of Parapsychology and Kirlian Photography*, Routledge & Kegan Paul, 1976.

28 Both published by Souvenir Press, London, 1972 and 1974 respectively.

29 See the Bibliography for the many books of Seth speaking through Jane Roberts. Bob Stewart also discusses Secret Masters in his new book *Celebrating Male Mysteries*, published in 1991. He considers such beliefs to be a barrier to true spiritual realisation and that they are based in patriarchal men's lust for power, longevity and immortality.

30 See *Clairvoyant Reality: Towards a General Theory of the Paranormal*, Turnstone Press, Wellingborough, Northants, 1980; also *From Newton to ESP: Parapsychology and the Challenge of Modern Science*, Turnstone Press, Wellingborough, Northants, 1984.

31 Chief Seattle of the Suwamish tribe wrote this in a letter to the President of the USA in 1854. The letter was quoted by Ed McGaa/Eagle Man in the Introduction to his book, *Mother Earth Spirituality*.
32 David Spangler, *Revelation: The Birth of a New Age*, Findhorn Press, Findhorn, 1975.
33 Both published by Findhorn Press 1977 and 1980, respectively.
34 David Spangler, *Explorations: Emerging Aspects of the New Culture*, pp. 70 and 87.
35 *Ibid.*, p. 61.
36 *Ibid.*, p. 98.
37 *Ibid.*, p. 164.
38 *Ibid.*, p. 99.
39 *Ibid.*, p. 93.
40 Sir John R Sinclair, *The Alice Bailey Inheritance*, pp. 88–90. On p. 89, Sinclair quotes DK as saying: 'Then, through the creative imagination and by an act of will, see untold and unlimited sums of money pouring into the hands of those who seek to do the Master's work' (From Alice Bailey, *Discipleship in the New Age*, vol. II, Lucis Press, London, 1944).
41 *Ibid.*, pp. 89–90.
42 Iona means 'dove', as does Columba. The dove was always sacred to the Goddess. The Christians adopted the dove as the sign of the Holy Ghost, which was originally Sophia or wisdom, God's female soul.
43 Findhorn Press, Findhorn, 1990.
44 Bhairava-Yamala in Ajit Mookerjee, *Tantra Art: Its Philosophy and Physics*, Kumar Gallery, New Delhi, New York and Paris, 1966–7.

5 Reclaiming the Dark Mother

1 Explored in depth in Monica Sjöö and Barbara Mor, *The Great Cosmic Mother: Rediscovering the Religion of the Earth*.
2 See Peter Redgrove and Penelope Shuttle, *The Wise Wound: Menstruation and Everywoman*, Gollancz, London, 1978. For information on the menstrual and lunar mysteries of ancient women, see *The Great Cosmic Mother*.
3 Professor P V Glob, *The Bog People*, Faber and Faber, London, 1969; see also, *The Mound People*, Faber and Faber, London, 1974.
4 Much of the information in this section on the sun and volcano/fire Goddess(es), as well as star goddesses, is from

Merlin Stone's *Ancient Mirrors of Womanhood*, vols. I and II, New Sibylline Books, New York, 1979.
5 Harper & Row, New York, 1983. Barbara Walker's many books (see the bibliography) are brimful of knowledge and witty information.
6 Cassell, London, 1976.
7 Explored further in *The Great Cosmic Mother*.
8 Serena Roney-Dougal, *Where Science and Magic Meet*, Element Books, Dorset, 1991.
9 James E Lovelock, *Gaia: A New Look at Life on Earth*.
10 Louise Lacy, *Lunaception*, Warner Books, New York, 1974.
11 Goblet d'Alviella, *The Mysteries of Eleusis*, Aquarian Press, Wellingborough, Northants, 1981.
12 Nigel Pennick, *Hitler's Secret Sciences – His Quest for the Hidden Knowledge of the Ancients*, p. 59.
13 Paul Deveraux, John Steele and David Kubrin, *Earthmind: Tuning into Gaia Theory*, Harper & Row, San Francisco, 1989.
14 Information about the vents has been taken from various articles published in issues of *New Scientist*, *Scientific American* and *National Geographic*, from 1979–1988. Betty Roszak, the feminist writer and thinker from San Francisco, first drew my attention to this extraordinary information in May 1990.
15 Paul Deveraux, *Earth Lights Revelation*.
16 See Bob Stewart's 'The Waters of the Gap: the Mythology of Aquae Sulis', Bath City Council, 1981. He comes from the magical tradition of bards and folksingers.
17 Ann Kent Rush, *Moon, Moon*, Random House, New York, 1976.
18 Arkana, Harmondsworth, 1985. Begg is a Jungian, and his book explores the locations of the black madonnas.
19 Bloomsbury, 1987.
20 This was discussed in conversation with Sig Lonegren, the Swedish-American dowser during an Oak Dragon Camp in 1989.

6 The Lord is a Consuming Fire

1 Alpine Fine Art collection, New York, USA, 1985.
2 Veronica Ions, *Indian Mythology*, Hamlyn, London, 1967.
3 Merlin Stone, *Paradise Papers*.
4 Andrée Collard, *Rape of the Wild*, The Women's Press, 1988.
5 See Vandana Shiva, *Women, Ecology and Development*, Zed Books, London, 1989.
6 Merlin Stone, *Ancient Mirrors of Womanhood*, 1976.

NOTES

7 Adele Getty, *Goddess – Mother of All Living*, Thames & Hudson, London, 1990.
8 Dictionary definition of eschatology: 'The science of the four last things: death, judgment, heaven and hell' – all of which seem appropriate here.
9 For further information about the history of the Roman Catholic Church, see Mary Condren's book *The Serpent and the Goddess: Women, Religion and Power in Celtic Ireland*.
10 See Monica Sjöö and Barbara Mor, *The Great Cosmic Mother: Rediscovering the Religion of the Earth*.
11 For further information on dowry murders, see recent issues of the Indian feminist journal *Manushi*, available in the UK and USA.
12 John Mitchell has been an initiator and prophet of the Earth Mysteries movement since the early 1970s. Unfortunately, like many writers on Earth mysteries, he uses patriarchal, phallocentric language. But his many books on ley lines and Earth mysteries are also full of very interesting and valuable knowledge.
13 Discussed in Merlin Stone's *Paradise Papers*. See also Marija Gimbutas, *Goddesses and Gods of Old Europe, 6500–3500 BC*, and *The Language of the Goddess*.
14 Merlin Stone, *Ancient Mirrors of Womanhood*, Sumerian section, p. 36.
15 *The Hymns of Zarathustra* (a translation of the *Gathas*), with an introduction and commentary by Jaques Duchesne Guillemin.
Murray, London, 1952; also, *The Teachings of The Magi: A Compendium of Zoroastrian Beliefs*, edited by Professor R C Zaehner, Allen & Unwin, London, 1956.
16 See above.
17 See R C Zaehner, p. 43.
18 Women were indeed 'men's adversaries' in early patriarchal societies. Many 'wives' of the then ruling Indo-European invaders would have belonged to the Aboriginal neolithic Goddess peoples and would have entered into enforced and unwanted marriages with memories of the destruction of their tribes and cultures vividly in their minds.
19 Veronica Ions, *Indian Mythology*.
20 See Jenny Randles, *Mind Monsters – Invaders from Inner Space*, Aquarian Press, Wellingborough, 1990.
21 Alexandra David-Neel, *Magic and Mystery in Tibet*, Souvenir Press, London, 1967. She was an extraordinary French woman who travelled alone in Tibet with her adopted Tib-

etan son, and was the first European woman to enter Lhasa in the 1920s. She was also an initiate and a scholar.

22 Dione Fortune was an initiate into the occult and a member of the Golden Dawn. She wrote many books on magic and the occult, including *Psychic Self-Defence: A Study of Occult Pathology and Criminality*, Aquarian Press, Wellingborough, 1985.

23 See the bibliography for some of H P Lovecraft's books.

24 The Crossing Press, Santa Cruz, 1987; see also Sonia Johnson, *Wildfire: Igniting the She/volution*, Wildfire Books, Alberqurque, New Mexico, 1989.

25 Stillpoint Publishing, Walpole, New Hampshire, 1985; Stillpoint Publishing, Walpole, NH, 1984, respectively.

26 The Aquarian Press, Wellingborough, 1985.

27 Hypnogogic means half waking, half sleeping – the in-between state before we fully awake or sleep, when spirits commune with us and we receive visions and sudden insights. As an artist, I know this state well. This is the time when my sons are able to reach me from the Otherworld.

28 See, for example, Judith Plant, (ed.), *Healing the Wounds: The Promise of Ecofeminism*, Greenprint, London, 1989; Leonie Caldecott and Stephanie Leland, (eds), *Reclaim the Earth: Women Speak Out for Life on Earth*, The Women's Press, London, 1983; Barbara Harford and Sarah Hopkins, *Greenham Common: Women at the Wire*, The Women's Press, London, 1984.

7 From the Rebirthing Movement to Biological Engineering

1 Carl and Stephanie Simonton, *Getting Well Again*, Bantam Books, New York, 1978.

2 I have told the story of Sean's illness and death in 'Tested by the Dark/Light Mother of the Otherworld', in the anthology *Voices of the Goddess: A Chorus of Sibyls*, Aquarian Press, Wellingborough, 1990, compiled and edited by Caitlin Matthews.

3 Celestial Arts, Berkeley, 1979.

4 With an introduction by W Y Evans-Wentz, the American Tibetan scholar. Rider, London, 1977.

5 From Leonard Orr, *Physical Immortality: The Science of Everlasting Life*, Inspiration University, Sierraville, California, 1980, p. 30.

NOTES

6 Now editor of *Self and Society*, the journal of the Humanistic Psychology Association.

7 *How to Feel Reborn? – Varieties of Rebirthing Experience*, Regeneration Press, London, 1985. There is only a limited edition of this book. I was told of its existence by John Rowan who, together with Jocelyn Chaplin, now runs the Serpent Institute giving counselling and psychotherapy based on Goddess spirituality.

8 This analysis of the Christian concept of rebirth is taken from Mary Condren's book *The Serpent and the Goddess: Women, Religion and Power in Celtic Ireland*.

9 Trinity Publications, San Francisco, 1978.

10 From Leonard Orr and Sondra Ray, *Rebirthing in the New Age*, Celestial Arts, Berkeley, 1979, p. 200.

11 Trinity Publications, San Francisco, 1983.

12 Wildwood House, Aldershot, 1975.

13 *Ibid.*, p. 24.

14 Explored in depth in Monica Sjöö and Barbara Mor, *The Great Cosmic Mother*.

15 Dick Read, *Childbirth Without Fear*, Harper & Row, New York, 1970.

16 Dr Arthur Janov, *The Primal Scream*, Abacus, London, 1973.

17 Sondra Ray, *Celebration of Birth*, Celestial Arts, Berkeley, California, 1983, p. 9.

18 Penguin, Harmondsworth, 1978; Pandora, London, 1988.

19 Trance/dream states in which visions, prophecy and wisdom were received, as well as powers of healing. Priestesses slept in underground womblike chambers in Malta, listening to the voices of the spirits or ancestors. In classical Greece until ca. 500 AD, sick pilgrims would still flock to temples of Asclepius, the god of healing, to take part in the incubation ritual. In their sleep, a strange state between sleeping and waking, the god would be seen and the disease would be healed or treatment advised.

20 See Ann Warren Davies, 'The Ancient Roots of Herbal Healing', article from 1980 issue of an alternative journal; Barbara Ehrenreich and Deirdre English, *Witches, Midwives and Nurses: A History of Women Healers*, Glass Mountain Pamphlets, The Feminist Press, New York, 1974; *Complaints and Disorders: The Sexual Politics of Sickness*, Glass Mountain Pamphlets, The Feminist Press, New York, 1974.

21 Attributed to the witchhunters Kramer and Sprenger in the fifteenth century, and taken from *Witches, Midwives and Nurses*, p. 11.

22 See Monica Sjöö and Barbara Mor, *The Great Cosmic Mother*.

23 Information from Gunnar Heinsohn, Rolph Knieper and Otto Steiger, *Menschenproduktion*, Surhkamp Verlag, Frankfurt am Main, 1979.
24 A recent critique of the alternative health and New Age movement, written from a very different perspective, is Rosalind Coward, *The Whole Truth: The Myth of Alternative Medicine*, Faber and Faber, London, 1989.
25 See Elisabeth Kübler-Ross, *On Death and Dying*, Tavistock, London, 1970; Dr Raymond Moody, *Life After Life*, Bantam Books, New York, 1975; Dr Raymond Moody, *Reflections on Life After Life*, Bantam Books, New York, 1978; Margot Grey, *Return from Death – An Exploration of the Near-Death Experience*, Arkana, Harmondsworth, 1985; David Lorimer, *Survival? Body, Mind and Death in the Light of Psychic Experience*, Routledge & Kegan Paul, London, 1984.
26 There is now a new translation called *The Awakening Osiris*, by Normande Ellis, Phanes Press, Boulder, Colorado, 1988.
27 Edited by W Y Evans-Wentz, Oxford University Press, Oxford, 1927.
28 Both books are published by Souvenir Press, London, 1975 and 1977, respectively.
29 See the bibliography for other books by Dr Elisabeth Kübler-Ross.
30 Thames & Hudson, London, 1980.
31 See Rita Arditti, Renate Duelli Klein and Shelley Minden (eds.), *Test Tube Women – What Future for Motherhood?*, Pandora, London, 1984; Patricia Spallone and Deborah Lynn Steinberg (eds.), *Made to Order – The Myth of Reproductive and Genetic Progress*, Pergamon Press, Oxford, 1986; Gina Corea, *The Mother Machine – Reproductive Technologies from Artificial Insemination to Artificial Wombs*, The Women's Press, London, 1985; also Patricia Hynes, *The Recurring Silent Spring*, Pergamon Press, Oxford, 1989.

8 Traditional Shamanism and its New Age Manifestations

1 This work, which I was told about in conversation with Geoffrey Ashe, can be found in the British Library.
2 Routledge & Kegan Paul, London, 1964.
3 Arkana, Harmondsworth, 1987.
4 Harper & Row, San Francisco, 1983; Harper & Row, San Francisco, 1991.
5 See the bibliography for Joan Halifax's books.

NOTES

6   Beacon Press, Boston, 1986. As Walter Williams is gay, I think he speaks with insight.
7   In the summer of 1990, I slept under Pentre Ifan capstone with three other women, on one dark and rainy night. As a result, my dreams were haunted by cromlechs for weeks afterwards and they inspired several of my paintings.
8   I have learnt what I know of Spider/Thought Woman and Corn Mother from Paula Gunn Allen's books, *The Sacred Hoop – Recovering the Feminine in American Indian Tradition*, and *The Woman Who Owned the Shadows*. Paula Gunn Allen is part Laguna/Pueblo/Sioux and teaches Native American Studies at the University of California in Berkeley. She is also the editor of *Spider Woman's Granddaughters*.
9   For further information, see Donald G Pike's *Anasazi: Ancient People of the Rock*, Harmony Books, New York, 1974. (Photos by David Muench.)
10 The Sinagua people lived near Sedona in Arizona from about 900–1400 AD when they deserted the settlements. According to legend they are ancestors of the Hopis.
11 The information about the 'Hopi Prophecies' was gleaned from articles in the *Glastonbury Communicator* prior to the Harmonic Convergence in 1987. It would seem that these are also not the ancient traditional Hopi prophecies – these are kept very secret and are guarded by the women Elders – but are prophecies which have been circulated since the end of the last war and were developed by a group of elders around Thomas Banyaca, the Hopi tribal chairman. It was Banyaca who gave Richard Cupidi Matthias Neitsch's paper. For additional information about the Hopis, their past and religious rituals, read Frank Waters, *The Book of the Hopis*, Penguin, Harmondsworth, 1977, which unfortunately is very patriarchal in its assumptions.
12 *Moonshine*, pagan journal.
13 For further information on US Native American history, see Jack Weatherford, *Indian Givers – How Indians of the Americas Transformed the World*, Fawcett Columbine, New York, 1988.
14 See the bibliography for a list of some of Carlos Casteneda's many books.
15 This paper was given to me in 1988 by Richard Cupidi, an Italian American who runs the radical Public House bookshop in Brighton. He in turn was given it by Thomas Bayaca, a Hopi elder, who was involved in evolving contemporary 'Hopi Prophecies'.
16 Bob Gustafson's Open Letter was sent to various US and

NEW AGE AND ARMAGEDDON

    UK journals and was published in *Wood and Water*, a London-based pagan journal, vol. 2, no. 18, summer 1986.
17 Marilyn Ferguson, *The Aquarian Conspiracy – Personal and Social Transformation in the 1980s*.
18 Waters also wrote *Mexico Mystique* in 1975 about the pre-Columbian cultures of Mexico and Guatemala.
19 See the bibliography for a list of Lynn Andrews' books.
20 She also wrote *Child of Her People*, Siren Books, London, 1987.
21 It was published in *Wood and Water*, vol. 2, no. 23, Samhain to winter solstice, 1987.
22 In this context, it is surprising just how many spirit guides of spiritualists, like Silver Birch and White Eagle, were/are 'Indian chiefs'.
23 It is ironic to note here that Anne Cameron has also since then been attacked by Native Canadian women at a Women's Book Fair in Canada.
24 Prentice-Hall, New Jersey, 1980.
25 Both published by Ballantine Books, New York, 1984 and 1983, respectively.
26 From a programme of 'Moon Owl Medicine, spring 1990', advertising seven workshops by her.
27 At the 'Challenging New Age Patriarchy' conference in Malvern, September 1990, a workshop was held entitled 'The Misuse of Sacred Sites', led by Jill Smith.
28 In this context, see *The Star People*, by Brad and Francie Steiger, Berkeley Books, New York, 1981.
29 Zed Books, London, 1989.
30 See Vandana Shiva, *Staying Alive: Women, Ecology and Survival in India*, Zed Books, London, 1988.
31 Ursula Parades and Georgina Ashworth, 'Development Crises and Alternative Visions', *Spare Rib*, London, 1990.

9 *The Harmonic Convergence*

1 Bear, New Mexico, 1987. See the bibliography for Arguelles' other books.
2 *Ibid.*, p. 36.
3 *Ibid.*, p. 33.
4 Published in the Findhorn-inspired journal *Link Up*, December 1988 and February 1989. I have heard nothing further of such a gathering.
5 The genuine and ancient Hopi Prophecies are kept secret by the women Elders, as I understand it, and have not been made public.

6 Jill and Peter First, *Pre-Columbian Art of Mexico*, Abbeville Press, New York, 1980.
7 Marija Gimbutas, *The Language of the Goddess*.
8 According to Jungian Erich Neumann in *The Great Mother: An Analysis of the Archetype*, Princeton University, Princeton Press, 1955.
9 *Ibid.*
10 *The Great Mother*, p. 208. Much of this information about Quetzalcoatl and the Goddess(es) of MesoAmerica comes from this book.
11 I find this very sinister and an outright threat to the Traditional Elders who are attempting to defend their people from exploitation by whites.
12 Note that this is the year of the Gulf War.
13 This 'Hopi Prophecy', subtitled 'A Rainbow Prophecy' was, according to the introduction by Harley Swiftdeer, 'channelled' by the women's societies of the Crystal Skull and the Black Widow. Grace Walkingstick and Ruby Morningstar are the women that Swiftdeer calls his 'grandmothers' and it would seem that the 'Prophecy' originated with the New Age 'tribe'.
14 1988.
15 It is true that Sunlight, a feminist lesbian crone, appears to have had a revelation at the time of the Harmonic Convergence in the USA, and she received a guide, or inner voice, that speaks of the Goddess. The guide told her that god is contained in Goddess and that the New Age is a way of living beyond patriarchy, that the 'new world will be one with the values and ways of women'. Sunlight has recorded her experiences and the voice of the guide in *Being: Guide to a New Way*, Earth Books, Redwood Valley, USA, 1988.
16 See Jill Smith, 'The Unharmonic Convergence', in *PAN* and *Ley Hunter* journal, 1987.
17 Roberts had a heart attack and died while walking on the Tor on 9 February, 1990 (which was the day of a lunar eclipse).
18 Fontana, London, 1981. Geoffrey Ashe quotes several pages in this book from an article I wrote called 'Treading the Maze at Glastonbury Tor', for the pagan Goddess journal, *Wood and Water*, 1981. He has written many books on the Arthurian legends, as well as *The Virgin: Mary's Cult and the Re-Emergence of the Goddess*, Arkana, Harmondsworth, 1988.
19 *The Glastonbury Tor Maze*, pamphlet, Glastonbury, 1980.
20 See the bibliography for a list of John Michell's books.
21 Nick Mann, in *The Cauldron and the Grail* and *Glastonbury Tor*,

both pamphlets published locally in Glastonbury in 1985 and 1986, respectively.

22 Jill Smith wrote an article, published in *PAN* and *Ley Hunter* journals, called 'The Unharmonic Convergence'. In it she discusses her misgivings concerning groups of American 'Metaphysical Jetsetters' who travelled the globe to sacred sites at the time of the 'Harmonic Convergence'. Such a group arrived at the Callanish stone circle on Lewis, where Jill lives in the Outer Hebrides, claiming to 'cleanse and heal' the stones. Jill felt this was an incredible arrogant affront to these magical stones which heal and awaken us if we but listen and dream.

10 False Transcendence: The Gurus or the Goddess?

1 Harrap, London, 1973.
2 Glastonbury, 1978. Unfortunately, it seems that Roberts considered the re-emerging Goddess movement a front for the return of the forces of darkness, characterising Black Isis as demonic, etc.
3 See the bibliography and chapter 5. Another book dwelling on occult horrors is Louis Pauwels and Jaques Bergier, *The Morning of the Magicians*, Avon Books, New York, 1961.
4 See Paul Deveraux, *Earth Lights Revelation*, and *Places of Power*.
5 My friend will have to remain anonymous because of possible danger to her.
6 Information from Doreen Valiente. See the bibliography for a list of her works.
7 No. 23, Spring, 1989.
8 This sign is, when used singly, which is how Zelleck uses it, the ancient sig rune which signifies the sun and flash from heaven journeying over the deep. It signifies the quest, revelation and shamanic descent.
9 Letter in January 1990.
10 Shekhinah Foundation, Australia, October, 1987.
11 Rupert Sheldrake, *A New Science of Life: The Hypothesis of Formative Causation*, Blond & Briggs, London, 1981. Not having read the book, I cannot comment on it.
12 The hundredth monkey syndrome: the story goes that a female monkey somewhere on an island somehow found out that to wash potatoes makes them more edible. Shortly afterwards, all the other monkeys on the island were also

washing their potatoes. It was, however, also found that when a fair number of monkeys were doing this, monkeys on other islands who had had no contact with the original potato-washing monkeys, also knew how to, and were doing, this. A certain critical mass had been reached in monkey consciousness. This is a very popular tale in the New Age movement.

13 The Fellowship of Isis is based in Ireland and has members all over the world.

Bibliography

Books

Adler, Margot, *Drawing Down the Moon*, Beacon Press, Boston, 1979.

Albery, Nicholas, *How to Feel Reborn? – Varieties of Rebirthing Experience*, Regeneration Press, London, 1985.

Alic, Margaret, *Hypatia's Heritage – A History of Women in Science from Antiquity to the Late 19th Century*, The Women's Press, London, 1986.

Allione, Tsultrim *Women of Wisdom*, Routledge & Kegan Paul, London, 1984.

d'Alviella, Goblet, *The Mysteries of Eleusis*, Aquarian Press, Wellingborough, Northants, 1981.

Andrews, Lynn, *Medicine Woman*, Harper & Row, San Francisco, 1981.

Flight of the Seventh Moon – the Teaching of the Shields, Routledge & Kegan Paul, London, 1984.

Jaguar Woman, Harper & Row, San Francisco, 1986.

Star Woman, Klein, 1986.

Teachings Around The Wheel, Harper & Row, San Francisco, 1980.

Arditti, Rita, Duelli Klein, Renate, Minden, Shelley (eds.), *Test Tube Women – What Future for Motherhood?*, Pandora Press, London, 1984.

Argüelles, José, *The Mayan Factor – Path Beyond Technology*, Bear, New Mexico, 1987.

Mandala, Shambhala, Berkeley, 1972.

The Transformative Vision: Reflections on the Nature and History of Human Expression, Shambhala, Berkeley, 1975.

Earth Ascending: An Illustrated Treatise on the Law Governing Whole Systems, Shambhala, Boulder, 1984.

BIBLIOGRAPHY

Ashe, Geoffrey, *Avalonian Quest*, Fontana, London, 1981.

Mythology of the British Isles, Methuen, London, 1990.

The Virgin: Mary's Cult and the Re-emergence of the Goddess, Routledge & Kegan Paul, London, 1976.

The Ancient Wisdom, Abacus Books, Tunbridge Wells, 1979.

Bailey, Alice, *A Treatise on Cosmic Fire*, Lucis Press, London, 1925; Lucis Publishing, New York, 1982.

Discipleship in the New Age, Lucis Press, London, 1944.

The Externalisation of the Hierarchy, Lucis Press, London, 1957.

Barbanell, Maurice, *The Case of Helen Duncan*, Spiritualist Press, London, 1945.

This is Spiritualism, Herbert Jenkins Ltd, London, 1959.

Begg, Ean, *The Cult of the Black Virgin*, Arkana, Harmondsworth, 1985.

Bell, Diane, *Daughters of the Dreaming*, George Allen & Unwin, Australia Pty Ltd, 1983.

Bender, George A, *Great Moments in Medicine*, Parke-Davis, Detroit, 1961.

Bernal, Martin, *Black Athena: The Afro-Asiatic Roots of Classical Civilisation*, Free Association Books, London 1987.

Besant, Annie, *An Autobiography*, Nasanta Press, Adyar, Madras, 1893–1983.

Blavatsky, Helena, *Isis Unveiled*, 1877.

The Secret Doctrine – the Synthesis of Science, Religion and Philosophy, Theosophist Society, Theosophy Co., Los Angeles, 1947.

Bloom, William, (ed.), *The New Age: An Anthology of Essential Writings*, Rider, London, 1991.

Board, Janet and Colin, *Sacred Waters – Holy Wells and Waterlore in Britain and Ireland*, Paladin Books, London, 1986.

Earth Rites – Fertility Practices in Pre-industrial Britain, Paladin Books, London, 1983.

Borgia, Anthony, *Life in the World Unseen*, Odhams Press, London, 1954.

More About the World Unseen, Psychic Press, London, 1956.

Boserup, Esther, *Women's Role in Economic Development*, Allen & Unwin, London, 1970.

Boucher, Sandy, *Turning the Wheel – American Women Creating the New Buddhism*, Harper & Row, San Francisco, 1988.

Brennan, Martin, *The Boyne Valley Vision*, Dolmen Press, London, 1980.

Brighton Women and Science Group, *Alice through the Microscope – the Power of Science over Women's Lives*, Virago, London, 1980.

Brown, Dee, *Bury My Heart at Wounded Knee – an Indian History of the American West*, Picador, London, 1972.

Budapest, Zsuzsanna, *The Holy Book of Women's Mysteries*, Part 1, Susan B. Anthony Coven, Oakland, CA, 1979.

The Holy Book of Women's Mysteries, Part II, Susan B Anthony, Coven, Los Angeles, CA.

The Grandmother of Time: A Woman's Book of Celebrations, Spells, and Sacred Objects for Every Month of the Year, Harper & Row, San Francisco, 1989.

Caddy, Eileen, *Flight to Freedom*, Element Books, Dorset, 1988.

God Spoke to Me, Findhorn Press, Findhorn, 1971

The Foundation of Findhorn, Findhorn Press, Findhorn.

Caldecott, Leonie and Leland, Stephanie, (eds), *Reclaim the Earth: Women Speak Out for Life on Earth*, The Women's Press, London, 1983.

Cameron, Anne, *Daughters of Copperwoman*, The Women's Press, London, 1984.

Child of Her People, Siren Books, London, 1987.

Capra, Fritiof, *The Tao of Physics*, Wildwood House, Aldershot, 1975.

Turning Point – Science, Society and the Rising Culture, Wildwood House, Aldershot, 1982.

Uncommon Wisdom – Conversations with Remarkable People, Rider, London, 1988.

Carson, Rachel, *The Silent Spring*, Houghton Mifflin, Boston, 1962.

Castenada, Carlos, *The Teachings of Don Juan: A Yaqui Way of Knowledge*, Penguin, Harmondsworth, 1970.

A Separate Reality, Penguin, Harmondsworth, 1973.

Journey to Ixtlan, Penguin, Harmondsworth, 1974.

Tales of Power, Arkana, Harmondsworth, 1990.

The Second Ring of Power, Arkana, Harmondsworth, 1990.

The Fire from Within, Transworld, London, 1985.

The Eagle's Gift, Penguin, Harmondsworth, 1982.

The Power of Silence, Transworld, London, 1987.

Chardin, Teilhard de, *The Future of Man*, Harper & Row, New York, 1964.

Churchill, Ward, (ed.) *Marxism and Native Americans*, South End Press, Boston, MA, 1982.

Collard, Andrée, (with Joyce Contrucci) *Rape of the Wild*, The Women's Press, London, 1988.

Condren, Mary, *The Serpent and the Goddess – Women, Religion and Power in Celtic Ireland*, Harper & Son, San Francisco, 1989.

Cook, Grace, *The Gentle Brother – White Eagle*, H. K. White Eagle Publications, Hampshire, 1968.

Prayers of the New Age, (published by the same) 1957.

The New Mediumship, (published by the same) 1965.

The Way of the Sun, (published by the same) 1982.

The Illumined Ones – Memories of Reincarnation, (published by the same) 1966.

Jesus, Teacher and Healer: from White Eagle's Teachings, (published by the same) 1986.

Sun Men of Americas, White Eagle Pub. Trust, Hampshire, 1988.

Cooke, Grace; Cooke, Ivan, *The Light of Britain: A Vision of the Ancient Spiritual Centres of Britain*, White Eagle Pub. Trust, Hampshire, 1985.

Corea, Gena, *The Mother Machine: Reproductive Technologies from Artificial Insemination to Artificial Wombs*, Harper & Row, San Francisco, 1985.

The Hidden Malpractice: How American Medicine Mistreats Women, Morrow, New York, 1977.

Embryos, Ethics and Women's Rights, Haworth, 1988.

Man Made Woman et al, Indianna University Press, Indianna 1987.

Coward, Rosalind, *The Whole Truth: the Myth of Alternative Health*, Faber and Faber, London, 1989.

Crowley, Aleister, *Magic in Theory and Practice*, Routledge & Kegan Paul, London, 1973.

Czaplicka, Marie Antoinette, *Aboriginal Siberia*, 1914.

Cumbey, Constance, *The Hidden Dangers of the Rainbow: The New Age Movement and our Coming Age of Barbarians*, Huntington House, Inc., Louisiana, 1983.

Dames, Michael, *Silbury Treasure – the Great Goddess Rediscovered*, Thames and Hudson, London, 1976.

Avebury Circle, Thames and Hudson, London, 1977.

David-Neel, Alexandra, *Magic and Mystery in Tibet*, 1931, Souvenir Press, London, 1967.

Davidson, Basil, *Africa in History* Paladin Books, London 1974.

Deren, Maya, *The Voodoo Gods/Divine Horsemen*, Thames and Hudson, London, 1953.

Deveraux, Paul, *Earth Lights Revelation*, Blandford Press, Dorset, 1989.

Earthmind: Tuning into Gaia Theory, with John Steele and David Kubrim, Harper & Row, New York, 1989.

Places of Power: Secret Energies at Ancient Sites, Blandford Press, Dorset, 1990.

Easlea, Brian, *Witch-hunting, Magic and the New Philosophy*, Harvester Press, Brighton, 1980.

Science and Sexual Oppression – Patriarchy's Confrontation with Woman and Nature, Weidenfeld & Nicolson, London, 1981.

Fathering the Unthinkable – Masculinity, Scientists and the Nuclear Arms Race, Pluto Press, London, 1982.

Ehrenberg, Margaret, *Women in Prehistory*, British Museum Publications, London, 1989.

Ehrenreich, Barbara; English, Deirdre, *Witches, Midwives and Nurses, A History of Women Healers*, Glass Mountain Pamphlets, Feminist Press, New York, 1974.

Complaints and Disorders – The Sexual Politics of Sickness, Glass Mountain Pamphlets, Feminist Press, New York, 1974.

For Her Own Good: 150 years of the Expert's Advice to Women, Anchor Press, 1978.

Eliade, Mircea, *Shamanism – Archaic Techniques of Ecstacy*, Routledge & Kegan Paul, London, 1964.

Myths, Dreams and Mysteries, Harvill Press, 1960.

Ellis, Normande, *The Awakening Osiris*, Phanes Press, Boulder, Colorado, 1988.

Enzensberger, Hans Magnus, *Raids and Reconstructions – Essays in Politics, Crime and Culture*, Pluto Press, London, 1976.

Ereira, Alan, *The Heart of the World*, Cape, London, 1990.

Evans, Arthur, *Witchcraft and the Gay Counterculture*, Fag Rag Books, Boston, USA, 1978.

Evans, Dr Christopher, *Cults of Unreason*, Harrap, London, 1973.

Evans-Wentz, W. Y., *The Fairy-Faith in Celtic Countries*, Colin Smyth, Buckinghamshire, 1988.

Tibet's Great Yogi, Milarepa – A Biography from the Tibetan (ed.), Oxford University Press, Oxford, 1969.

The Tibetan Book of the Dead/Bardo Thödol or Liberation by Hearing on The After-Death Plane (ed.), Oxford University Press, Oxford, 1927.

Ferguson, Marilyn, *The Aquarian Conspiracy – Personal and Social Transformation in the 1980s*, Paladin Books, London, 1982.

First, Jill and Peter, *Pre-Columbian Art of Mexico*, Abbeyville Press, New York, 1980.

Fortune, Dione, *Psychic Self-defence, a Study of Occult Pathology and Criminality*, Aquarian Press, Wellingborough, Northants, 1985.

Through The Gates of Death – Spiritualism in the Light of Occult Science, Aquarian Press, Wellingborough, Northants, 1987.

George, Susan, *How the Other Half Dies: the Real Reasons for World Hunger*, Penguin Books, Harmondsworth, 1976.

A Fate Worse than Debt, Penguin Books, Harmondsworth, 1988.

The Hunger Machine, with John Bennett, Polity Press, London, 1987.

Getty, Adele, *Goddess – Mother of All Living*, Thames & Hudson, London, 1990.

Gimbutas, Marija, *Goddesses and Gods of Old Europe, 6500–3500 BC*, Thames and Hudson, London, 1982.

The Language of the Goddess, Harper & Row, San Francisco, 1989.

The Civilization of the Goddess: The World of Old Europe, edited with Joan Marler, Harper & Row, San Francisco, 1991.

Glaeson, Judith, *Oya – In Praise of the Goddess*, Shambhala, Boston, 1987.

Glob, P. V., *The Bog People*, Faber and Faber, London, 1969.

The Mound People, Faber and Faber, London, 1974.

Graves, Robert, *The White Goddess – a Historical Grammar of Poetic Myth*, Faber and Faber, London, 1948.

Grey, Margot, *Return from Death – an Exploration of the Near-Death Experience*, Arkana, Harmondsworth, 1985.

Grof, Stanislaf; Halifax, Joan, *The Human Encounter with Death*, Souvenir Press, London, 1977.

Realms of the Human Unconscious – Observations from LSD Research, Souvenir Press, London, 1975.

Beyond Death – the Gates of Consciousness, with Christina Grof, Thames and Hudson, London, 1980.

Gunn Allen, Paula, *The Sacred Hoop – Recovering the Feminine in American Tradition*, Beacon Press, Boston, 1986.

The Woman Who Owned the Shadows, Spinsters ink, San Francisco, 1983.

(ed.) *Spider Woman's Granddaughters*, The Women's Press, London, 1990.

Gyatso, Janet, *Feminine Ground: Essays on Women in Tibet*, Snow Lion Publications, New York, 1989.

Halifax, Joan, *Shamanic Voices: the Shaman as Seer, Poet, and Healer*, Penguin Books, Harmondsworth, 1980.

Shaman – The Wounded Healer, Thames and Hudson, London, 1982.

Harford, Barbara; Hopkins, Sarah, *Greenham Common Women at the Wire*, The Women's Press, London, 1984.

Hitching, S, Francis, *Earth Magic*, Cassell & Co., London, 1976.

Pendulum: the PSI Connection, Fontana, London, 1977.

Hynes, Patricia, *The Recurring Silent Spring*, Pergamon Press, Oxford, 1989.

Ions, Veronica, *Indian Mythology*, Hamlyn, London, 1967.

Jamal, Michelle, *Shape Shifters – Shaman Women in Contemporary Society*, Arkana, Harmondsworth, 1987.

Janov, Dr Arthur, *The Primal Scream*, Abacus, London, 1973.

The Anatomy of Mental Illness, Abacus, 1978.

Johnson, Sonia, *Going Out of Our Minds: the Metaphysics of Liberation*, The Crossing Press, Santa Cruz, 1987.

From Housewife to Heretic, Doubleday, New York, 1981.

Wildfire: Igniting the She/volution, Wildfire Books, New Mexico, 1989.

Kitzinger, Sheila, *The Experience of Childbirth*, Penguin, Harmondsworth, 1978.

The New Pregnancy and Childbirth, Penguin Books, Harmondsworth, 1980.

The Midwife Challenge, (ed.) Pandora Press, London, 1988.

Kübler-Ross, Elisabeth, *On Death and Dying*, Tavistock, London, 1970.

Death: The Final Stages of Growth, Prentice-Hall, New Jersey, 1978.

Lacy, Louise, *Lunaception*, Warner Books, New York, 1974.

Laut, Phil, *Money is My Friend*, Trinity Publications, San Francisco, 1978.

Leboyer, Frédéric, *Birth without Violence*, Wildwood House, Aldershot, 1975.

Leonard, Jim, Laut, Phil, *Rebirthing – the Science of Enjoying All of Your Life*, Trinity Publications, San Francisco, 1983.

Le Shan, Lawrence, *Clairvoyant Reality – Towards a General Theory of the Paranormal*, Turnstone Press, Wellingborough, 1980.

From Newton to ESP – Parapsychology and the Challenge of Modern Science, Turnstone Press, Wellingborough, 1984.

How to Meditate, Wellingborough, 1974.

Einstein's Space and Van Gogh's Sky – Physical Reality and Beyond, with Henry Margenau, MacMillan, New York, 1982.

Lorimer, David, *Survival? Body, Mind and Death in the Light of Psychic Experience*, Routledge & Kegan Paul, London, 1984.

Lourde, Audre, *The Cancer Journals*, Sheba, London, 1989.

Lovecraft, H. P., *The Haunter of the Dark and other Tales of Horror*, Panther Books, London, 1963.

The Shadow out of Time and other Tales of Horror, Gollancz, London, 1968.

Lovelock, James E., *Gaia: A New Look at Life on Earth*, Oxford University Press, Oxford, 1979.

Lurker, Manfred, *The Gods and Symbols of Ancient Egypt – an Illustrated Dictionary*, Thames and Hudson, London, 1980.

McCrickard, Janet, *Eclipse of the Sun*, Gothic Image, Glastonbury, 1990.

McGaa, Ed/Eagle Man, *Mother Earth Spirituality*, Harper & Row, San Francisco, 1989.

McLuhan, Marshall, *Understanding Media: The Extensions of Man*, McGraw Hill, New York, 1965.

Mann, Nick, *The Cauldron and the Grail*, Annenterprise, Glastonbury, 1985.

Glastonbury Tor, Pamphlets published in Glastonbury, 1986.

Sedona Sacred Earth, Zurah, Arizona, 1989.

Manning, Matthew, *The Link – the Extraordinary Gifts of a Teenage Psychic*, Colin Smythe, Gerrards Cross, Bucks, 1974.

The Strangers – my Conversations with a Ghost, W. H. Allen, London, 1974.

Matthews, Caitlin, *The Elements of the Goddess*, Element Books, Dorset, 1989.

The Celtic Tradition, Element Books, Dorset, 1989.

Voices of the Goddess: A Chorus of Sibyls, (ed.), Aquarian Press, Wellingborough, Northants, 1990.

Sophia, Goddess of Wisdom, Thorsons, London, 1991.

Matthews, Caitlin; Jones, Prudence, (eds), *Voices from the Circle*, Aquarian Press, Wellingborough, Northants, 1990.

Matthews, Caitlin and John, *The Western Way: a Practical Guide to the Western Mystery Tradition*, Arkana, an imprint of Penguin Books Ltd, Harmondsworth, 1985.

Merchant, Carolyn, *The Death of Nature: Women, Ecology and the Scientific Revolution*, Harper & Row, New York, 1980.

Michell, John, *The New View Over Atlantis*, Abacus, an imprint of Sphere Books Ltd, London, 1973.

City of Revelation – a Book of Forgotten Wisdom, Ballantine Books 1972.

The Earth Spirit: Its Ways, Shrines and Mysteries, Thames & Hudson, London, 1975.

Mode, Heinz and Chandra, Subodh, *Indian Folk Art*, Alpine Fine Art Collection, New York, 1985.

Moody, Dr Raymond, *Life after Life*, Bantam Books, New York, 1975.

Reflections on Life after Life, Bantam Books, New York, 1978.

Mookerjee, Ajit, *Tantra Art: Its Philosophy and Physics*, Kumar Gallery, New Delhi, New York and Paris, 1966–7.

Kali: The Feminine Force, Thames & Hudson, London, 1988.

Monroe, Robert A., *Journeys Out of the Body*, Souvenir Press, London, 1972.

Far Journeys, Souvenir Press, London, 1974.

Moss, Dr Thelma, *The Probability of the Impossible – Scientific Discoveries and Explorations in the Psychic World*, Routledge & Kegan Paul, London, 1976.

The Body Electric: A Personal Journey into the Mysteries of Parapsychology and Kirlian Photography, Routledge & Kegan Paul, London, 1976.

Neumann, Erich, *The Origins and History of Consciousness*, Princeton University Press, Princeton, 1970.

The Great Mother: an Analysis of the Archetype, Princeton University Press, Princeton, 1955.

Nietzsche, Friedrich, *Thus Spake Zarathustra*, Everyman's Library, an imprint of J. M. Dent & Sons Ltd, London, 1958.

Noble, Vicki, *Motherpeace – a Way to the Goddess Through Myth, Art and Tarot*, Harper & Row, San Francisco 1983.

Shakti Woman, Harper & Row, San Francisco, 1991.

Noyes, Ralph (ed.) *The Crop Circle Enigma: grounding the phenomenon in science, culture and metaphysics*, Gateway Books, Bath, 1990.

Orr, Leonard, *Physical Immortality: The Science of Everlasting Life*, Inspiration University, Sierraville, California, 1980–8.

Orr, Leonard and Ray, Sondra, *Rebirthing in the New Age*, Celestial Arts, Berkeley, 1979.

Owen, Alex, *The Darkened Room – Women, Power and Spiritualism in Late Victorian England*, Virago, London, 1989.

Pagels, Elaine, *The Gnostic Gospels*, Penguin Books, Harmondsworth, 1982.

Patai, Raphael, *The Hebrew Goddess*, Avon Books, New York, 1978.

Pauwels, Louis, Bergier, Jacques, *The Morning of the Magicians*, Avon Books, New York, 1961.

Pennick, Nigel, *Hitler's Secret Sciences – his Quest for the Hidden Knowledge of the Ancients*, Neville Spearman, an imprint of the C. W. Daniel Company Ltd, Saffron Walden, 1981.

The Subterranean Kingdom – a Survey of Man-made Structures Beneath the Earth, Turnstone Press, London, 1981.

The Ancient Science of Geomancy, Thames and Hudson, London, 1979.

Pike, Donald G, *Anasazi: Ancient People of the Rock*, Harmony Books, New York, 1974.

Plant, Judith, (ed.), *Healing the Wounds: The Promise of EcoFeminism*, Greenprint, London, 1989.

Mind Monsters – Invaders from Inner Space, Aquarian Press, Wellingborough, Northants, 1990.

Plaskow, Judith, *Standing Again at Sinai, Judaism from a Feminist Perspective*, Harper & Row, San Francisco, 1990.

Ray, Sondra, *Celebration of Birth*, Celestial Arts, Berkeley, CA, 1983.

Read, Dick, *Childbirth Without Fear*, Harper & Row, New York, 1970.

Redgrove, Peter, *The Black Goddess and the Sixth Sense*, Bloomsbury, London, 1987.

Redgrove, Peter and Shuttle, Penelope, *The Wise Wound: Menstruation and Everywoman*, Gollancz, London, 1978.

Richardson, Alan, *The Magical Life of Dion Fortune*, Aquarian Press, Wellingborough, Northants, 1987.

Riddell, Carol, *The Findhorn Community – Creating a Human Identity for the Twenty-First Century*, Findhorn Press, Findhorn, 1990.

River, Lindsay and Gillespie, Sally, *The Knot of Time – Astrology and Female Experience*, The Women's Press, London, 1987.

Robbins, Don, *The Secret Language of Stone*, Rider, London, 1988.

Circles of Silence, Souvenir Press, London, 1985.

Roberts, Anthony, and Gilbertson, Geoff, *The Dark Gods*, Hutchinson, London, 1980.

Roberts, Estelle, *Fifty Years as a Medium*, 1969.

Roberts, Jane, *The Seth Material*, Prentice-Hall, New Jersey, 1970.

Seth Speaks: The Eternal Validity of the Soul, Prentice-Hall, New Jersey, 1972.

The World View of Paul Cézanne: a Psychic Interpretation, Prentice-Hall, New Jersey, 1977.

The Nature of the Psyche: Its Human Expression, Prentice-Hall, New Jersey, 1979.

Robinson, Hilary (ed) *Visibly Female: Feminism and Art Today*, Camden Press, London, 1987.

Roney-Dougal, Serena, *Where Science and Magic Meet*, Element Books, Dorset, 1991.

Rush, Ann Kent, *Moon, Moon*, Random House, New York, 1976.

Russell, Peter, *The Earth Awakening – the Global Brain*, Arkana, an imprint of Penguin Books, Ltd, Harmondsworth, 1988.

Saunders, Lesley, (ed.) *Glancing Fires: An Investigation into Women's Creativity*, The Women's Press, London, 1987.

Shucman, Helen *A Course in Miracles*, Arkana, Harmondsworth, 1976.

Schure, Edouard, *The Great Initiates: A Study of the Secret History of Religions*, Rudolf Steiner Publications/Harper & Row, San Francisco, 1961.

Shallis, Michael, *The Electric Shock Book*, Souvenir Press, London, 1988.

Sheldrake, Rupert, *A New Science of Life: the Hypothesis of Formative Causation*, Blond & Briggs, London, 1981.

Shiva, Vandana, *Staying Alive: Women, Ecology and Survival in India*, Zed Books, London, 1988.

Women, Ecology and Development, Zed Books, London, 1989.

Simonton, Carl and Stephanie, *Getting Well Again*, Bantam Books, New York, 1978.

Sinclair, Sir John R., *The Alice Bailey Inheritance*, Turnstone Press, London, 1984.

Sinnett, A. P., *The Occult World*, Theosophical Publishing Society, London, 1906.

Esoteric Buddhism, Theosophical Publishing Society, Madras, 1898.

Letters from the Masters of Wisdom, Theosophical Society, Adywar, India, 1925.

Sjöö, Monica and Mor, Barbara, *The Great Cosmic Mother: Rediscovering the Religion of the Earth*, Harper & Row, San Francisco, 1987. Extended by Barbara Mor from *The Ancient Religion of the Great Cosmic Mother of All* (published 1981 by Rainbow Press in Trondheim, Norway). Original pamphlet by Monica Sjöö, written in 1976.

Spallone, Patricia and Steinberg, Deborah Lynn (eds), *Made to Order – The Myth of Reproductive and Genetic Progress*, Pergamon Press, Oxford, 1986.

Spangler, David, *Revelation: The Birth of New Age*, The Findhorn Press, Findhorn, 1975.

Towards a Planetary Vision, Findhorn Press, Findhorn, 1977.

Explorations: Emerging Aspects of the New Culture, Findhorn Press, Findhorn, 1980.

Starhawk, *The Spiral Dance: A Rebirth of the Ancient Religion of the Great Goddess: Rituals, Invocations, Exercises, Magic,*, Harper & Row, San Francisco, 1989.

Dreaming the Dark: Magic, Sex and Politics, Beacon Press, Boston, 1982.

Truth or Dare: Encounters with Power, Authority and Mystery, Harper & Row, San Francisco, 1987.

Steiger, Brad; Steiger, Francie, *The Star People*, Berkeley Books, New York, 1981.

Steiner, Rudolf, *Christianity as Mystical Fact and the Mysteries of Antiquity*, Steiner Press, London 1972.

Christ and the Spiritual World: Search for the Holy Grail, Steiner Press, London, 1965.

Stewart, Bob, *The Underworld Initiation: A Journey Towards Psychic Transformation*, Aquarian Press, Wellingborough, Northants, 1985.

Stewart, B. ed., *Psychology and the Spiritual Tradition*, Element Books, London, 1990.

Stewart, R. J. *Robert Kirk: Walker Between the Worlds*, Element Books, London, 1990.

Celtic Gods, Celtic Goddesses, Blandford Press, Dorset, 1990.

The Mystic Life of Merlin, Arkana, Harmondsworth, 1987.

The Prophetic Vision of Merlin, Arkana, Harmondsworth, 1987.

Celebrating Male Mysteries, 1991.

Prophecy, Element Books, Dorset, 1990.

Stewart-Park, Angela and Cassidy, Jules, *We're Here: Conversations with Lesbian Women*, Quartet Books, London, 1977.

Stone, Merlin, *Paradise Papers (When God was a Woman)*, Virago, London, 1976.

Ancient Mirrors of Womenhood, vols I and II, New Sibylline Books, New York, 1979.

Storm, Hyemeyohsts, *Seven Arrows*, Ballantine Books, New York, 1985.

Song of Heyoehkah, Ballantine Books, 1983.

Storm, Stella (ed.), *The Philosophy of Silver Birch*, Psychic Press, London; reprinted 1989.

Sun Bear and Wabun, *Buffalo Hearts*, Bear Tribe Publishing, New Jersey, 1988.

The Medicine Wheel – Earth Astrology, Prentice-Hall, New Jersey, 1980.

Sunlight, *Being: Guide to A New Way*, Earth Books, Redwood Valley, USA, 1988.

Swaffer, Hannen, *Teachings of Silver Birch*, Psychic Press, London, 1938.

Teish, Luisah, *Jambalaya – the Natural Woman's Book of Personal Charms and Practical Rituals*, Harper & Row, San Francisco, 1988.

Teubal, Savina J., *Sarah the Priestess – the First Matriarch of Genesis*, Swallow Press, Athens, Ohio, 1984.

Thom, Alexander, *Megalithic Lunar Observatories*, Oxford University Press, Oxford, 1971.

Thompson, William Irwin, *Passages about the Earth – an Exploration of the New Planetary Culture*, Rider, London, 1973.

The Time Falling Bodies Take to Light: Mythology, Sexuality and the Origins of Culture, St Martin's Press, New York, 1981.

Timms, Moira, *The Six o'Clock Bus: A Guide to Armageddon and the New Age*, Turnstone Books, London, 1971.

Trevelyan, Sir George, *Operation Redemption*, Stillpoint Publishing, Walpole, New Hampshire, 1985.

A Vision of the Aquarian Age, Stillpoint Publishing, Walpole, New Hampshire, 1984.

Summons to a High Crusade, The Findhorn Press, Findhorn.

Magic Casements, Coventure Ltd, London, 1980.

Valiente, Doreen, *Witchcraft for Tomorrow*, Robert Hale, London, 1978.

The ABC of Witchcraft, Abacus, an imprint of Sphere Books Ltd, London, 1972.

The Rebirth of Witchcraft, Robert Hale, London, 1989.

Walker, Barbara, *The Woman's Dictionary of Symbols and Sacred Objects*, Harper & Row, San Francisco, 1988.

The Woman's Encyclopedia of Myths and Legends, Harper & Row, San Francisco, 1983.

The Crone: Woman of Age, Wisdom and Power, Harper & Row, San Francisco, 1985.

The Sceptical Feminist – Discovering the Virgin, Mother and Crone, Harper & Row, San Francisco, 1987.

The Book of Sacred Stones – Fact and Fallacy in the Crystal, Harper & Row, San Francisco, 1989.

Women's Rituals, Harper & Row, San Francisco, 1990.

Waters, Frank, *The Book of Hopis*, Penguin Books, Harmondsworth, 1977.

Weatherford, Jack *Indian Givers: How the Indians of the Americas Transformed the World*, Fawcett Columbine, New York, 1988.

Williams, Walter, L., *The Spirit and the Flesh – Sexual Diversity in American Indian Culture*, Beacon Press, Boston, 1986.

Wilson, Colin, *Rudolf Steiner, the Man and His Vision*, The Aquarian Press, Wellingborough, 1985.

Mysteries – an Investigation into the Occult, the Paranormal and the Supernatural, Grafton Books, London, 1979.

The Occult – the Ultimate Book for Those Who Would Walk with the Gods, Panther Books, London, 1979.

Wilson, Peter Lamborn, *Angels*, Pantheon Books, New York, 1980.

Yogananda, Paramhansa, *Autobiography of a Yogi*, Rider, London, 1977.

Zaehner, R. C., *The Hymns of Zarathustra* (A translation of the *Gāthās*) by Jacques Duchesne-Guillermin, John Murray, London, 1952.

The Teachings of the Magi: A Compendium of Zoroastrian Beliefs, Allen & Unwin, London, 1956.

Articles and Papers

Argüelles, José, *Open Letter to the World Community regarding UFOs*, Link Up, December 1988.

Ashe, Geoffrey, 'The Glastonbury Tor Maze', pamphlet, Glastonbury, 1980.

Bahdarage, Asoka, 'Spirituality, Politics and Feminism', *Women of Power*, journal, 1986.

'Beware of the New Age', *Faerie Fire*, journal, New York.

Berenholtz, Jim, paper on sacred sites, 25 December, 1986. 'The Harmonic Convergence and International Sacred Sites Festival of 1987: a Commemorative Book', Jim Berenholtz, California, 1988.

Cameron, Anne, 'A Message to those who would Steal Native Traditions', *Wood and Water*, and *Moonshine* journals, 1985.

Fell, Alison, 'All a girl needs is a guru', *Spare Rib*, London, 1970s.

Francis, Daphne, 'New Age or New Right, Findhorn, a feminist view', *Greenline*, journal, 1985.

Findhorn Community, 'The Plan of Light' research papers, Findhorn Community, 1970s.

Goodman, Jenny, 'Are These Things done on Albion's Shores?', *PAN*, *Wood and Water*, *Greenline*.

Gustafson, Bob, 'Open Letter to the Pagan Community', *Faerie Fire*, New York, *PAN Journal*.

Halifax, Joan, 'Shamanism, Mind and No-Self', 1986.

Kornegger, Peggy, 'The Spirituality Rip-off', *Second Wave*, 1976.

Women Working for a Nuclear-Free and Independent Pacific, pamphlets, 1987.

McCrickhard, Janet, 'Ungrounded Glastonbury', *Glastonbury Communicator* journal, October 1985.

Neitsch, Matthias, 'Paper to the third conference of European Indian supporters', given in Vienna, 1987.

Remy, Val, 'Anti-feminist Troublemakers in Glastonbury', *PAN* journal, 1986.

Selleck, Vincent, *Resonance Returning*, pamphlet, Shekinah Foundation, Australia, 1987.

Sjöö, Monica, *Women are the Real Left/Wider We* journal/pamphlet by Monico Sjöö and Keith Motherson.

Matri/anarchy 1979, Bristol. (assorted articles including 'Feminist Arts, Manifesto, by Monica Sjöö and Anne Berg).

'Towards a Revolutionary Feminist Art', stencilled newsletter, 1971–73. 'Some Thoughts on Feminist Art', stencilled newsletter 1970/3.

'The History of Contraception and Abortion', (given as a paper at the first WACC conference in Liverpool 1971.)

Published as a pamphlet and included in the anthology *Body Politics* (see under Books in bibliography) in 1972 in an edited version and called there 'A Woman's Right to her Body'.

'Journeying through the Underworld', published in *Arachne*

Matriarchy journal in 1986 and in an edited version called 'Journey into Darkness' in the anthology *Glancing Fires*, (see under Books in bibliography) in 1987.

'The Goddess/es of the North' published in two parts in *Arachne*, 1984.

'Some Thoughts on the New Age Movement', article published in *PAN* journal 1989 and same year in *Wood and Water*, and in an edited version in *Greenline* titled 'The Goddess and the New Age'.

Interview in *We're Here: Conversations with Lesbian Women*, Angela Stewart-Park and Jules Cassidy, (eds.), Quartet Books, London, 1977.

All Work and No Pay, Falling Wall Press, USA, 1975.

'A Woman's Right Over Her Body' in *Body Politics – Women's Liberation in Britain 1969–72*, Michelene Wandor, ed., Stage 1, London, 1972.

Walking on the Waters – Women talk about Spirituality, (eds.), Jo Garcia and Sara Maitland, Virago Press, London, 1983.

'Journey into Darkness' in *Glancing Fires – an Investigation into Women's Creativity*, Lesley Saunders, ed., The Women's Press, London, 1987.

'Tested by the Dark/Light Mother of the Otherworld', in *Voices of the Goddess: a Chorus of Sibyls*, Caitlin Matthews, ed., Aquarian Press, Wellingborough, Northants, 1990.

Moira Vincentelli's interview with Monica Sjöö in Wales in 1984 in *Visibly Female – Feminism and Art Today*, Hilary Robinson, ed., Camden Press, London, 1987.

The Sexual Perspective – Homosexuality and Art in the last 100 years in the West, Emmanual Cooper, Routledge & Kegan Paul, London, 1986.

Framing Feminism – Art and the Women's Movement 1970–85, Rozsika Parker and Griselda Pollock, (eds.), Pandora Press, London, 1987.

'New Age, Same Old Story', article in *Everywoman* journal in December 1989.

'Journeying across Salisbury Plain' published in *Pan* and edited in *Greenline* 1985.

'Pilgrimage to USA: Goddess Women I Met There and Feminist Books I Read', published in two parts in *Wood and Water*, 1989.

Assorted articles, poems and images (paintings and drawings) by Monica Sjöö have appeared over the years in:

The UK:
From the Flames, c/o Vron, 42 Mapperley Road, Nottingham, NG3 5AS

Peace News (Nottingham): *Arachne* – Matriarchy journal (c/o 14 Hill Crest, Sevenoaks, Kent); Matriarchy Research and Reclaim Network Newsletter (MRRN – subscriptions to Blanche, Cloverly House, Erwood, Builth Wells, Powys LD2 3EZ, Cymru); *PAN (Pipes of Pan or Pagans Against Nukes)* (c/o Blaenberem, Mynyddcerrig, Nr. Llanelli, Dyfed, Wales/Cymru); *Wood and Water*, a Goddess-inclined eco-pagan magazine; *Greenline* (c/o 34 Cowley Road, Oxford, OX4 1HZ); *Ley Hunter: Journal of Geomancy and Earth Mysteries* (c/o PO Box 92, Penzance, Cornwall, TR1 2XL); *Everywoman* (c/o 34, Islington Green, London N1 8BU)

The USA:
Womanspirit (no longer published but back issues available from Jean Mountaingrove, 2000 King Mountain Trail, Sunny Valley, Oregon 97497); WeMoon (an astrological Moon calendar) (c/o Mother Tongue Ink, 37010 SE Snuffin Rd., Estacada, Oregon, 97023); *Calyx: a journal of Art and Literature for Women* (c/o 216 S.W. Madison PO Box B, Corvallis, Oregan 97339); *Women of Power Journal* (c/o PO Box 827, Cambridge, Massachusetts, 02238); article 'New Age or Armegeddon?' in *Women of Power* journal March 1990, USA; from 1970–76 assorted shorter articles in the magazine *Enough*, published by the Women's Liberation group in Bristol and in *Move*, the newsletter of the Gay Women's group in Bristol.

Smith, Jill, *The Unharmonic Convergence*, *PAN* and *Ley Hunter* journal, 1987.

Stewart, R. J. 'The Waters of the Gap: The Mythology of Aquae Sulis', Bath City Council, Bath, 1981.

Swiftdeer, Harley Reagan, *A Hopi Prophecy*, pamphlet, Acorn Publications, Glastonbury.

Tickwell, Alawn, 'Shamanism in Britain: Being our Grandfathers', *Moonshine* journal, Birmingham.

Further Reading

Journals

Arachne, Matriarchy Journal, c/o 14 Hill Crest, Sevenoaks, Kent.
Brain-Mind Bulletin, ed. Marilyn Ferguson, c/o PO Box 4211, Los Angeles, CA 90042.
Cosmic Voice, Aetherius Society, 757 Fulham Road, London SW6 5UU.
Everywoman, 34 Islington Green, London N1 8BU.
The Fountain, Fountain International, PO Box 915, Seaford, East Sussex BN25 1TW.
Greenline, c/o 34 Cowley Road, Oxford, OX4 1HZ.
Ley Hunter: Journal of Geomancy and Earth Mysteries, PO Box 92, Penzance, Cornwall, TR182XL.
Link Up, 51 Northwick Business Centre, Blockley, Gloucester, GL56 9RF.
Manushi, cl/202 Laipat Nagar 1, New Delhi 110024, India.
Media Watch, 803 Mission Street, Santa Cruz, California 95060.
Medicine Ways, c/o Alawn Tickhill, Galdraheim, 35 Wilson Avenue, Deal, Kent, CT14 9NL.
Moccasin Line, Northwest Indian Women's Circle, USA.
Pandora's Jar, formerly *PAN* (Pagans Against Nukes), c/o Blaenberem, Mynyddcerrig, Nr Llanelli, Dyfed, Wales/Cymru.
Psychic News, c/o Psychic News Bookshop, 20 Earlham Street, London WC2H 9LW.
Second Wave
Shaman's Drum, journal, PO Box 2636 Berkeley, California 94702.
Snake Power, journal, Vicki Noble, 5856 College Avenue, 138, Oakland, California 94618.
Spare Rib, 27 Clerkenwell Close, London EC1R 0AT.
Reproductive and Genetic Engineering: Journal of International Feminist Analysis, vol. 1, Pergamon Press, 1988.
Wood and Water, Pagan Journal, c/o 4 High Tow Close, Babbacombe Road, Bromley, Kent, BR1 3LQ.
Women of Power journal, Cambridge, Massachusetts 02238, USA.

Poetry

Barbara Mor, *Mother Tongue*, Athena Press, San Diego, 1976.
Winter Ditch and other Poems, Second Porcupine Press, Santa Fe, New Mexico, 1982.

Jill Smith, *Awakening: the Tale of a Journey through the Landscape of the Sacred Centres of the Body of this Land*, published by Jill Smith, 1983.
The Gipsy Switch: a Year-long Journey round Britain, PAN, 1986.
First Circle: a First Year Lived on the Isle of Lewis, published by Jill Smith, 1988.